“Readers are sure to find this multi-faceted analysis of the constellation of social and legal questions surrounding religious liberty powerfully illuminative. These vital issues have recently assumed increasing importance, domestically and internationally, and this penetrating coverage of the terrain deserves both its place in the literature and a wide readership.”

David Baggett, Professor of Philosophy, Liberty University, USA

“Dr. Menuge has assembled an impressive and diverse group of contributors to address one of the most pressing issues of the day: religious liberty and the law. The book’s survey of legal, religious, and philosophical traditions around the world make this a must read for any serious student of the subject.”

John Bursch, Bursch Law PLLC

“While everyone else is running around talking about secondary issues, this book raises the questions that matter most: Is religious liberty a basic human need, and what assumptions about the universe and human nature are necessary to justify it? *Religious Liberty and the Law* cuts through both popular hysteria and superficial ideology to show us what is really at stake in these debates.”

Greg Forster, Trinity International University, USA

Religious Liberty and the Law

Questions of religious liberty have become flashpoints of controversy in virtually every area of life around the world. Despite the protection of religious liberty at both national and supranational levels, there is an increasing number of conflicts concerning the proper way to recognize it – both in modern secular states and in countries with an established religion or theocratic mode of government.

This book provides an analysis of the general concept of religious liberty along with a close study of important cases that can serve as test beds for conflict resolution proposals. It combines the insights of both pure academics and experienced legal practitioners to take a fresh look at the nature, scope and limits of religious liberty. Divided into two parts, the collection presents a blend of legal and philosophical approaches, and draws on cases from a wide range of jurisdictions, including Brazil, India, Australia, the USA, the Netherlands and Canada.

Presenting a broad range of views, this often provocative volume makes for fascinating reading for academics and researchers working in the areas of law and religion, legal philosophy and human rights.

Angus J. L. Menuge is Professor and Chair of Philosophy, Concordia University, Wisconsin, USA. His teaching and research interests are in the areas of philosophy of mind and philosophy of science. He has published widely on these and related issues.

Applied Legal Philosophy Series

General Editor: Tom D. Campbell, Professional Fellow,
Centre for Applied Philosophy and Public Ethics,
Charles Sturt University, Canberra

The principal objective of this series is to encourage the publication of books which adopt a theoretical approach to the study of particular areas or aspects of law, or deal with general theories of law in a way which is directed at issues of practical, moral and political concern in specific legal contexts. The general approach is both analytical and critical and relates to the socio-political background of law reform issues.

This series includes studies of all the main areas of law, presented in a manner which relates to the concerns of specialist legal academics and practitioners. Each book makes an original contribution to an area of legal study while being comprehensible to those engaged in a wide variety of disciplines. Their legal content is principally Anglo-American, but a wide-ranging comparative approach is encouraged and authors are drawn from a variety of jurisdictions.

Self-Constitution of European Society: Beyond EU politics, law and governance
Jiří Přibáň
9781472458506 (hbk)

Sovereignty in Post-Sovereign Society: A Systems Theory of European Constitutionalism
Jiří Přibáň
9781472460875 (hbk)
9781138701496 (pbk)

Principled Engagement: Negotiating Human Rights in Repressive States
Morten B. Pedersen and David Kinley
9781409455387 (hbk)
9781138250659 (pbk)

Legitimizing Human Rights: Secular and Religious Perspectives
Angus J. L. Menuge
9781409450023 (hbk)

Legisprudence: Practical Reason in Legislation
Luc J. Wintgens
9781409419815 (hbk)
9781138256866 (pbk)

Constitutional Life and Europe's Area of Freedom, Security and Justice
Alun Howard Gibbs
9781409402695 (hbk)
9781138256767 (pbk)

The Vantage of Law: Its Role in Thinking about Law, Judging and Bills of Rights
James Allan
9781409430605 (hbk)
9781138261488 (pbk)

Religious Liberty and the Law

Theistic and Non-Theistic Perspectives

Edited by
Angus J. L. Menuge

Routledge
Taylor & Francis Group
LONDON AND NEW YORK

First published 2018 by Routledge

2 Park Square, Milton Park, Abingdon, Oxfordshire OX14 4RN
52 Vanderbilt Avenue, New York, NY 10017

Routledge is an imprint of the Taylor & Francis Group, an informa business

First issued in paperback 2019

British Library Cataloguing-in-Publication Data
A catalogue record for this book is available from the British Library

Library of Congress Cataloging-in-Publication Data
Names: Menuge, Angus J. L., editor.
Title: Religious liberty and the law : theistic and non-theistic perspectives / Angus J. L. Menuge.
Description: Abingdon, Oxon ; New York, NY : Routledge, 2017. | Series: Applied legal philosophy series | Includes bibliographical references and index.
Identifiers: LCCN 2017002090 | ISBN 9781138244474 (hardback) | ISBN 9781351982672 (web pdf) | ISBN 9781351982665 (epub) | ISBN 9781351982658 (mobipocket/kindle)
Subjects: LCSH: Freedom of religion. | Religion and state. | Religion and law.
Classification: LCC K3258 .R455 2017 | DDC 344/.096--dc23
LC record available at https://lccn.loc.gov/2017002090

ISBN: 978-1-138-24447-4 (hbk)
ISBN: 978-0-367-27343-9 (pbk)

Typeset in Galliard
by Taylor & Francis Books

Contents

Illustrations

Figures

Tables

Contributors

Vito Breda (LLB Milan, LLM Brussels, PhD Edinburgh) is Research Leader of the Comparative Law Group at the School of Law of the University of Southern Queensland. He held a tenure position in Cardiff. His publications include *The Objectivity of Judicial Decisions: A Comparative Analysis of Nine Jurisdictions* (Peter Lang, 2016) and various articles in the *Journal for the Semiotics of Law, European Law Journal, Modern Law Review, International Journal for the Semiotics of Law* and *Res Publica*.

John Calvert trained as a geologist, and became a lawyer in 1968. He specialized in stock fraud for 32 years with the firm of Lathrop and Gage in Kansas City, Missouri. In 1999, he switched his practice to the study of the religious liberty of parents and children in public education and became the managing director of an organization that seeks institutional objectivity in origins science. Since then, he has advocated the objective teaching of origins science in public education. In 2011, he became counsel for Citizens for Objective Public Education Inc. (COPE). In 2013, he filed a case for COPE and 15 parents and 21 children that deals with K-12 public education about our origins. The case was presented to the Supreme Court of the United States in August 2016.

Paul Cliteur is Professor of Jurisprudence at Leiden Law School. Paul has obtained degrees in law and philosophy. His research focuses on ethics and the philosophical foundations of the law, in particular moral dilemmas concerning the multicultural society and the relationship between law and religion. Paul is the author of *The Secular Outlook: In Defense of Moral and Political Secularism* (Wiley-Blackwell, 2010) and "A Secular Critique of Religious Ethics and Politics" (in Phil Zuckerman and John Shook, eds., *The Oxford Handbook of Secularism* [Oxford Handbooks, 2017], 389–400). He was co-editor, with Tom Herrenberg, of *The Fall and Rise of Blasphemy Law* (Leiden University Press, 2016).

Paul Copan (PhD Marquette) is Professor and Pledger Family Chair of Philosophy and Ethics at Palm Beach Atlantic University in West Palm Beach, Florida. He is the author or editor of over 30 books, including *The Routledge Companion to Philosophy of Religion* (Routledge, 2007) and *The Rationality of Theism*

(Routledge, 2003), and he is the author of many journal articles and book chapters. He and his wife, Jacqueline, have six children and live in West Palm Beach. His website is www.paulcopan.com.

Hendrik Kaptein is Associate Professor of Jurisprudence at Leiden Law School. He has lectured and published on legal ethics, on (legal) logic and argumentation, and on criminal justice. Key publications include *Kwade zaken? De moraal van het juridisch beroep* (Ars Aequi, 2006, on legal ethics), chapters in *Crime, Victims and Justice* (Ashgate, 2004, edited in cooperation with Marijke Malsch) and in *Legal Evidence and Proof: Statistics, Stories, Logic* (Ashgate, 2009, edited in cooperation with Henry Prakken and Bart Verheij). Throughout his career, he has been active in both faculty and university management. He is a board member of various non-profit organizations, and he is the chief bell-ringer of the Old Church in Amsterdam.

Laura Kittel is a PhD student at the University of Notre Dame Australia. She received a BA in history and religion from St. Olaf College and an MA in human rights practice from Curtin University. She published "Healing Heart and Mind: The Pursuit of Human Rights in Engaged Buddhism as Exemplified by Aung San Suu Kyi and the Dalai Lama" (*International Journal of Human Rights,* 2011, 15(6): 905–925). She has worked at the International Campaign for Tibet in Washington, DC, and presented her research at the United Nations in New York. Originally from Guam and the United States, she lives in Perth, Western Australia. Her current research focuses on human rights, happiness and virtue ethics.

Katya Kozicki is Full Professor of Law at the Pontifical Catholic University of Parana and the Federal University of Parana (Brazil), teaching in their undergraduate and graduate programs. She holds a PhD in juridical science from the Federal University of Santa Catarina. She was a visiting research associate at the Centre for the Study of Democracy (CSD), University of Westminster, London, UK, from 1998 to 1999, and visiting research scholar at the Benjamin N. Cardozo School of Law, Yeshiva University, New York, USA, from 2012 to 2013. She is a research fellow for the National Council for Scientific and Technological Development (CNPq) in Brasilia, Brazil.

Angus J. L. Menuge is Professor and Chair of Philosophy at Concordia University Wisconsin and President of the Evangelical Philosophical Society. He is author of many journal articles and book chapters on the philosophy of mind and has broad interests in philosophical and theological anthropology. He is the editor of several books, including *Reading God's World* (Concordia Academic Press, 2004) and *Legitimizing Human Rights: Secular and Religious Perspectives* (Ashgate, 2013), and is the author of *Agents under Fire: Materialism and the Rationality of Science* (Rowman and Littlefield, 2004). With J. P. Moreland and Jonathan Loose, he is currently editing *The Blackwell Companion to Substance Dualism* (Wiley-Blackwell, forthcoming).

Dallas K. Miller has been a federal trial judge in Alberta, Canada, for more than 10 years. In addition to his JD, Justice Miller has degrees in history and theology and holds the *Certificat* from the International Institute of Human Rights, Strasbourg, France. He is a fellow of the Society of Advanced Legal Studies in London and teaches human rights at the university level. Justice Miller volunteers for a human rights organization (www.ijm.ca) which seeks to bring justice to the poor in the developing world by providing judicial training programs to countries like Bolivia and Uganda.

Dwight Newman is Professor of Law and Canada Research Chair in Indigenous Rights in Constitutional and International Law at the University of Saskatchewan. He completed his BA and JD in Canada and his BCL and DPhil at Oxford University, with his DPhil focused on legal philosophy. He has also studied at the Hague Academy of International Law and at Regent College. He was a 2015-2016 Visiting Fellow in the James Madison Program at Princeton University. He has published around 75 articles or book chapters and 10 books, including most recently an edited collection, *Religious Freedom and Communities* (LexisNexis, 2016).

Ray Pennings is Co-Founder of Cardus, a Canadian public and social policy think tank (www.cardus.ca) and currently serves as its executive vice-president. He is a respected voice in Canadian politics, and has held senior positions on campaign teams at the municipal, provincial and federal levels. Ray's BA is from McMaster University and he holds an MA in religion from Puritan Theological Seminary. His grasp of applied public theology is evident through his writings, but also through his volunteer efforts. He has served on the boards of charities, universities and community groups, and on boards in his church community. Ray and his wife, Kathy, have one adult son.

William Soares Pugliese holds a PhD and an LLM from the Federal University of Paraná (Brazil), where he is currently Substitute Professor of Constitutional Law, State Theory and Political Science. He previously served as a visiting scholar at the Max Planck Institute for Comparative Public Law and International Law (Germany). He is also the coordinator of the Civil Procedural Law Specialization Program at the Academia Brasileira de Direito Constitucional (ABDConst). He is an attorney-at-law and a member of the Constitutionalism and Democracy Research Group and the Comparative Civil Procedural Law Research Group at the Federal University of Paraná Law School.

James K. A. Smith is Professor of Philosophy at Calvin College, Editor-In-Chief of *Comment* magazine and author of *How (Not) to Be Secular: Reading Charles Taylor* (Eerdmans, 2014). A native of Embro, Ontario, James studied at Emmaus Bible College in Dubuque, Iowa; the University of Waterloo; the Institute for Christian Studies in Toronto; and Villanova University, where he earned his PhD. Working at the intersection of philosophy, theology and cultural criticism, James is an award-winning author of a number of books. His latest book is *You Are What You Love: The Spiritual Power of Habit* (Brazos, 2016).

Christian Vandergeest is a former research assistant at Cardus, where his research focused on religious freedom in Canadian Supreme Court decisions. He holds a Master of Global Affairs degree from the University of Toronto and completed his undergraduate studies at Redeemer University College. He is currently pursuing a JD at Harvard Law School.

Mary Anne Waldron has been a faculty member in the Faculty of Law at the University of Victoria since 1976. She is the author of *Free to Believe: Rethinking Freedom of Conscience and Religion in Canada* (University of Toronto Press, 2013). Her teaching interests include contracts, commercial law, legal skills and legal ethics. From 2009, she has been a visiting fellow at the Centre for Studies in Religion and Society at the University of Victoria. She was appointed to Queen's Counsel in 2004.

Thom Wolf (PhD Andrews University) is Professor of Global Studies, University Institute, New Delhi; Research Professor at the Centre for Social Research, National Institute of Social Work and Social Sciences, Bhubaneswar; and Visiting Professor at Nagpur University. He is a life member of the Indian Sociological Society; a contributing editor to *Forward Press*, India's only Hindi-English news magazine; and was an international consultant for *The Oxford Encyclopaedia of South Asian Christianity* (Oxford University Press, 2012). His *India Progress-Prone: The Baliraja Proposal of Mahatma Phule* (University Institute – New Delhi, 2008) and *Phule: In His Own Words* (University Institute – New Delhi, 2007) are also available in Hindi and Marathi; and his "Mahayana Buddhism: Tipping Point Buddhism," written for the Government of India's 2,550-anniversary Buddha commemoration, is also available in Tibetan.

Introduction

Angus J. L. Menuge

Religious liberty in the balance

All around the world, questions of religious liberty have become flashpoints of controversy in virtually every area of life. Both the 1948 United Nations Universal Declaration of Human Rights (Article 18) and the 1953 European Convention on Human Rights (Article 9) recognize religious liberty (in the form of freedom of both conscience and action) as a fundamental human right, and many countries include more specific protections within their constitutions or other legislation. Yet in practice, we find an increasing number of conflicts concerning the proper way to recognize religious liberty arising both in modern secular states and in countries with an established religion or theocratic mode of government.

At the extremes of the debate, a minority perceive religion monolithically as either bane or blessing. Some of the New Atheists contend that, on the whole, religion is both irrational and a harmful influence on society, and maintain that religious freedom should be confined to the privacy of people's minds and places of worship. At the other extreme, some maintain a broadly libertarian conception of religion, according to which the state has no legitimate business regulating religion because what counts as religious liberty must be defined by the consciences of those within the religions themselves.

It is fair to say that most thoughtful students of this topic would reject both of these extreme positions. The first appears either naïve or disingenuous in maintaining that critics of major religions are themselves religiously neutral, and runs the serious risk of allowing a favored ideology or religion (such as secular humanism) to be established by the state. The second has no resources to curb the public dangers posed by religions that promote harms either to those within a religion (for example, by discouraging the use of life-saving medical treatments) or to those outside a religion (for example, by punishing apostasy or criminalizing the evangelistic efforts of rival religions or ideologies).

So what is the way forward? It appears that we must explore the *via media* between a chauvinistic and dismissive approach to religious liberty that advances the religious liberty of some at the expense of others, and an uncritical support of all kinds of religious liberty that undermines basic principles of a civilized society. We must find a way to balance the legitimate scope of religious liberty as part of the personal and social flourishing of human beings with the limits rightly imposed when harms become evident.

On the one hand, a positive case needs to be made that religious liberty is not the trivial or optional preference of some people, but a basic need of all human beings to orient their lives around ultimate values. It appears that humans alone among other living creatures have a sense not only of the immediate goods required for their survival, but of the ultimate goods that they believe give their lives meaning. To deprive human beings of religious liberty would be, in an important sense, to deprive them of their humanity. Yet, on the other hand, the right to religious liberty, like any right, may come into conflict with other rights claims. For example, in many countries today there is an increasing assertion that various gender identities and relationships must be recognized by all, regardless of the religious conscience of individuals or organizations such as churches and many private universities. So are there rights that sometimes trump the right to freedom of religion? And, in the other direction, there are clashes between the religious assertion that some statement or artwork should be curtailed as blasphemous and claims of the right to freedom of expression. So does freedom of religion sometimes trump other rights?

The goals of this collection

This collection has several major goals, which are reflected in the organization of the volume. In the first section of the book, "The Nature of Religious Liberty," several writers grapple with such basic questions as the proper ontological grounding of religious liberty, whether "religion" is really the most helpful term to use, and why we should think that "religious liberty" is beneficial to human flourishing. In the second and much longer section, "The Scope and Limits of Religious Liberty," contributors examine a number of historical and contemporary cases in which conflicts arise over the proper extent of religious freedom. Just how far does the right of religious liberty extend? Should religious liberty have narrow scope in order to protect the secular sphere from intrusion? Or is it in the secular state's interest to permit a rich and expansive exercise of religious liberty? What is the proper understanding of both the religious and the secular spheres needed in order that a secular state can permit without endorsing appropriate expressions of religious freedom? How does that play out in such contested cases as sex education, the conduct codes of religious schools and universities, and government funding of religious ministries?

This second section also explores the limits of religious liberty. If religion is narrowly defined in terms of theistic belief, will that unfairly favor theistic beliefs in cultures with an established theistic religion or unfairly discriminate against theistic beliefs in secular cultures, where non-theistic religions can pose as neutral? At what point can we say that religious expression should be limited because it comes into conflict with other basic human rights, such as freedom of expression, freedom of association, and the opportunity for education and personal and social development?

It emerges from the various chapters that the religious liberties that deserve legal protection are those which make positive contributions to human flourishing, to the well-being and development of individuals and societies. To be sure, this does not resolve all of the difficult issues, since there are different, competing visions of what constitutes human flourishing that are themselves far from religiously neutral. Most fundamentally, there is a conflict between the rights of *autonomy* and self-determination, and *heteronomy*, or governance by external standards. Do humans flourish when they are set free from external constraints to achieve as many as possible of their self-chosen goals? Or do they flourish when they live in humble obedience to a higher authority that requires them to sacrifice many personal desires – to see them as misdirected, selfish or even perverse – so that they develop the capacity for serving others and perhaps also their god or gods?

Yet, despite these difficulties, it is possible for proponents of a particular religion to appeal to secular reason and secular data (for example, data drawn from history and the social sciences) to make the case that their religion has made a positive contribution to individuals and society. In this way, a secular state, one that is committed to religious neutrality, can, without prejudice, draw some conclusions about which religious traditions are supportive of the goods of society. And, on the negative side, a secular state can also have reason to curb religious practices that undermine security or other important freedoms to which it has an equal or stronger commitment.

The nature of religious liberty

In the opening chapter, Paul Copan considers the basic grounds for such fundamental human rights as religious liberty. Having elsewhere argued that Christian theism provides the best ontological foundation for these rights, Copan here considers the evidence of history. He finds that "religion" has become an unhelpful term due to its vagueness, ambiguity and unfair privileging of Enlightenment assumptions as "secular," and so he proposes that a more consistent approach is to consider the right to adopt or reject a *worldview*. Next, he surveys a variety of historical contributions to civilization, including modern science, bioethics, democracy and major moral reforms, which he argues depended on a biblical worldview. And finally, Copan shows that a biblical worldview has provided a grounding for human rights and liberties that is superior to competing alternatives.

In the next chapter, Laura Kittel considers the nature of human flourishing. The US Declaration of Independence expresses this idea in terms of "life, liberty and the pursuit of happiness." But Kittel argues that our current understanding of these important words has been debased by consumerism and myopic hedonism, and that it would serve us well to recover their original meaning. Rather than pitting personal freedoms against the social good, and willfulness against responsibility, it would help us to see that humans flourish best in a community of virtue. Without this idea, it is inevitable that "rights" are reduced to wants instead of being seen as liberties that support the well-being of society. On this understanding, liberty (including religious liberty) is properly granted not as a license to do as one pleases, but as a means of fostering the public good.

In a fascinating essay, Hendrik Kaptein mines the writings of the ancient philosopher Epictetus and concludes that a central and neglected insight is that liberty *itself* is a deeply religious concept. Whether one takes Epictetus's views literally or not, he teaches us that there is a sense in which human freedom is godlike: human beings have a kind of "omnipotence," not, to be sure, in what they can do, but in how they choose to interpret life. And it is by recognizing their godlike nature that they can see why all human beings have tremendous value. This liberty, Epictetus thinks, is part of who we are and does not require the support of institutionalized religion.

But what of the legal situation? In the closing chapter of this section, Dallas K. Miller surveys the history of religious liberty as a human right, and focuses on a rather disturbing fact. While religious liberty is explicitly listed in the 1948 Universal Declaration of Human Rights, and although more than 50 years have passed, it is the only basic human right that has not been protected by a convention. This means that the freedom to practice, adopt or change a religion recognized by the UDHR is not legally protected, as it should be, a fact which has encouraged extensive religious persecution in many countries. So Miller argues that there is an urgent need to negotiate a binding convention on the freedom of religion or belief.

The scope and limits of religious liberty

In the opening chapter of this section, I argue that although a secular state is committed to neutrality among religious options, it can have good reason not merely to permit, but to *promote* the freedom of religious expression and action when these contribute social goods that it can recognize using secular standards. For example, the state benefits from liberty of thought, which includes religious thought, as it prevents dangerous claims of infallibility; moreover, due to its transcendent perspective, some religious thought is especially valuable to the welfare of the state, as it provides the critical distance necessary to recognize and resist trends that might otherwise issue in totalitarianism. And religious institutions foster many goods in the state, such as care for the poor and the modeling of a harmonious yet diverse community in a manner which the state cannot by itself adequately replicate.

In the next chapter, Mary Anne Waldron, James K. A. Smith, Ray Pennings and Christian VanderGeest examine the difficult question of the proper definition of the secular, charting the development of that notion in Canadian legal decisions. The authors draw on Charles Taylor's seminal work, *A Secular Age* (2007), which distinguishes three notions of a "secular" society. That can mean a society which (1) is governed by secularism; (2) has diminished religious belief and participation; or (3) is genuinely neutral and pluralistic, allowing a range of religious options, where none are assumed and all can be contested. They argue that recent

Canadian Supreme Court decisions suggest that it is moving from the second to the third understanding of "secular," helping the cause of religious liberty, although many clashes with other rights and the claims of "expressive humanism" remain to be adjudicated.

Some of these clashes are found at religious institutions themselves. Dwight Newman considers the Canadian debate over the potential opening of a Christian law school at Trinity Western University (TWU). The debate arises because TWU has a covenant requiring students to act according to traditional Christian understandings of sexuality and marriage, but since 2005 Canada has recognized the legality of same-sex marriage. Newman points out that there is a challenging parallelism between rights claims based on sexual identity and those based on religious identity. Will the recognition of religious identity rights require the recognition of sexual identity rights – a problem for institutions like TWU? And, will the recognition of sexual identity rights require the recognition of religious rights – a problem, perhaps, for some secularists? Newman suggests that humility and respectful engagement will be necessary to negotiate these difficult questions.

But clashes are also evident in public institutions. Moving to the US context, John Calvert considers whether public school education meets the constitutional standard of religious neutrality. This concerns the religious liberty of parents – their right to direct the religious education of their children – and the religious rights of students not to be indoctrinated by a particular religious view. Following his previous work, Calvert argues that religious neutrality can only be achieved if the state adopts an unbiased definition of "religion" that includes all worldviews that address questions of ultimate origins, meaning and purpose. Referencing such examples as the teaching of evolution and sex education, Calvert argues that current educational practices are not neutral, because they favor non-theistic over theistic religions, and he suggests a number of different ways that progress could be made toward the goal of more objective education in public schools.

Changing our focus to Australia, Vito Breda considers the case of the secular funding of chaplaincy programs. The High Court of Australia (HCA) ruled that such a program could not be justified as meeting a "human want." Breda argues, however, that there was no proper analysis of what constitutes a "human want," and that it is hard to see how uncoerced access to pastoral care could not address the wants of some students even in a secular setting. He provides a detailed analysis to show that the HCA appears to have misread the case.

What about the religious claim that certain kinds of expression are blasphemous, and that those who make them can expect the threat (or reality) of violent reprisals? Focusing on a variety of European cases, ranging from the *fatwah* on Salman Rushdie in 1989 to the murder of the *Charlie Hebdo* cartoonists in 2015, Paul Cliteur makes the case that religiously inspired violence ("theoterrorism") has resulted in a new variant of the ancient practice of hostage-taking. While people from one population have taken people hostage from rival populations for centuries by abducting them and imprisoning them, usually in a different country, modern hostage-taking does not require these elaborate measures. By issuing a credible death threat toward offenders against religious codes of expression, theoterrorists make those individuals prisoners in their own country. The victims of terrorism are stripped indefinitely of the normal civic freedoms they previously enjoyed, and must live anonymously and in seclusion under a secure watch. Cliteur provides a clear case of the sort of religious liberty – the absolute right not to be offended and the correlative right to deprive offenders of their basic rights – that does not merit legal protection (e.g., in the form of anti-blasphemy laws) in a civilized society.

And, while theoterrorism provides an extreme illustration of the damage to individuals and society that religion can do, it is not hard to provide other examples. Thom Wolf applies a society-as-a-culture-tree metaphor to Nepal and India that allows one to trace the impact of their worldviews on society from "roots" to "shoots" to "fruits." In these cultures, traditional religious beliefs had the tragic consequence of fostering discrimination against women and the denial of basic human rights to members of lower castes (viewed as subhuman). At the same time, he shows how Mahatma Jotirao Phule, a 19th-century Indian activist, fought against what he saw as the "prison houses" of superstitious belief and bigotry and in favor of broader liberties and universal education. While significant progress has been made, many of Phule's ideals are still not fulfilled.

Finally, Katya Kozicki and William Soares Pugliese consider religious liberty in the Brazilian legal system. The Brazilian Constitution makes due reference to freedom of conscience, and insists that no-one may be deprived of any right on the basis of religious belief or conviction. And many more specific protections of religious liberty can be found therein. In practice, however, Kozicki and Pugliese argue that courts have typically operated with an inadequate, narrow definition of "religion," one that requires a text, a hierarchy and a God. As a result, non-standard expressions of religion in the broader sense of a worldview that orients life around a system of ultimate values (including Umbanda, Spiritualism and Masonry) are often discriminated against. So in practice, what the Brazilian system tends to support is a truncated religious liberty: liberty for the religions that the state recognizes. The solution to this is not merely legal: it requires the state to become better informed about the nature and diversity of religion.

It is interesting to note that a common theme emerging from these chapters is that the ideals of a truly secular state cannot be attained in a climate of religious ignorance. The state will have to become acquainted with accurate, fair general definitions of religion and, at least on some occasions, the specific teachings of particular religions in order to protect religious liberty.

The origin of the collection

Several of the contributors to this volume collaborated on a special workshop on the foundations of human rights at the 2011 IVR[1] World Congress in Frankfurt, Germany. Papers drawn from that gathering were combined with several outside contributions, culminating in the volume *Legitimizing Human Rights* that was published by Ashgate in 2013 (and since acquired by Routledge). Having considered human rights in general, we decided that one of the particular rights most under threat, and most in need of careful conceptual and legal analysis, was the right of religious liberty. With an expanded group that included some of the outside contributors to *Legitimizing Human Rights*, such as Paul Copan and Paul Cliteur, and many new contributors, such as Laura Kittel, Katya Kozicki, Dwight Newman, Ray Pennings and William Soares Pugliese, we formed a special workshop on religious liberty for the 2015 IVR World Congress in Washington, DC. In the end, all but one of the chapters was developed from material originally presented at that meeting. But we observed that a crucial deficiency of the book was its lack of coverage of religious liberty in an Asian context, and Thom Wolf's chapter was the remedy. One contributor to our 2015 meeting, John Warwick Montgomery, decided to publish his essay elsewhere.

Acknowledgments

I would like to thank the IVR World Congress, and all of the contributors to the 2015 workshop and to this book. I am also very grateful to Taylor and Francis for keeping this project going through the transition from Ashgate to Routledge. Finally, I would also like to thank my kind and patient wife, Vicki, who has put up with my long hours of editing and who made invaluable contributions by proofreading the manuscript and checking the index.

Note

1 IVR stands for the German name for the International Society for the Philosophy of Law and Social Philosophy (http://ivronlineblog.wordpress.com/about).

Part I
The nature of religious liberty

1 The biblical worldview context for religious liberty[1]

Paul Copan

Introduction: Nietzsche's madman and human rights

Many scholars are familiar with Friedrich Nietzsche's "Parable of the Madman." The madman – who represents the "prophetic" voice of Nietzsche himself – comes running into the marketplace, lantern in hand, crying "I seek God! I seek God!" His fellow atheists there – unaware of the weighty implications of God's non-existence – mock and laugh at him: Is he lost? Is he hiding? Has he gone on a voyage? No:

> *We have killed him* – you and I. All of us are his murderers. But how did we do this?...Do we hear nothing as yet of the noise of the gravediggers who are burying God? Do we smell nothing as yet of the divine decomposition? Gods, too, decompose. God is dead. God remains dead. And we have killed him.

The madman continues his lament and then falls silent. His listeners are dumbstruck, staring at him in astonishment. He throws down his lantern, and then exclaims:

> I have come too early...my time is not yet. This tremendous event is still on its way, still wandering; it has not yet reached the ears of men. Lightning and thunder require time; the light of the stars requires time; deeds, though done, still require time to be seen and heard. This deed is still more distant from them than most distant stars – *and yet they have done it themselves.*
>
> (Nietzsche 1974, 181–182)

As the madman himself, Nietzsche here is rightly exposing the earth-shattering consequences of Western civilization's shift away from belief in God (the "killing" of God), although most Westerners (the ignorant atheists in the marketplace) have not begun to grasp the implications of God's non-existence ("I have come too early").

Aside from the biblical faith's actual *historical* influence on human rights discourse in the West, the latter's increasing rejection of the *metaphysical* foundation of God's existence as a means to ground human worth (the *imago Dei*) leaves us with a kind of edifice complex: the house of human rights and religious liberties cannot be properly sustained without the proper metaphysical footing to uphold them. Nietzsche acknowledged this: "Moral judgments agree with religious ones in believing in realities which are no realities.... *There are altogether no moral facts.*" Indeed, he contends, morality "has truth only if God is the truth – it stands or falls with faith in God" (Nietzsche 1968, 55, 70) – or to be more precise, it stands or falls with whether God exists or not, which is an *ontological* matter, not merely an *epistemological* one ("faith in God").

Nietzsche is not alone in seeing the moral implications of God's absence. Atheist philosopher Kai Nielsen puts it this way:

> We have not been able to show that reason requires the moral point of view or that all really rational persons, unhoodwinked by myth or ideology, not be individual egoists or classic amoralists. Reason doesn't decide here.
>
> The picture I have painted for you is not a pleasant one. Reflection on it depresses me....The point is this: pure practical reason, even with a good knowledge of the facts, will not take you to morality.
>
> (Nielsen 1984, 90)

Jean-Paul Sartre found these implications distressing too:

> It [is] very distressing that God does not exist, because all possibility of finding values in a heaven of ideas disappears along with Him; there can no longer be an *a priori* Good, since there is no infinite and perfect consciousness to think it. Nowhere is it written that the Good exists, that we must be honest, that we must not lie; because the fact is we are on a plane where there are only men. As Dostoievsky [*sic*] said, "If God didn't exist, everything would be possible."
>
> (Sartre 1957, 22)

And atheist philosopher and former moral realist Joel Marks also acknowledges the connection between God and morality:

> I have thrown over my previous commitment to Kantianism. In fact, I have given up morality altogether!...The long and the short of it is that I became convinced that atheism implies amorality; and since I am an atheist, I must therefore embrace amorality....The religious fundamentalists are correct: without God, there is no morality.
>
> (Marks 2015)

Then there is Bertrand Russell, who notes that we are "but the outcome of accidental collocations of atoms" and that "only on the firm foundation of unyielding despair, can the soul's habitation henceforth be safely built" (Russell 1963, 41). And cognitive scientist Steven Pinker says, with regard to nihilism, that "it can only say that love, beauty, morality, and all that we hold precious, are just figments of a brain pursuing selfish evolutionary strategies" (Pinker 2006, 7). Pinker brings us back to Nietzsche's point – that an atheism that still affirms objective moral values and intrinsic human dignity engages in a hijacking of theistic metaphysics.

In this essay, my primary focus is on the *historical* question of the connection between the biblical faith and its immense democratizing influence in the West and elsewhere. I only indirectly mention the intrinsic *metaphysical* point – namely, the connection between the existence of a good God and intrinsic human value, and thus the non-arbitrary basis for human rights. Non-theistic alternatives simply fail to account for objective human values and duties, and for personal responsibility (I extensively address this metaphysical argument elsewhere; see Copan 2008, 2012, 2013a, 2013b, 2013c).

To support my claim, I make the following four points. First, I give a brief word on "rights." A right is a relational title and therefore requires an ultimate ground or justification. Second, the concept of "religion" must be revisited. As many scholars have observed, the term "religious" is itself vague, unhelpful and even problematic. For example, the Enlightenment "religious-secular" compartmentalization is deeply flawed. Also, traditional "religions" like classical Buddhism reject belief in God or divinity – a common assumption about religion. A more consistent approach would be to speak of the right or freedom to hold and change one's worldview – the personal embrace of what one takes to be ultimate, including beliefs regarding origins, destiny, human nature, and meaning – without fear of punitive legal measures. Third, I consider various historical gains for humanity that have been shaped by devotion to a biblical worldview; these include modern science, bioethics, human rights, democracy and key moral reforms. And fourth, I explore some possible historical alternatives to explain the emergence of human rights (and "religious liberty") discourse – the "democracy" of ancient Greece, the Renaissance or the Enlightenment. I argue that each of these is inadequate. Our human rights language is the legacy of the Judeo-Christian tradition of the *imago Dei*, the notion that human dignity and worth are divinely bestowed. Furthermore, such dignity and worth are not mere cultural by-products or historical inventions. The discourse of freedom of conscience and other human liberties has been nourished by persons transformed and inspired by this biblical vision. To assume that existing legislative reforms and/or judicial decisions can adequately prop up a vision of human dignity and effectively buttress human rights discourse is to overlook the deeper and broader leavening effect that has shaped Western civilization.

1. Rights and religious liberty

The United Nations Universal Declaration on Human Rights of contains this critical affirmation:

> Everyone has the right to freedom of thought, conscience, and religion; this right includes the freedom to change his religion or belief, and freedom, either alone or in community with others and in public or private, to manifest his religion or belief in teaching, practice, worship and observance.
>
> (Article 18)

What is a right? A right – including that of religious liberty – is a kind of *title* or *legitimate claim to something.* A right is what is *due* to a person – the right to be treated in a particular way by others. Moreover, these rights are bound up with corresponding *duties.* A professor owes or has a duty to her student to give him a just grade – a mark reflecting the student's quality of work, to which the student is entitled; this is the student's right. Also, we may need to distinguish between *prima* and *ultima facie* duties. We have a duty not to harm a person unless that purported (*prima facie*) "harm" is part of a larger moral framework that is aimed at the overall or ultimate flourishing for that person (*ultima facie*). Further, while we are always duty-bound to rights-bearers, we may have duties concerning non-rights-bearing objects. For example, while sequoia or redwood trees do not have rights, I am duty-bound not to wantonly raze such a forest to the ground.

If rights "are what respect for worth requires" (Wolterstorff 2012, 45), what is the *source* or *justification* of the title or claim in question? True, a right entails the worth or excellency of the rights-bearer. But the right – the claim or title – must be *rooted in* or *spring from* some authority or source that bestows such a status; a right is not self-standing but is rather a relational title, requiring a ground or justification that is not merely free-floating. This title requires a metaphysical grounding to make sense of this entitlement (Montgomery 1986, 78–80; Wolterstorff 2012). A Kantian or Rawlsian ethical stance, say, may offer epistemological insights into making moral judgments (e.g., Kant 1996a, 1996b; Rawls 1999; see Copan 2013a), but, as such, it is metaphysically incomplete, as this stance simply takes for granted human dignity and freedom without justification.

2. The problem of defining "religion"

What is "religion"? In his book *When Religion Becomes Evil*, Charles Kimball claims that religion has caused more violence than any other "institutional force in human history" (Kimball 2002, 1). Mark Juergensmeyer's *Terror in the Mind of God* makes similar claims, insisting that religion is violent by its very nature because it tends to "absolutize and to project images of cosmic war," and thus what is needed to produce peace and harmony instead is the rational, humanizing influence of Enlightenment values (Juergensmeyer 2000, 159, 242–243). Perhaps we could make a few comments on the "religious" and the "secular."

First, an irony for such "pro-Enlightenment" claimants is *that they are typically not clear on what "religion" is.* Someone like Kimball insists that we can all tell the difference between the religious and the secular, between faith and unbelief: "We all know [religion] when we see it" (Kimball 2002, 15). Within the US legal system, "religion" is a "deeply personal" matter. Though we are not told what religion is, it is often treated with suspicion, as potentially divisive, and certainly cannot be considered a knowledge tradition (Beckwith 2006).

So, does belief in "God" or "the divine" constitute what is "religious"? No, it is not so tidy. Certainly, classical Buddhists – though considered traditional religionists – would reject belief in the divine. Indeed, even "secular" political visions may have strongly "religious" overtones. Political leaders have been deified throughout history. Consider how the philosopher Martin Heidegger not only joined the Nazi Party, wore the swastika, "heiled" Hitler, and sang Nazi songs with much spirit, in one speech he declared: "Do not let principles and ideas be the rulers of your existence. The Führer himself, and he alone is the German reality of today, and of the future, and its law" (cited in Ward 2004, 165). Or think of the devotion to Communist dictators such as Stalin, North Korea's Kim Jong-Il, or Mao Zedong (in the Chinese Communist song "The East Is Red," Zedong is called "the people's savior"). And what of the "Unabomber" – the serial killer Ted Kaczynski? He terrorized and harmed people through the use of pipe bombs, and he was *not* affiliated with any traditional religion. And Juergensmeyer even admits to the existence of "secular nationalism," which embraces a "doctrine of destiny" and which he claims "*is* a religion" (Juergensmeyer 1993, 15).

Historian William Cavanaugh points to University of Chicago "religion" scholar Martin Marty, who informs us that "religion divides" and that we need to separate politics from religion. However, given that there are at least 17 definitions of "religion," he admits that "scholars will never agree on the definition of religion" (cited in Cavanaugh 2009, 28). Cavanaugh wryly comments: "If one is trying, as is Marty, to convince the reader that 'religion divides' and 'religion can be violent,' then one ought to be clear about what religion is" (Cavanaugh 2009, 28). Cavanaugh considers the "myth of religious violence" to be part of the "folklore of Western societies" (Cavanaugh 2009, 226).

Second, it would seem anachronistic to blame pre-Enlightenment "religion" for all kinds of evils when the ecclesiastical and political in the West had hitherto been intertwined. The intellectuals of the Enlightenment (1650–1800) often attempted to separate the religious from the secular and the church from the state. However, the problem was not "religion" per se, but the exertion of political power in the name of religion. The same is true with the many atrocities carried out in the name of atheism or allegedly "secular" political structures. Thus Cavanaugh advises those who write books entitled *When People Do Bad Things in the Name of Religion* to be more economical and accurate by using a more appropriate title, *When People Do Bad Things* (Cavanaugh 2009, 26). We could add here that Cavanaugh persuasively argues that, contrary to the received view of post-Enlightenment critique, Europe's "religious wars" of Catholics, Lutherans, Zwinglians and Calvinists were not divided along sectarian lines but on political ones; so Catholics might fight against other Catholics, or Protestants might fight with Catholics against other Catholics (Cavanaugh 2009, 142–151).

Third, we should question the category "secular" or "non-religious" as the default stance by which any "religious" claim – say, "humans have dignity because they are created in the image of God" – might be judged. One problem with the secular-as-default position is this: which version or "denomination" of secularism will serve as the foundation to anchor and affirm intrinsic human dignity on which rights such as religious liberty are based? Will it be that of the optimistic "secular humanist" who takes for granted human rights and the duty to aspire to our highest ideals? Or will it be that expressed by Berkeley philosopher John Searle and Harvard evolutionary biologist Richard Lewontin?

According to Searle, we must reject our most fundamental intuitions in favor of physicalism:

> Physical events can have only physical explanations, and consciousness is not physical, so consciousness plays no explanatory role whatsoever. If, for example, you think you ate because you were consciously hungry, or got married because you were consciously in love with your prospective spouse, or withdrew your hand from the flame because you consciously felt a pain, or spoke up at a meeting because you consciously disagreed with the main speaker, you are mistaken in every case. In each case the effect was a physical event and therefore must have an entirely physical explanation.
>
> (Searle 1997, 154)

In another work, Searle explicitly states what his – and most of his professional academic peers' – "religion" is:

> There is a sense in which materialism is the religion of our time, at least among most of the professional experts in the fields of philosophy, psychology, cognitive science, and other disciplines that study the mind. Like most traditional religions, it is accepted without question and it provides the framework within which other questions can be posed, addressed, and answered.
>
> (Searle 2004, 48)

Meanwhile, Lewontin talks about naturalistic fideism – an "*a priori* adherence to material causes to create an apparatus of investigation and a set of concepts that produce material explanations, no matter how counter-intuitive, no matter how mystifying to the uninitiated" (Lewontin 1997).

Is *this* the "secular" default position to which we should subscribe? Should we take confidence in these knowledge claims – as though they are inherently superior to traditionally "religious" ones? If we are the products of a naturalistic universe and processes that are non-rational, non-conscious, valueless, materialistic and deterministic, what then grounds our common affirmations and the intuitions by which we live – namely, objective moral values and duties, human dignity, knowledge, rationality, consciousness, free will, personal responsibility, and the like? (see Copan 2013a, 2013c; Baggett and Walls 2011; Hare 2007; Smith 2009; and Plantinga 2010). Shall we merely adhere to a "secularist" vision for society, even if the metaphysical grounding of those assumed values better fits with the biblical theistic tenet that a good Creator exists and has made humans with dignity?

Fourth, we are better served by thinking along the lines of *worldview* than along the lines of some vague *religious-secular* categorization. As we have just noted, those traditionally labeled as "secularists" and "religionists" alike can divinize, absolutize or render ultimate any number of things (e.g., the state, nature, science, the self), and thus they can correspondingly engage in all kinds of evils in their name. The wiser course would be to speak in terms of worldview or philosophy of life instead of the nebulous term "religion." After all, what has been commonly taken to be "religious" is a fundamental personal commitment to some outlook or narrative that shapes our lives and identities – a commitment that could just as easily be "secular."

Philosopher Paul Griffiths describes "religion" as "a form of life that seems to those who inhabit it to be comprehensive, incapable of abandonment, and of central importance" (Griffiths 2001, 7), though this description could equally apply to "worldview." By *form of life*, Griffiths has in mind a pattern of activity that appears to its practitioners to have boundaries and particular actions bound up with it. This form of life is *comprehensive* – a framework in which all of life's particularities (marriage, moral actions, relationships) can be placed. It is also *incapable of abandonment* – not that a person could never change his outlook, but this form of life that gives shape to a person's identity would not be lightly dismissed – much like the deep embeddedness of a mother tongue. And it is *of central importance*, that is, it addresses issues of paramount significance concerning what is real, what is to be valued, and what one's purpose is – issues that cut to the very heart of our humanness (Griffiths 2001, 2–12).

"Religion" is commonly understood as an attempt to answer fundamental questions: ultimate origins (of the universe and of life itself); destiny (what happens when we die); and human nature and purpose (how life should be lived). But certainly the atheist or the naturalist has her own metaphysical views and convictions about these questions (Calvert 2013).

So as we speak about "the right of *religious* liberty," we should speak in a more robust or encompassing manner. We should refer to the legal protection for holding *any* worldview – theistic or naturalistic or pantheistic or polytheistic or solipsistic. Each view on this spectrum holds to a metaphysical and axiological perspective concerning what is ultimate – of origins, of death (and what, if anything, comes thereafter), and of human nature and life's meaning. I am not here defending a worldview free-for-all (e.g. the "right" of those with a jihadist worldview to blow up a bus of children), but sketching out the parameters and limits is not my aim here, and other participants in this project will be addressing such matters as rights, responsibilities and respect. (But for a start, see Guinness 2012.)

3. The fruits of biblical theism

Thom Wolf – a sociologist and contributor to this volume – asks why certain worldviews will more likely produce life-fettering results, while others will produce life-flourishing results. Some will be progress-resistant, while others will be progress-prone. Some will more likely lead to humanitarian reforms, while others will more likely perpetuate oppression.

He proposes the horticultural imagery of "roots, shoots, and fruits" (Wolf 2014). This image illustrates what he designates "WV3: worldvoice, worldview, and worldvenue" (Wolf 2012). The "roots" are the metaphysical outlook that concern origins, human nature, meaning and destiny; this outlook is commonly expressed by certain authoritative "worldvoices" such as Marx, Nietzsche,

Buddha, Krishna, Jesus and Muhammad. The "shoots" are the "worldviews," the elaborations of adherents who seek to live in light of the "voice" they have heard – with all of their communal practices, institutions, and avenues of cultural engagement. The "fruits" are the "worldvenues" – the kinds of moral and social outcomes and patterns that become embedded in a community or culture or civilization (Wolf 2012).

While certain practitioners may deviate from this "voice" – that is, live in a manner inconsistent with their espoused ideals – the more fundamental question that concerns us here is this: what outcomes ("fruits") should we rightly expect when the adherents ("shoots") live in a manner consistent with the "root" or authoritative "voice"? For example, does one's metaphysical or worldview concept promote or inhibit the recognition of human equality, education for all, information for the masses (not just social elites), affirm the dignity of the girl-child, support the equal worth of both high-caste Brahmins and those in the lowest or "backward" castes (*shudra*) or no-caste (*atishudra* or *dalit*), and care for the disabled and diseased (Wolf 2012, 2014)?

As we look at the world around us, we can detect some common threads being woven into a pattern we should not ignore. That is, the metaphysical roots of the biblical faith have issued forth in the fruits of modern science, human rights, bioethics, political democracy and other democratizing gains. I briefly review these below.

Modern science

Though not related to religious liberty, modern science is significant, as it raises the broader metaphysical and historical considerations of how a worldview shapes a certain practice. A common cultural myth is that belief in God and the practice of sound science are inherently conflicting enterprises. This is unfortunate. Indeed, the "warfare" model of God and science is a relatively recent invention that has been fairly well rejected by historians of science (e.g., Lindberg 2003).

Modern science arose through belief in a rational God who created a predictable, orderly universe that could be studied by rational humans made in God's image. Even the Bible-reading shapers of modern science were not deterred from their study of nature given their acceptance of the miraculous – public displays of divine action in the world not predictable by natural processes. (For credible – including medical – documentation of hundreds of miraculous accounts in today's world and throughout church history, see Keener 2011.) Indeed, divinely appointed authorities cited in the Bible routinely – and quite often incidentally and even off-handedly – appeal to publicly verifiable and accessible signs and the role of eyewitnesses as (at least partial) vindication of their message (see, for example, Deuteronomy 34:11; Acts 2:32 ["we are all witnesses", 3:15, 5:32, 10:39, 26:26 ["this has not been done in a corner"]; Romans 15:18–19; 1 Corinthians 15:3–9, 13–14; 2 Corinthians 12:12 ["signs and wonders and miracles" that were "performed among you"]; and Hebrews 2:2–4 ["{the gospel message} confirmed to us...both by signs and wonders and miracles"]). According to

St. Paul's argument for the historicity of Jesus' bodily resurrection, if Jesus' body rotted in the tomb, then the Christian faith is false and Christians are false witnesses (1 Corinthians 15:12–19).

Such appeals to publicly accessible evidence and eyewitness testimony underscore the biblical faith as a knowledge tradition. And the common biblical appeal to miracles as public evidences to reinforce the Bible's revelatory status highlights the importance of historicity, objectivity, reason, empirical observation and (in principle) falsification – a unique feature among traditional world religions – which is also quite in keeping with many of the ideals of modern science.

J. J. Thomson, who identified and characterized the electron and was the Cavendish Professor of Physics at Cambridge University, placed over his door in the Cavendish Laboratory a verse from the Bible: "Great are the works of the LORD. They are studied by all who delight in them" (Psalm 111:2). Other biblically inspired pillars of modern science include Isaac Newton, Johannes Kepler, Nicholas Copernicus, Galileo Galilei, Robert Boyle, Michael Faraday, James Clerk Maxwell, William Henry Perkin, George Stokes and William Thomson/Lord Kelvin. Indeed, remove them, and we have virtually nothing left (Schaefer 2013, 7–33). Even Charles Darwin himself, in his *On the Origin of Species*, makes reference to "laws impressed on matter by the Creator," who "originally breathed" life "into a few forms or into one" (Darwin 1860, 460, 459).

Noted physicist Paul Davies makes this connection between science and religion clear: "Science began as an outgrowth of theology, and all scientists, whether atheists or theists...accept an essentially theological worldview" (Davies 1995, 96). Famed scientist Robert Oppenheimer likewise attributes the growth of modern science to the Christian faith, observing that the study of science was a Christian expression of good "works" – an effort and a "duty" to better the human condition (Oppenheimer 1962, 5). Sociologist Rodney Stark points out that the roots of science have "rested entirely on religious foundations, and the people who brought it about were devout Christians" (Stark 2005, xi; see also Jaki 1988).

Human rights

The modern doctrine of human rights is closely connected to belief in the existence of a good God and humans made in God's image (Genesis 1:26–28). Historically, the cradle for human rights discourse has been the biblical worldview (Stark 2005; Reed 2007). America's Declaration of Independence (1776) emphasizes that God is the foundation for human dignity and worth: "All men are created equal, that they are endowed by their Creator with certain unalienable rights." These include life, liberty and the pursuit of happiness – the latter being the pursuit of well-being and virtue and freedom of thought (McCullough 2003). France's Declaration of the Rights of Man and of the Citizen (1789) acknowledges these rights in the presence of "the Supreme Being." Both of these documents indicate a deep connection between God, human dignity, and rights.

The influential figure behind such landmark social contracts is philosopher John Locke, who himself grew up under the influence of a Calvinistic (Puritan)

Protestantism. He wrote that "all mankind" are "all equal and independent" and that "no one ought to harm another in his life, health, liberty, or possessions." The reasoning behind this is that all humans are "the workmanship of one omnipotent, and infinitely wise maker" (Locke 1960, 271).

Another leading document is the United Nations Universal Declaration on Human Rights (1948). Forged in the wake of Nazi and Japanese atrocities during World War II, it affirms "the inherent dignity" and "the equal and inalienable rights of all members of the human family." Harvard's Mary Ann Glendon documents how the chief movers behind this document were church coalitions and individual Christian leaders such as the Lebanese Orthodox Christian Charles Habib Malik, who helped draft the document and who would later become the United Nations' General Secretary and work closely with some Jewish rabbis (Glendon 2001). Princeton human rights scholar Max Stackhouse makes the strong point that "intellectual honesty demands recognition of the fact that what passes as 'secular,' 'Western' principles of basic human rights developed nowhere else than out of key strands of the biblically rooted religion" (Stackhouse 2004, 2005).

Bioethics

Connected to the theme of human rights is the development of the bioethics movement. The beginning of this movement ("fruits") was led by strategic shapers ("shoots") who were themselves inspired by the biblical worldview that affirms that all humans being are made in God's image ("roots"). The Tuskegee syphilis experiments (1932–1972) and the *Roe v. Wade* abortion decision (1973) prompted Daniel Callahan (a founder of the modern bioethics movement and co-founder of the Hastings Center) to say that when he first began the movement, the only resources available were theological and "heavily shaped by religion" (Callahan 1990, 2–4).

Though bioethics has become more secularized since then, Albert R. Jonsen's account of the "birth of bioethics" gives chief credit to the "Judeo-Christian religious tradition" and its emphasis on the sanctity of life (Jonsen 1998, 7). Ethicist, bioethics pioneer and Methodist professor Paul Ramsey stated that human value is "ultimately grounded in the value God is placing on it" and that the fetus and the adult human have an equal sanctity: "No one is ever much more than a fellow fetus" (Ramsey 1971, 12–13). Biblical theism has provided a suitable worldview context for bioethics (see Copan 2013b).

Political democracy, moral reforms, and education

Political scientist Robert Woodberry of the National University of Singapore has marshalled impressive documentation showing how "conversionary Protestant" Christians – that is, "missionaries" – have been uniquely responsible for remarkable democratizing gains throughout the world. Here are some of them: "the development and spread of religious liberty, mass education, mass printing, volunteer organizations, most major colonial reforms [including abolishing slavery, widow-burning, foot binding, female circumcision, marriage of pre-pubescent girls, etc.], and the codification of legal protections for nonwhites in the nineteenth and early twentieth centuries" (Woodberry 2012, 244–245; see also Mangalwadi 2012; Schmidt 2004).

During this period, European Protestant missionaries often sought to protect indigenous peoples from abusive colonial powers. They were selected to act as judges to punish or reprimand military officials or magistrates in cases of murder, land seizure and forced labor. These missionaries sought to apply the same legal standards for whites and non-whites. They often documented atrocities through detailed information, later through photographs. Without Protestant missionaries and ministers, mobilizing mass protests would have been difficult. These missionaries helped create a kind of "cocoon in which non-violent, indigenous political movements could develop" to press for democracy and decolonialization (Woodberry 2012, 254).

The documentation for the impact of Protestant missionaries throughout the world is quite thorough, and the results are clear and persuasive. Woodberry challenges his readers to look at any map: where Protestant missionaries have been, there you will find more printed books and more schools per capita. And you will discover that in Africa, the Middle East, and parts of Asia, "most of the early nationalists who led their countries to independence graduated from Protestant mission schools" (cited in Dilley 2014, 41).

Wherever these Protestant missionaries would go, the following phenomena would invariably accompany them: literacy and education (to promote the reading of "God's Word" – the Bible), mass printing and print technology (in order to spread God's Word), and democracy / civil society (the result of educating all rather than merely social elites). Woodberry's research also shows that countries with more Protestants are more democratic and have more stable democratic transitions (Woodberry 2012). This is not surprising, given the democratizing roots of the Protestant Reformation. Protestantism emphasized the priesthood of every believer before God; the right of every believer to study the Bible for himself in his own language; and the appropriateness of pursuing any honest vocation to the glory of God (see Ozment 1980, 182–438; 1991; see also Wolf 2014).

Woodberry's claims concerning Protestant missionaries as moral and social change agents have held up under rigorous scrutiny, which has repeatedly tested his theory and its many variables. The summary article of his findings in the *American Political Science Review* required an additional 192 pages of supporting documentation. And this article has received several awards, including the prestigious Luebbert Article Award in 2012 for the best article in comparative politics (Dilley 2014, 41). Here is a summary of Woodberry's well-documented findings: "Areas where Protestant missionaries had a significant presence in the past are on average more economically developed today, with comparatively better health, lower infant mortality, lower corruption, greater literacy, higher educational attainment (especially for women), and more robust membership in nongovernmental associations" (Dilley 2014, 39).

4. Influence on human rights discourse: Ancient Greece, Renaissance, or Enlightenment?

Various scholars have suggested that historical roots *other* than the biblical worldview – namely, ancient Greek "democracy," the Renaissance, or the Enlightenment – sufficiently explain modern democracy and human rights discourse. Let us review them briefly.

Ancient Greece

Greece's elitist version of democracy was very different from modern democracy. In Book 5 of his *Republic*, Plato argued for the rule of philosopher-kings; ordinary citizens were not capable of such rule. He advocated selective breeding between philosopher-kings and intelligent women to create intelligent offspring. As for Aristotle, he believed that some humans were slaves by nature: "A slave is an animated tool, and a tool an inanimate slave, whence there is nothing in common" between the master and the slave (*Nicomachean Ethics* 8.11; also *Politics* 1.14). Both thinkers considered manual labor undignified – a kind of semi-slavery. Furthermore, the writings of Greek philosophers such as Plato and Aristotle were widely read in the medieval Muslim world, though without the democratizing effects therein.

Agnostic philosopher Luc Ferry offers this summary:

> The Greek world was fundamentally an aristocratic world, a universe organised as a hierarchy in which those most endowed by nature should in principle be "at the top," while the less-endowed saw themselves occupying inferior ranks. And we should not forget that the Greek city-state was founded on slavery.
>
> (Ferry 2011, 72–73)

Likewise, philosopher Peter van Inwagen reminds us that "we must remember that no Greek *polis*, if it existed today, would be described as a democracy" (van Inwagen 1994, 55–56). Indeed, the "concept of universal human rights and its embodiment in working constitutions and the rule of law (law as opposed both to the momentary will of the sovereign and unalterable custom)" are in his view the result of Christian influence. Ancient Greece, then, with Athens as the "cradle of democracy" is inadequate to account for modern human rights and the notion of equality before the law.

Renaissance

Certain scholars have appealed to the paganized "humanism" of the Renaissance (1300–1550) as the historical soil in which individual human rights gained traction. Swiss historian Jakob Burckhardt, for instance, has claimed that Renaissance "humanism" was an anthropological decentering of the theological, but this thesis is incorrect. Late Renaissance scholar Paul Oskar Kristeller effectively showed that the Renaissance was fundamentally Christian in its outlook, concluding that the "view that the humanist movement (of the Renaissance) was essentially pagan or anti-Christian cannot be sustained" (Kristeller 1961, 74).

"Humanism" was a cultural and educational program whose rallying cry was "*Ad fontes!*" – "To the sources!" of Greek and Latin literature. This program comprised grammar, rhetoric, poetry, history and moral philosophy – *studia humanitatis*, or what we would call *humanities*, which was taught by a *humanista*; it was not a human-centered "philosophical tendency or system" (Kristeller 1961, 10). Indeed, the only philosophical discipline in the humanities was moral philosophy. Thus logic, natural philosophy (what later came to be called "science"), metaphysics, theology and law were not included in humanism. This, according to Kristeller, furnishes "irrefutable evidence against repeated attempts to identify Renaissance humanism with the philosophy, the science, or the learning of the period as a whole" (Kristeller 1961, 10; see also Kristeller 1965).

This return to the sources was not only to classical Greek and Latin literary sources, but to the Bible and the writings of the church fathers as well (Kristeller 1961, 75). The Renaissance was a "fundamentally Christian age" (Kristeller 1961, 73), and few, if any, thinkers "seriously thought of reviving ancient pagan cults" (Kristeller 1961, 74–75). Noted Renaissance humanist Lorenzo Valla engaged in groundbreaking historical research that exposed the Donation of Constantine as a forgery. And though he opposed philosophical methods of medieval scholasticism, he was dedicated to Christian orthodoxy, which defended the Trinitarian doctrine (Trinkaus 1996). Valla even considered philosophy "the seedbed of heresy" (Trinkaus 1996, 28)!

When accused of theological compromise, the famed Florentine humanist Coluccio Salutati wrote in his defense of liberal studies: "Let the mob of philosophers run after Aristotle or Plato or the pestilent Averroes.…I am satisfied with Jesus Christ alone" (Salutati 1965, 17). We could add to this that 19th-century historian Henry Thode has made a persuasive case that Renaissance painting was strongly influenced by Francis of Assisi and the prominence he ascribed to God's creation (Thode 1904). Charles Trinkaus' study of Italian Renaissance humanism makes a strong case that the biblical view of the image of God as the basis for human dignity informed this intellectual movement: "Renaissance humanists… find it almost impossible to define man and to discuss him except in terms of his relationship to the nature of the divine and its influence and actions in this world. 'Anthropology' and 'theology' belong together in Renaissance thought" (Trinkaus 1995, 1.3). These Renaissance humanists "remained deeply religious" (Barzun 2000, 49), and their references to pagan mythology, history and geography were no more a theological compromise than those of the Puritan poet John Milton (Barzun 2000, 52).

The Enlightenment

What about the European Enlightenment as the historical grounding explanation for human rights? Some scholars have preferred this alternative, but again it is inadequate. Consider, for starters, how formative an influence was the Calvinist education or family background of the following Enlightenment-era democratic theorists and practitioners: Hugo Grotius, John Locke, Jean-Jacques Rousseau, Benjamin Franklin, John Adams, Patrick Henry, James Madison and Alexander Hamilton (Woodberry 2012, 248).

Even the US Constitution and Bill of Rights are modeled on previous colonial compacts that utilized theological and biblical terms – well before the publications of the notable social contract theorists Thomas Hobbes (1588–1679) and John Locke (1632–1704). The works of these social contractarian philosophers were not as groundbreaking as many have thought. These thinkers were preceded by Puritan and Protestant Nonconformist arguments that pressed for the equality of all persons. As Woodberry points out: "Even between 1760 and 1805, political writings quoted the Bible more often than either Enlightenment or classical thinkers (34% versus 22% and 9%, respectively)" (Woodberry 2012, 248).

We have already noted how the Enlightenment's "secular" challenge to Europe's "religious wars" is a flawed rendering of the merits of secularism. These battles were far more political than sectarian.

Perhaps we should mention here that leading atheistic European intellectuals have acknowledged the close historical connection between the shaping influence of the biblical worldview and modern human rights discourse. Philosopher Jürgen Habermas acknowledges the inescapable and profound debt that human rights discourse, democracy and equality today owe to the biblical worldview:

> Christianity has functioned for the normative self-understanding of modernity as more than just a precursor or a catalyst. Egalitarian universalism, from which sprang the ideas of freedom and a social solidarity, of an autonomous conduct of life and emancipation, the individual morality of conscience, human rights, and democracy, is the direct heir to the Judaic ethic of justice and the Christian ethic of love. This legacy, substantially unchanged, has been the object of continual critical appropriation and reinterpretation. To this day, there is no alternative to it. And in light of current challenges of a postnational constellation, we continue to draw on the substance of this heritage. Everything else is just idle postmodern talk.
>
> (Habermas 2006, 150–151)

Likewise, the postmodern atheistic thinker Jacques Derrida made the same kind of affirmation about the Christian faith:

> Today the cornerstone of international law is the sacred, what is sacred in humanity. You should not kill. You should not be responsible for a crime against the sacredness, this sacredness of man as your neighbor...made by God or by God made man....In that sense, the concept of crime against humanity is a Christian concept and I think there would be no such thing in the law today without...the biblical heritage.
>
> (Derrida 2001, 70)

French philosopher Luc Ferry likewise affirms that the Christian idea of human equality was "unprecedented at the time, and one to which our world owes its entire democratic inheritance" (Ferry 2011, 72). Former Oxford (now Harvard) historian Niall Ferguson sees the same connection between Protestantism and six "killer apps" that propelled the West forward as a civilization: work ethic, civilizational competition, science, modern medicine, property rights and a free market. Indeed, this worldview has begun to influence rising economies like China's (Ferguson 2012).

Likewise, historian Stephen Hopgood asserts that the post-Enlightenment use of "human rights" has been a secularization of its biblical roots: "Humanism (the cultural precondition for Human Rights) was a secular replacement for the Christian god" (Hopgood 2013, x).

We should not be surprised that, because dedicated Christians follow a suffering Savior, they have often identified with the less fortunate, the disempowered and the suffering. Political scientist Guenter Lewy, an agnostic himself, offers this penetrating contrast between the mindset of the dedicated Christian and the ethic of the "secularist":

> Adherents of [a secularist] ethic are not likely to produce a Dorothy Day or a Mother Teresa. Many of these people love humanity but not individual human beings with all their failings and shortcomings. They will be found participating in demonstrations for causes such as nuclear disarmament but not sitting at the bedside of a dying person. An ethic of moral autonomy and individual rights, so important to secular liberals, is incapable of sustaining and nourishing values such as altruism and self-sacrifice.
>
> (Lewy 1996, 137)

Canadian Broadcasting Corporation (CBC) journalist Brian Stewart recounts his experience about the practical impact of the Christian faith, which persuaded him to embrace it:

> I've found there is no movement, or force, closer to the raw truth of war, famines, crises and the vast human predicament, than organized Christianity in action. And there is no alliance more determined and dogged in action than church workers, ordained and lay members, when mobilized for a common good. It is these Christians who are right "on the front lines" of committed humanity today and when I want to find that front, I follow their trail.
>
> It is a vast front, stretching from the most impoverished reaches of the developing world to the hectic struggle to preserve caring values in our own towns and cities. I have never been able to reach these front lines without finding Christian volunteers already in the thick of it, mobilizing congregations that care, and being a faithful witness to truth – the primary light in the darkness, and so often, the only light.
>
> Now this is something the media and government officials rarely acknowledge, for religion confuses many and anyway, we all like to blow our own horns. So front line efforts of Christianity do not usually produce headlines,

> and unfortunately this feeds the myth that the church just follows along, to do its modest bit.
>
> Let me repeat, I've never reached a war zone, or famine group or crisis anywhere where some church organization was not there long before me: sturdy, remarkable souls, usually too kind to ask: "What took you so long?"…
>
> …Now I came to this admiring view slowly and reluctantly. At the start of my career, I'd largely abandoned religion for I, too, regarded the church as a rather tiresome irrelevance. What ultimately persuaded me otherwise, and I took a lot of persuading, was the reality of Christianity's mission, physically and in spirit, before my very eyes…
>
> …I'm often asked if I lost belief in God covering events like Ethiopia, then called "the worst hell on earth." Actually, like others before me, it was precisely in such hells that I rediscovered religion. I saw so many countless acts of human love and charity, total respect for the most forsaken, for all life.
>
> (Stewart 2003)

Concluding remarks

In a 1988 speech, then British Prime Minister Margaret Thatcher offered an apt summary of what I have argued in this essay:

> The truths of the Judaeo-Christian tradition are infinitely precious, not only, as I believe, because they are true, but also because they provide the moral impulse which alone can lead to that peace, in the true meaning of the word, for which we all long….There is little hope for democracy if the hearts of men and women in democratic societies cannot be touched by a call to something greater than themselves. Political structures, state institutions, collective ideals – these are not enough….When all is said and done, the politician's role is a humble one….[The church's] success matters greatly – as much as to the temporal as to the spiritual welfare of the nation.
>
> (Thatcher 1998)

I believe Thatcher was correct, and historical research has borne out her point.

Human rights – including the right of religious liberty – are taken for granted by many who consider themselves "secular." Yet this brings us back to Nietzsche's madman, who was Nietzsche's mouthpiece emphasizing what God's absence truly entailed. His contemporaries who mocked him were unknowingly living off the borrowed metaphysical capital of a biblical worldview. Likewise, the "secularist" who adheres to a naturalistic worldview is doing some heavy *philosophical* and *historical* borrowing from the capital of the biblical faith; this worldview offers metaphysical grounds for human dignity and its attendant rights (including that of religious liberty), as well as a demonstrable historical connection between the affirmation of these rights and faithful Christians whose lives have had a leavening effect on the societies in which they have lived, particularly Western civilization. Thus, any discussion about religious liberty will be misguided if it fails to understand the rich biblical soil in which the aforementioned democratizing gains were nourished.

I have *not* tried to sketch out the practical outworkings of religious liberty in a pluralistic society or global village. I have only attempted to look at the *historical* connection between the biblical faith and remarkable humanizing, democratizing advances. Of course, I am assuming (and argue elsewhere) that theism – unlike naturalism – provides the metaphysical foundation to support human dignity (the image of God) and offers a historical connection to today's human rights discourse and important democratizing gains.

A few final remarks are now in order. First, though atheist Christopher Hitchens' claim that "religion poisons everything" is partly correct in pointing to abuses in the name of traditional "religion," *we should point out that much harm has been wrought by adherents to a naturalistic or atheistic ("secular") worldview.* As argued above, atheism or naturalism is not a neutral, default worldview by which all other worldviews or "religions" are to be judged. Naturalism has a metaphysic (materialism), an etiology (determinism) and an epistemology (scientism), and these positions must be argued for and defended, not simply presumed.

Second, *not all traditional religions are alike, and some are more likely to be a threat to human rights and religious liberty than others.* We have noted how the biblical faith is more conducive to the notion of religious liberty than, say, naturalism, which has no metaphysical room for intrinsic human dignity (and the rights derived from this status), rationality, free will, knowledge and the like (see Copan 2008, 2012, 2013a, 2013b and 2013c). By contrast, apart from the biblical worldview's robust metaphysical resources, the gift of the gospel message is freely offered, and it can be freely received or rejected (Proverbs 1:24; Isaiah 55:1–3; Matthew 23:37; John 6:37; 7:37–38); the gospel *invites* rather than coerces, which is fundamental to religious liberty. True enough, wrongs have been done in the name of Jesus by professing Christians, but such hypocrisy hardly entails the falsity of the claims and credentials of the Christian faith – a commonly committed genetic fallacy.

Another worldview significantly less conducive to the affirmation of universal human rights, including religious liberty, would be Islam, at least throughout its history and in much of its present condition. Though we can be grateful for many peace-loving, democratically minded Muslims, we should consider the broader worldview of Islam. Consider how Muhammad himself engaged in dozens of military campaigns, asserting in his farewell speech: "I was ordered to fight all men until they say, 'There is no God but Allah'"; his immediate successors continued to spread Islam in the same fashion – by military force – and in largely Christianized lands. Indeed, exactly 100 years after Muhammad's death, Muslims were battling against Charles Martel in Tours, France. In addition to Islam's military expansion under Muhammad, and then his successors, Islam's history has largely been one of the subjugation of "dhimmis" (see Ye'or 1985, 1997 and 2002), and Muslims by and large live under the long shadow of anti-apostasy laws. Islam's history and present condition evince a broad-based acceptance of capital punishment – at best ostracism from family and community – for those who apostatize from Islam (see the Quran, Surah 4:90–91 and Bukhari Hadith 9.84.57, in which Muhammad says, "Whoever changed his Islamic religion, then kill him"; see also Chapter 21 in Copan and Flannagan 2014, and Durie 2010). In Western and various other countries, freedom to de-convert from a "religion" is a basic human right; in the lion's share of Islamic communities, to do so is a basic human wrong.

Third, *reason is not the presumed domain of the self-proclaimed "secularist," who may give the impression of inhabiting a neutral, objective, unbiased "default position."* Professing adherents to *any* worldview can do great harm – whether naturalist, Christian, Hindu or Buddhist. Thus the practitioners of any worldview should, in humility, take seriously historical, philosophical/rational and ethical scrutiny – whether from within or without. *Any* worldview adherent would benefit from such deeper self-scrutiny and cross-examination. An atheist or agnostic, Buddhist or Christian, should give thoughtful consideration to the degree to which her metaphysical foundations are adequate for explaining human value, what the worldview's historical defects or present inconsistencies are, and what her misunderstandings or misrepresentations of other views may be. As she seeks the truth, as she humbly and charitably engages with her detractors in conversation and friendship, as she candidly acknowledges deficiencies and problems in her worldview, she can truly profit from such self-examination and perhaps adjust – or even abandon – it.

An example of a needed worldview correction is the Crusades – and this applies to the adherent to the Christian faith and the outsider to the faith: we should abandon naïve acceptance of cultural, often-hackneyed myths surrounding this or that particular worldview. For example, a largely flawed interpretation that sees "Christian aggression" as having inspired the Crusades has become the received view, although Crusades historians such as Jonathan Riley-Smith and Thomas Madden have sought to correct it (Riley-Smith 2008, 2009; Madden 2013). Unfortunately, many of their well-grounded arguments have been unheard or ignored.

In a noteworthy cross-worldview conversation, atheist philosopher Jürgen Habermas and theologian Joseph Ratzinger affirmed the need for "reason" and "revelation" to engage with each other and to learn from one another. As noted above, Habermas humbly and freely acknowledges the West's indebtedness to the biblical faith that gave shape to democracy, equality before the law, and human rights discourse. And he points out that "philosophy has good reasons to be willing to learn from religious traditions" (Habermas and Ratzinger 2006, 42). He adds that the biblical concept of "man in the image of God" has now been translated into "the identical dignity of all men that deserves unconditional respect" – that is, "the substance of biblical concepts" has been made "accessible to a general public that also includes those who have other faiths and those who have none" (Habermas and Ratzinger 2006, 45).

For his part, Ratzinger points out "*pathologies in religion*" that are dangerous and require "the divine light of reason as a 'controlling organ.'" He goes on to say that "religion must continually allow itself to be purified and structured by reason, and this was the view of the Church Fathers too" (Habermas and Ratzinger 2006, 77).

Yet there are also "*pathologies of reason*" – expressions of human hubris like weapons of mass destruction that pose a severe threat to humanity, or like the degradation of humanity as a mere "product": "This is why reason, too, must be warned to keep within proper limits, and it must learn a willingness to listen to the great religious traditions of mankind. If it cuts itself completely adrift and rejects this willingness to learn, this relatedness, reason becomes destructive" (Habermas and Ratzinger 2006, 78).

Of course, Ratzinger takes "reason" to be some human or "secular" ideology. But again, the notion of "secular versus religious" is mistaken, vague and misleading. I have noted that *all* worldviews hold as ultimate a host of things – whether it is nature, science, self or God (however construed). As we have noted, *any* worldview proponent must be self-scrutinizing and self-correcting, utilizing the tools of philosophy, historical analysis and ethical scrutiny.

Fourth, *while God offers the best metaphysical foundation for human dignity / human rights, and while the lived-out biblical faith has clearly been the source of human rights discourse and other democratizing gains, one need not be a Bible believer to benefit from such foundations.* As we just cited from Habermas above, the biblical concepts of human dignity, rights, and respect have been made "accessible to a general public that also includes those who have other faiths and those who have none" (Habermas and Ratzinger 2006, 45). One need not be a Bible believer to know objective moral truths or to recognize human dignity and worth. Put in philosophical language, we can distinguish between the *ordo cognoscendi* ("the order of knowing") and the *ordo essendi* ("the order of being"). As it applies here, people can readily know or recognize human dignity or press for human rights, even though they are unaware of the actual metaphysical grounds for that dignity or for those rights.

Fifth, *this perspective on human rights is no mere "Western" understanding of human rights that "Easterners" cannot understand.* No, we are speaking about a fundamental universality that cuts across cultures. For one thing, even the charge of "ethnocentrism" suggests an objective (negative) universal value. Also, the biblical text itself emerged from the ancient Near *East* / Middle *East*. Further, despite differing metaphysical perspectives and communal concerns, surely Cambodian killing fields, Soviet gulags and Nazi concentration camps are rightly still a horror. All languages and nations have terms for and laws against "sacrilege, disrespect, lying, cheating, stealing, murder, rape, [and] exploitation" (Stackhouse 2002). We can think of a host of human dignity violations that humans can recognize even though they do not believe in a good, personal God: sexual slavery / human trafficking, honor killings of raped women, arbitrary imprisonment, forced military conscription of young boys, coerced "religious conversion," forced marriages, exploitation and oppression of ethnic groups, wife-beating. More positively, this universal dignity calls for the right to convert to another religious perspective or worldview, to form a family, to find a life's vocation or calling, to undergo a fair trial, and so on (Stackhouse 2005, 36–38).

Indeed, the biblical worldview not only offers a rich metaphysic for making sense of human dignity and thus human rights, it also, when faithfully lived out by adherents to the Scriptures, has made a pronounced moral difference in the world – a difference of which we are all beneficiaries, whether Bible believers or not.

Note

1 I would like to thank Thom Wolf, Paul Cliteur and Paul Tiedemann for their questions and comments on an earlier draft of this essay.

Bibliography

Aikman, David. 2003. *Jesus in Beijing: How Christianity Is Transforming China and Changing the Global Balance of Power*. Washington, DC: Regnery.

Baggett, Dave, and Jerry L. Walls. 2011. *Good God: The Theistic Foundations of Morality*. New York: Oxford University Press.

Barzun, Jacques. 2000. *From Dawn to Decadence*. New York: HarperCollins.

Beckwith, Francis J. 2006. "Taking Theology Seriously: The Status of Religious Beliefs of Judicial Nominees." *Notre Dame Journal of Law, Ethics and Public Policy* 20(1): 455–471.

Callahan, Daniel. 1990. "Religion and the Secularization of Bioethics." *Hastings Center Report* 20(4): 2–4.

Calvert, John H. 2013. "Human Rights in a Secular State Will Depend on its Legal Definition of Religion." In *Legitimizing Human Rights: Secular and Religious Perspectives*, ed. Angus J. L. Menuge. Burlington, VT: Ashgate, 103–125.

Cavanaugh, William. 2009. *The Myth of Religious Violence: Secular Ideology and the Roots of Modern Conflict*. Oxford: Oxford University Press.

Cliteur, Paul. 2010. *The Secular Outlook: In Defense of Moral and Political Secularism*. Oxford: Wiley-Blackwell.

Cliteur, Paul. 2013. "Theism and Human Rights." In *Legitimizing Human Rights: Secular and Religious Perspectives*, ed. Angus J. L. Menuge. Burlington, VT: Ashgate, 33–56.

Copan, Paul. 2008. "Theism, Naturalism, and the Foundations of Morality." In *The Future of Atheism: Alister McGrath and Daniel Dennett in Dialogue*, ed. Robert Stewart. Minneapolis: Fortress Press, 141–162.

Copan, Paul. 2012. "The Naturalists Are Declaring the Glory of God: Discovering Natural Theology in the Unlikeliest Places." In *Philosophy and the Christian Worldview: Analysis, Assessment and Development*, ed. David Werther and Mark D. Linville. New York: Continuum, 50–70.

Copan, Paul. 2013a. "Grounding Human Rights: Naturalism's Failure and Biblical Theism's Success." In *Legitimizing Human Rights: Secular and Religious Perspectives*, ed. Angus J. L. Menuge. Burlington, VT: Ashgate, 11–31.

Copan, Paul. 2013b. "A Protestant Perspective on Human Dignity." In *Human Dignity in Bioethics: From Worldviews to the Public Square*, ed. Stephen C. Dilley and Nathan J. Palpant. London: Routledge, 67–85.

Copan, Paul. 2013c. "Ethics Needs God." In *Debating Christian Theism*, ed. Chad V. Meister, Khaldoun A. Sweis, and J. P. Moreland. Oxford: Oxford University Press, 85–100.

Copan, Paul, and Matthew Flannagan. 2014. *Did God Really Command Genocide? Coming to Terms with the Justice of God*. Grand Rapids: Baker.

Darwin, Charles. 1860. *The Origin of Species.* New York: Thomas Y. Crowell.

Davies, Paul. 1995. *Are We Alone?* New York: Basic.

Derrida, Jacques. 2001. "To Forgive: The Unforgivable and Imprescriptible." In *Questioning God*, ed. John D. Caputo, Mark Dooley and Michael J. Scanlon. Bloomington, IN: Indiana University Press, 21–51.

Dilley, Andrea P. 2014. "The World the Missionaries Made." *Christianity Today* (January/February): 34–41.

Durie, Mark. 2010. *The Third Choice: Islam, Dhimmitude and Freedom.* n.p.: Deror Books.

Ferguson, Niall. 2012. *Civilization: The West and the Rest.* New York: Penguin.

Ferry, Luc. 2011. *A Brief History of Thought: A Philosophical Guide to Living.* New York: Harper Perennial.

Glendon, Mary Ann. 2001. *The World Made New: Eleanor Roosevelt and the Universal Declaration of Human Rights.* New York: Random House.

Griffiths, Paul J. 2001. *Problems of Religious Diversity.* Oxford: Blackwell.

Guinness, Os. 2012. *The Global Charter of Conscience.* Accessed October 21, 2016. http://www.osguinness.com/wp-content/uploads/2016/02/The-Global-Charter-of-Conscience.pdf.

Habermas, Jürgen. 2006. *Time of Transitions*, trans. Ciaran Cronin and Max Pensky. Cambridge: Polity.

Habermas, Jürgen and Joseph Ratzinger. 2006. *The Dialectics of Secularization: On Reason and Religion.* San Francisco: Ignatius.

Hare, John E. 2007. *God and Morality: A Philosophical History.* Oxford: Blackwell.

Hopgood, Stephen. 2013. *The Endtimes of Human Rights.* Ithaca, NY: Cornell University Press.

Jaki, Stanley. 1988. *The Savior of Science.* Washington, DC: Regnery.

Jonsen, Albert R. 1998. *The Birth of Bioethics.* Oxford: Oxford University Press.

Juergensmeyer, Mark. 1993. *The New Cold War? Religious Nationalism Confronts the Secular State.* Berkeley: University of California Press.

Juergensmeyer, Mark. 2000. *Terror in the Mind of God.* Berkeley: University of California Press.

Kant, Immanuel. 1996a. "Religion within the Boundaries of Mere Reason 1793." In *Religion and Rational Theology*, trans. Allen W. Wood and George Di Giovanni. Cambridge: Cambridge University Press, 39–216.

Kant, Immanuel. 1996b. "The Conflict of the Faculties 1798." In *Religion and Rational Theology*, trans. Allen W. Wood and George Di Giovanni. Cambridge: Cambridge University Press, 233–328.

Keener, Craig S. 2011. *Miracles: The Credibility of the New Testament Accounts*, 2 Vols. Grand Rapids: Baker.

Kimball, Charles. 2002. *When Religion Becomes Evil.* San Francisco: HarperCollins.

Kristeller, Paul O. 1961. *Renaissance Thought: The Classic, Scholastic, and Humanistic Strains.* New York: Harper and Row.

Kristeller, Paul O. 1965. "The Moral Thought of Renaissance Humanism." In *Renaissance Thought II: Papers on Humanism and the Arts.* New York: Harper and Row, 20–68.

Lewontin, Richard C. 1997. "Billions and Billions of Demons." *The New York Review of Books* (January 9). Accessed June 10, 2015. http://www.nybooks.com/articles/archives/1997/jan/09/billions-and-billions-of-demons/.

Lewy, Guenter. 1996. *Why America Needs Religion.* Grand Rapids: Eerdmans.

Lindberg, David. 2003. *When Science and Christianity Meet.* Chicago: University of Chicago Press.

Locke, John. 1960. *Two Treatises of Government*, ed. Peter Laslett. Cambridge: Cambridge University Press.

Madden, Thomas F. 2013. *The New Concise History of the Crusades.* Lanham, MD: Rowman and Littlefield.

Mangalwadi, Vishal. 2012. *The Book that Made Your World.* Nashville: Thomas Nelson.

Marks, Joel. 2015. "An Amoral Manifesto (Part 1)." *Philosophy Now* 80. Accessed October 21, 2016. https://philosophynow.org/issues/80/An_Amoral_Manifesto_Part_I.

McCullough, David. 2003. "The Course of Human Events." *The Jefferson Lecture*, National Endowment for the Humanities. Accessed March 5, 2013. http://www.neh.gov/about/awards/jefferson-lecture/david-mccullough-lecture.

Montgomery, John W. 1986. *Human Rights and Human Dignity.* Grand Rapids: Zondervan.

Nielsen, Kai. 1984. "Why Should I Be Moral? Revisited." *American Philosophical Quarterly* 21(1): 81–92.

Nietzsche, Friedrich. 1968. *Twilight of the Idols and the Anti-Christ.* New York. Penguin.

Nietzsche, Friedrich. 1974. *The Gay Science*, ed. Walter Kaufmann. New York: Vintage.

Oppenheimer, Julius R. 1962. "On Science and Culture." *Encounter* 19: 3–10.

Ozment, Steven. 1980. *The Age of Reform, 1250–1550: An Intellectual and Religious History of Late Medieval and Reformation Europe.* New Haven: Yale University Press.

Ozment, Steven. 1991. *Protestants: The Birth of a Revolution.* New York: Doubleday.

Pinker, Steven. 2006. "The Blank Slate." *The General Psychologist* 41(1): 1–8.

Plantinga, Alvin. 2010. "Naturalism, Theism, Obligation, and Supervenience." *Faith and Philosophy* 27(3): 247–272.

Ramsey, Paul. 1971. "The Morality of Abortion." In *Moral Problems: A Collection of Philosophical Essays*, ed. James Rachels. New York: Harper and Row, 1–27.

Rawls, John. 1999. *Theory of Justice*, 2nd ed. Cambridge: Harvard University Press.

Reed, Esther D. 2007. *The Ethics of Human Rights: Contested Doctrinal and Moral Issues.* Waco: Baylor University Press.

Riley-Smith, Jonathan. 2008. *The Crusades, Christianity, and Islam.* New York: Columbia University Press.

Riley-Smith, Jonathan. 2009. *What Were the Crusades?* 4th ed. San Francisco: Ignatius.

Russell, Bertrand. 1963. "A Free Man's Worship." In *Mysticism and Logic and Other Essays.* London: Allen and Unwin, 40–47.

Salutati, Coluccio. 1965. "Letter in Defense of Liberal Studies." In *The Italian Renaissance*, ed. Werner L. Gundersheimer. Englewood Cliffs, NJ: Prentice-Hall, 13–24.

Sartre, Jean-Paul. 1957. *Existentialism and Human Emotions.* New York: Philosophical Library.

Schaefer, Henry F. 2013. "Scientists and their Gods." In *Science and Christianity: Coherence or Conflict?* Athens, GA: University of Georgia Press, 7–33.

Schmidt, Alvin. 2004. *How Christianity Changed the World.* Grand Rapids: Zondervan.

Searle, John R. 2004. *Mind: A Brief Introduction.* Oxford: Oxford University Press.

Searle, John R. 1997. *The Mystery of Consciousness.* New York: New York Review of Books.

Smith, Christian. 2009. "Does Naturalism Warrant a Moral Belief in Universal Benevolence and Human Rights?" In *The Believing Primate: Scientific, Philosophical, and Theological Reflections on the Origin of Religion*, ed. Jeffrey Schloss and Michael J. Murray. Oxford: Oxford University Press, 292–317.

Stackhouse, Max L. 2002. "Covenantal Justice in a Global Era." *Lecture.* The Institute for Reformed Theology (January). Accessed October 21, 2016. http://reformedtheology.org/SiteFiles/PublicLectures/StackhousePL.html.

Stackhouse, Max L. 2004. "A Christian Perspective on Human Rights." *Society* 41(2): 23–28.

Stackhouse, Max L. 2005. "Why Human Rights Needs God: A Christian Perspective." In *Does Human Rights Need God?* ed. Elizabeth M. Bucar and Barbra Barnett. Grand Rapids: Eerdmans, 24–40.

Stark, Rodney. 2005. *The Victory of Reason*. New York: Random House.

Stewart, Brian. 2003. "Christians Are on the Front Lines of Compassion." Accessed June 10, 2015. http://www.reformedevangelism.com/library/library03-article-cbc.html.

Thatcher, Margaret. 1988. "Speech to the General Assembly of the Church of Scotland." Accessed June 5, 2015. http://www.margaretthatcher.org/document/107246.

Thode, Henry. 1904. *Franz von Assisi und die Anfänge der Kunst der Renaissance in Italien*. Berlin: G. Grote'sche.

Trinkaus, Charles. 1995. *In Our Image and Likeness: Humanity and Divinity in Italian Humanist Thought*, 2 Vols. Notre Dame: University of Notre Dame Press.

Trinkaus, Charles. 1996. "Lorenzo Valla on the Problem of Speaking about the Trinity." *Journal of the History of Ideas* 57(1): 27–53.

van Inwagen, Peter. 1994. "Quam Dilecta." In *God and the Philosophers: The Reconciliation of Faith and Reason*, ed. Thomas B. Morris. New York: Oxford University Press, 31–60.

Ward, Ian. 2004. *Introduction to Critical Legal Theory*, 2nd ed. Portland: Cavendish Publishing.

Wolf, Thom. 2012. "WV3: Worldvoice, Worldview, and Worldvenue." In *Social Change and Development: A Research Template*. New Delhi: University Institute, 13–23.

Wolf, Thom. 2014. "Development and its Implications for the Indian Social System: A WV3 Case Study of Jotirao Phule." *The National Seminar on Globalization and Social Development in India: Issues and Challenges*. New Delhi: University Institute.

Wolterstorff, Nicholas. 2012. "Christianity and Human Rights." In *Religion and Human Rights: An Introduction*, ed. John Witte, Jr. and M. Christian Green. Oxford: Oxford University Press, 42–55.

Woodberry, Robert D. 2012. "The Missionary Roots of Liberal Democracy." *American Political Science Review* 106(2): 244–274.

Ye'or, Bat. 1985. *The Dhimmi: Jews and Christians under Islam*. Teaneck, NJ: Fairleigh Dickinson University Press.

Ye'or, Bat. 1997. *The Decline of Eastern Christianity under Islam: From Jihad to Dhimmitude*. Teaneck, NJ: Fairleigh Dickinson University Press.

Ye'or, Bat. 2002. *Islam and Dhimmitude: Where Civilizations Collide*. Teaneck, NJ: Farleigh Dickinson University Press.

2 Thomas Jefferson and the pursuit of happiness

Rethinking what the right means for us today[1]

Laura Kittel

Pursuing happiness appears as a right alongside life and liberty in the US Declaration of Independence, but since the 18th century its significance has diminished in both theory and practice. Whereas the founders of America saw the pursuit as commensurate with an ethical approach to life and liberty, now society tends to see happiness as best quantified, measured and accumulated in material or psychological terms. Scholars today cite the right of pursuit in a variety of contexts, such as the science of subjective well-being (happiness), positive psychology, sociology and economics. Although many of these disciplines contribute to our knowledge of ethical behavior and altruism, their approach is different from that of philosophy and religion, so that what tends to legitimize ethics and altruism is their physiological impact on human beings, rather than their relationship to justice. For example, the United Nations (UN) *World Happiness Reports* (2012, 2013 and 2015) maintain that the scientific measurement of happiness is one of the most important considerations in understanding happiness, and that happiness can be "assessed, correlated with observable brain functions and related to the characteristics of an individual and the society" (Sachs 2012, 7–9). Rather than asking about how individuals' happiness relates to a just state of affairs in the world today, "[l]ooking over scientists' shoulders in their pursuit of happiness in human lives informs our personal pursuit of happiness" (Myers 1992, 16).

People are adept at viewing happiness from a variety of angles, especially over the shoulders of scientists, but not from the pursuit's original position in Western society in ethics, and in American society within the context of rights (as universal moral norms or entitlements that one has by virtue of being human).[2] Even the UN now "connects well-being and the pursuit of happiness" with sustainable development, rather than human rights (Un.org 2015a). Gone is Jefferson's voice that highlights the moral significance of pursuing happiness as a right, that humans must also factor into their personal calculations of desires that its pursuit is the equal right of other human beings as well. For the most part, people do not now see why viewing happiness outside rights and ethics could be problematic, or that, over time, the pursuit of happiness has indeed become problematic on account of being changed by these scientific and economic perspectives.

Happiness has gone from the *virtuous* pursuit of both personal priorities *and* the public good, to what Jeffrey Sachs identifies as the egoistic pursuit of hyper-commercialism (Sachs 2013, 91–92). This means that even if people pursue happiness in non-material ways, such as psychologically or socially, the economic approach still tends to predominate. While a broader vision of happiness is on the horizon, Sachs writes, "I would argue that the ethicists are still mostly overlooked" (Sachs 2013, 82). Indeed, in the *World Happiness Reports*, the UN leaves the discussion of ethics to economists, not moral philosophers. While investigating the change in the ethos of happiness from moral to amoral and immoral, then, the present inquiry invites reengagement with ethics by asking: how *ought* humanity to pursue happiness? We shall begin by looking over the shoulder of Thomas Jefferson.

The pursuit of happiness at the founding of America

When Jefferson penned the Declaration of Independence in 1776, he did not specify the exact meaning of pursuing happiness (McMahon 2006, 314), but Jefferson did have specific views on happiness, as did the Americans of his time. Though multifaceted, these views were also unifying. Jefferson explained that the Declaration's very strength lay in bringing together the "harmonizing sentiments of the day" and therefore the people as well:

> This was the object of the Declaration of Independence. Not to find out new principles, or new arguments, never before thought of, not merely to say things which had never been said before; but to place before mankind the common sense of the subject, in terms so plain and firm as to command their assent, and to justify ourselves in the independent stand we are compelled to take. Neither aiming at originality of principle or sentiment, nor yet copied from any particular and previous writing, it was intended to be an expression of the American mind, and to give to that expression the proper tone and spirit called for by the occasion. All its authority rests then on the harmonizing sentiments of the day, whether expressed in conversation, in letters, printed essays, or in the elementary books of public right, as Aristotle, Cicero, Locke, Sidney, &c.
>
> (Jefferson 1950, 802)

Jefferson gave voice to the American mind as a whole, even on the subject of happiness, and set its pursuit within the proper tone and spirit called for in creating a new nation. But what was the concept of happiness befitting such an occasion?

Jefferson's selected views on happiness

Jefferson's mention of Aristotle gives us our first clue. In *Nicomachean Ethics*, Aristotle defined happiness as "activity of soul exhibiting virtue, and if there are more than one virtue, in accordance with the best and most complete" (*NE* 1.7, 1098a.15–20). In his own copy of *Nicomachean Ethics*, Jefferson underlined that definition as well as Aristotle's observation that this happiness was "in a complete life" (O'Toole 2005, 28). Like the Greeks, Jefferson likely saw happiness as the aim or overall goal of life and, along with virtue, as touching every aspect of life. In other words, happiness was not a momentary emotion or discrete occurrence. Rather than being a thoroughgoing Aristotelian as one scholar argues, however, Jefferson more likely followed Aristotle's vision of happiness in general.[3] Based on his letters, Jefferson's thoughts on happiness were particularly shaped by John Locke, Jesus and Epicurus, the latter of whom was a younger contemporary of Aristotle in ancient Greece. In a letter to William Short, his private secretary, Jefferson writes: "I too am an Epicurian" (Jefferson 1975, 564). The founding father felt at home in the materialist metaphysics of Epicurus and included at the end of his letter a syllabus of Epicurean doctrines, some of which are:

> Happiness [is] the aim of life.
> Virtue [is] the foundation of happiness.
>
> | | | | | |
> |---|---|---|---|---|
> | Virtue consists in: | 1. Prudence | 2. Temperance | 3. Fortitude | 4. Justice |
> | to which are opposed: | 1. Folly | 2. Desire | 3. Fear | 4. Deceit. |
>
> (Jefferson 1975, 567)

Epicurean happiness sought the tranquility of the mind and the health of the body, aligning with medicine rather than with politics as in Aristotle; however, Epicurus still shared the wider Greek vision of happiness as living life in accordance with the virtues Jefferson outlines above (DeWitt 1947). [4]

The first issue of concern in ancient ethics is: "How ought I to live? or, What should my life be like?" (Annas 1993, 27). This question framed the discussion about happiness, which was acknowledged by most ancient Greeks and Romans as the aim of life. They saw the "good life" as one in which happiness was as a way of life founded on virtue, especially moral virtue. Other people could to a certain extent see whether one was living the good life, as the virtues were tangible behavioral manifestations. The good life was thus not so much a subjective evaluation of one's life as one that lent itself to an objective standard (by observing a code of ethics or a set of moral norms, which today could correspond to human rights). Many 18th-century Americans shared this objective orientation toward happiness, though it was Christianity that heavily influenced their views on living virtuously (McMahon 2006).

Today, however, happiness is predominantly seen not as an ethical way of life, but as an emotion, as a material possession, or as the fulfilment of personal desires. In contrast to the earlier philosophical formulation, psychologists now conceive of the "good life" as answering the question, "What is it that makes life desirable?" (Diener 2009, 1). Ed Diener, the American pioneer of contemporary happiness studies, reports that one answer "is that a person feels and thinks his or her life is desirable regardless of how others see it. This phenomenon has come to be called *subjective well-being*, which refers to the fact that the person subjectively believes his or her life is desirable, pleasant, and good" (Diener 2009, 1). According to this view, it no longer really matters that life is lived virtuously, that one's life exhibits virtue that is visible to others or that conforms to an objective moral standard. Virtue is no longer the foundation of happiness.

Ironically, happiness studies now center on desire, which Jefferson lists as the vice opposed to temperance. Rather than satisfaction of desires, however, for Jefferson happiness seems ultimately to be a pursuit: "Perfect happiness, I believe, was never intended by the Deity to be the lot of one of His creatures in this world; but that He has very much put in our power the nearness of our approaches to it, is what I have steadfastly believed" (Jefferson 2004, 7). The expression of the American mind has certainly changed over time. Where once the focus was wisely and virtuously striving for happiness, the focus has shifted to the issue of whether people have enough pleasant feelings or satisfied desires. The nation has forgotten its heritage.

Harmonizing sentiments of happiness

Recovering what 18th-century Americans thought about pursuing happiness is critical for a number of reasons, not least of which is that it does not resemble what Americans currently think about happiness. But unlike "cultural critics who wish to manipulate the past for the sake of the present," all we must do is history, to recreate the past on its own terms, and see in what ways it "does tell us how we might live in the world" (Wood 2009, 4). During this re-creation, a number of concepts will come to light that will be important for rethinking what happiness means for us as a society today. Although these concepts might seem too good to be true, they are not extrapolations or inventions; rather, they are rendered here as they appeared in history, or as close to it as can be discerned. In other words, a genuine interpretation of the past is sought, which could have the effect of informing us about how people might live better in the world today.

In 18th-century America, the Declaration of Independence expressed not only Thomas Jefferson's own thoughts, but those that were widely held among the people. According to historian Darrin McMahon, several concepts of happiness existed during that time and could overlap within the same person, as appears to be the case with Jefferson (McMahon 2006, 325). Let us now turn to four main strands of happiness.

Lockean liberalism

John Locke is seen as one of the major influences on the Declaration of Independence, with some thinkers hypothesizing that Jefferson substituted Locke's "property" with the "pursuit of happiness" so as to mask the founders' true materialistic intentions (McMahon 2006, 316–317). But as McMahon points out, Locke himself never listed property alongside life and liberty, though he did refer to estate and fortunes. The relationship between happiness and property was indeed a close one for many 18th-century Americans. Property even featured alongside happiness in several state constitutions: Virginia (1776), Pennsylvania (1776), Vermont (1777), Massachusetts (1780) and New Hampshire (1784). But happiness appears without property in the constitutions of Georgia (1777), North Carolina (1776), New Jersey (1776) and New York (1777) (McMahon 2006, 318–319). Property and happiness were not synonymous, and in the end happiness, not property, was chosen for the Declaration.

Locke discusses the pursuit of happiness in his *Essay Concerning Human Understanding* (1689), where human beings are to make a "careful and constant pursuit of true and solid happiness," to choose the good, which is furthermore the "necessary foundation of our *liberty*" (Locke 1975, 266). For Locke, happiness equals pleasure, though orientated toward Christian ends. It remains unclear, though, how individuals are supposed to overcome their hedonistic self-regard in order to pursue those Christian ends. Further complicating matters, Christianity defines happiness not as pleasure, but as knowing and loving God (Augustine) and ultimately as beholding God in the afterlife (Aquinas).

Characterized as pleasure, however, happiness gains sanction as a free pursuit in another of Locke's great works. In the *Two Treatises of Government* (1690), Locke argues that political power originally derives from people who are in "a *State of Perfect Freedom* to order their Actions, and dispose of their Possessions, and Persons as they think fit, within the bounds of the Law of Nature, without asking leave, or depending upon the Will of any other Man" (Locke 1970, 287). Government is supposed to facilitate this freedom and preserve as much of it as possible. Notwithstanding Locke's thoughts on careful discernment in the quest for true happiness, then, the pursuit of personal pleasure however people see fit was born. This is the current definition of happiness according to Lockean liberalism.

Classical republicanism

Historians contend that Aristotle, Cicero and Algernon Sidney, whom Jefferson includes above among the day's "harmonizing sentiments," have in common the tradition of classical republicanism. The Greek philosopher, Roman Stoic, and English politician, respectively, were part of a "language of liberty" that extended through history, which promoted liberty as "active devotion to the public good (civic virtue)" (McMahon 2006, 323–324). In contrast to Locke's focus on the individual's pleasure and freedom from constraints, according to classical republicanism participating in public life for the good of others leads to both individual and social happiness. Classical republicans saw the egotism and hedonism that could arise from the individual's pursuit of pleasure as a threat to the well-being of the person and society. As Darrin McMahon (2006) reports, their vision of happiness often involved self-sacrifice and willingness to withstand pain.

The republican vision of social relations transformed American society during the American Revolution (1775–1783), which, historian Gordon Wood (1991, 6) argues, created a culture that was not only different from that of colonial times, but that was unique in the world. The Revolution involved not only the overthrow of Great Britain's rule of the 13 colonies and the establishment of the United States, but a transformation of thought among the people regarding the type of society they wished to establish in furtherance of their rights. Americans wanted to supplant the "kinship, patriarchy and patronage" of British monarchical society with new egalitarian "bonds of love, respect, and consent," and to set up a government based on moral virtue and impartial leadership (Wood 1991, 229–230). Many 18th-century Americans agreed that personal desire needed limits and that people should not focus only on themselves. At the same time, leaders began to question whether people possessed the virtue necessary to follow through with these changes. People were becoming competitive, individualistic and self-absorbed. Wood explains that the "[e]xpectations of raising one's standard of living – if only to buy new consumer goods – seeped deeper and deeper into the society and had profound effects on the consciousness of ordinary people" (Wood 1991, 229–230). He thus concludes that "the Revolution was the source of its own contradictions." As with Lockean liberalism, tension in republican values was evident from the beginning.

Selected Enlightenment ideas

Still, active devotion to the public good was seen as an important value within society, and there were other strands of thought besides classical republicanism that promoted this value. Among them were Enlightenment theories such as Francis Hutcheson's "moral sense." Hutcheson expanded Locke's views on sensation, adding to touch, taste, sight, smell and sound the idea that human beings have a "moral sense, a capacity to respond pleasurably to goodness in others and in ourselves" (McMahon 2006, 326). This theory maintained that people could most reliably ensure their own happiness by behaving virtuously toward others. Hutcheson's Lockean formulation and the notion that one could enjoy virtue and pleasure at the same time resonated with many Americans. Further accounting for its appeal, moral sense theory reaffirmed the view that, when human beings live in environments free from superstition, prejudice and ignorance, they are more readily able to express benevolence toward one another (McMahon 2006).

Other ideas, especially from the Scottish Enlightenment, which included not only Hutcheson, but David Hume and Adam Smith as well, were also influential during this period. Smith, the purported father of capitalism, observes in the *Theory of Moral Sentiments* (1759) that wealth does not produce real and lasting happiness, though the illusion that wealth does drives the progress of civilization (McMahon 2006, 328–329). He describes the phenomenon in terms of the poor man's son, who gives up peace and contentment to pursue the wealth he thinks will lead to happiness, only to discover in old age after his body is wasted and his mind "galled and ruffled" that "wealth and greatness are mere trinkets of frivolous utility no more adapted for procuring ease of body or tranquility of mind than the tweezer cases of the lover of toys" (Smith 1853, 259–261). Throughout his life, the son did not stop to "consider what it is that is really wanting to his happiness" (Smith 1853, 262).

Christianity

Although Christianity is not explicitly referred to in Jefferson's (1950) letter to Henry Lee as an influence on the Declaration, it is undeniably one of the major influences of the day. Jefferson even mentioned the Creator as the one who bestows upon us our inalienable rights. Many Americans saw Jesus' teachings on morality and happiness as authoritative for their own pursuits. Jefferson himself thought that from Jesus "we have the outlines of a system of the most sublime morality which has ever fallen from the lips of man" (Jefferson 1975, 565). Throughout the nation, Christian pastors in their sermons "linked social welfare and the pursuit of happiness to the pursuit of Christian ethics" (McMahon 2006, 322). Whereas Christianity previously emphasized happiness that would be obtained in the afterlife, during this period happiness was brought down to earth and God was seen as its guarantor. People could have happiness in this life by cultivating their moral qualities, living an upright life and relying on God. Moreover, "they concurred that to think of happiness without love of one's neighbor – without Christian charity, denial, and constraint – was profane" (McMahon 2006, 322). The religion played a significant role in the success of the new nation, an idea that will be explored in more depth below. First, however, we will look at how these four concepts functioned together in early American society.

Double meaning of the pursuit of happiness

There were many ways of formulating the pursuit of happiness at the founding of America, but together they held a double meaning: one of private freedoms and pleasures, and the other of civic virtue for the sake of others. Classical virtue, republican values, the moral sense and religious faith regulated Lockean liberalism and the unfettered pursuit of a happiness often understood as self-centered satisfaction. Many 18th-century Americans thought it imperative to have a public-minded pursuit of happiness so that people did not become engrossed in their own concerns at the expense of the society they were creating, regardless of which of these virtuous, altruistic lines of thought they followed (McMahon 2006, 330–331).

While there was tension at the outset between personal liberty and public good in the pursuit of happiness, including the risk that people would choose only the personal version, the idea that private interests and public welfare could be harmonized with one another was not a problem for many, including Thomas Jefferson. Darrin McMahon explains that Jefferson's belief "reflected a wider eighteenth-century assumption and article of faith: that individual interest and the greater good, private and public happiness, could be reconciled" (McMahon 2006, 330–331). In the 20th century, this article of faith would be challenged, especially by postmodern thinkers. Jacques Derrida (1986) deals directly with the US Declaration in "Declarations of Independence," but challenges a different article of faith. Richard Rorty, on the other hand, more directly targets the 18th-century notion that reconciliation between private and public is possible in his book

Contingency, Irony, and Solidarity (1989). Rorty (1989, xv) proposes that "we drop the demand for a theory which unifies the public and private" and be "content to treat the demands of self-creation and of human solidarity as equally valid, yet forever incommensurable." Today, many Americans, like Rorty, see the private and public realms as representing two "truths" that are fundamentally incompatible with one another; they see their own quest for happiness as something unrelated to or superseding public welfare, something which I will demonstrate below.

Divorcing private from public happiness was not the intention of the generation of people that founded America, leaders and lay alike. Nor was it the legacy they wanted to leave future generations, since they realized that such a mentality would have corrosive effects on society. Each individual, rather, was responsible for regulating the inherent tension between their personal interests and the public good. While Jefferson and the other founders intended to provide people with the freedom to pursue happiness however they chose, the founders also charged them with restraining themselves in that pursuit and actively working toward the public good – not only their own interests (McMahon 2008, 89). For "a disinterested devotion to the public cause first achieved [our independence] and a disinterested sacrifice of private interests will now maintain [it]" (Jefferson 2004, 43). The ethos of happiness during the 18th century was one of regular and accommodating self-discipline, properly ordering desires, and practicing moral virtues such as those Jefferson listed above: prudence, temperance, fortitude and justice. Individuals were tasked with mediating their passions and resolving any conflicts they had between their own interests and the public's welfare (McMahon 2006, 327–331). Furthermore, this mediation was seen not as an undue burden, but a normal, logical part of life. At the nation's beginning, the pursuit of happiness was established on virtue – not self-interest or personal pleasure – thereby imparting a solid foundation to liberty and to life.

A culture of self-interest rightly understood supported by the spirit of religion

When French political theorist Alexis de Tocqueville visited America (1831–1832), he found that these values manifested themselves in the form of two principles that seemed to account in large part for the nation's success: (1) the "principle of self-interest rightly understood" and (2) the "spirit of religion" (Tocqueville 1952, 392–397, 229–255; McMahon 2006, 338). The expectation that people would sacrifice some of their private interests for the sake of others was not unreasonable or idealistic; in 18th-century America, it was actual practice. Tocqueville explains in *Democracy in America* (1835) that, wherever he went, Americans "almost always manage to combine their own advantage with that of their fellow citizens" (Tocqueville 1952, 392). People were aware that they could not escape the influence of their individual egos, but were devoted to directing their own interests toward the benefit of others. "They therefore do not deny that every man may follow his own interest," Tocqueville elaborates, "but they endeavor to prove that it is in the interest of every man to be virtuous" (Tocqueville 1952, 392).

Remarkably, happiness was pursued according to the principle of self-interest rightly understood:

> The Americans, on the contrary, are fond of explaining almost all the actions of their lives by the principle of [self-]interest rightly understood; they show with complacency how an enlightened regard for themselves constantly prompts them to assist each other, and inclines them willingly to sacrifice a portion of their time and property to the welfare of the State.
>
> (Tocqueville 1952, 393)

Tocqueville further notes that people were more concerned with living a life that was true to their altruistic philosophy than with honoring themselves.

On a daily basis, individuals demonstrated that the success of others was integral to their own success by undertaking small acts of self-sacrifice:

> The principle of [self-]interest rightly understood is not a lofty one, but it is clear and sure...it lies within the reach of all capacities, everyone can without difficulty apprehend and retain it...[The principle] produces no great acts of self-sacrifice, but it suggests daily small acts of self-denial. By itself it cannot suffice to make a man virtuous, but it disciplines a number of citizens in habits of regularity, temperance, moderation, foresight, self-command; and, if it does not lead men straight to virtue by the will, it gradually draws them in that direction by their habits.
>
> (Tocqueville 1952, 393–394)

Significantly, Tocqueville regarded the principle of self-interest rightly understood to be America's main insurance against the pursuit of happiness deteriorating into self-centered hedonism, and thus the decline of society, wherein people would act predominantly on the basis of their own interests (Tocqueville 1952, 394–395). In the future, this logic would be reversed as the pursuit of happiness would come to be defined by self-centered hedonism, which would be billed as an improvement on the economy and society. By the 20th century, acting almost solely on the basis of one's own interests would come to be seen as normal and unproblematic.

Returning to Tocqueville's 18th-century observations, it is important to note that he credits, in addition to self-interest rightly understood, the Christian "spirit of religion" with the flourishing of democracy in America. In his view, one of the reasons for this was that, while the political world was often unpredictable, the moral world remained "fixed and determinate" (Tocqueville 1952, 234). Tocqueville was struck by the fact that Christianity and liberty were passionately intertwined in the American mind and even buttressed one another, with faith enabling people to use their liberty wisely (18th-century philosophers had predicted the demise of religion with the rise of liberty, but America disproved that theory). Christianity's egalitarianism also prepared people for democratic institutions. Further, the faith inspired people to behave morally in their dealings, restrain their desire for earthly pleasures, and orient themselves toward the future, infusing life with a steadfast hope that "work[ed] 'as much in favor of happiness in this world as of felicity in the next'" (McMahon 2006, 340–341).

Religious liberty

Curious about what caused religion to thrive alongside liberty – in France, the two were opposed – Tocqueville interviewed Roman Catholic priests, who informed him that the success of religion was due to religious liberty, or the separation of church and state (Tocqueville 1952, 234–238). Unlike their counterparts in Europe, American religious leaders did not exercise political power: they did not hold public office, were not represented in the legislature, and did not engage in public debate. Pastors were content with keeping faith separate from politics. They discovered that, in people's lives, faith flourished of its own accord without being imposed on them by the state. Tocqueville concluded that religion did not need political power to survive and that it was actually stronger without it: "[Religion, rather than politics,] is the only one of them that can hope for immortality; but if [religion is] connected with their ephemeral [political] authority, it shares their fortunes, and may fall with those transient passions which supported them for a day" (Tocqueville 1952, 234–239).

Establishing religious liberty in the new nation was also a project dear to Thomas Jefferson, so much so that among the three accomplishments he wanted emblazoned on his tombstone was his authorship of the Virginia Statute for Religious Freedom (1786), which was a precursor to the First Amendment of the US Constitution.[5] Prior to the American Revolution (1775–1783), numerous colonies possessed established religions that regulated life among their inhabitants, outlawed certain denominations, and punished people with imprisonment or execution for unorthodox beliefs, even after the conclusion of the Revolutionary War. The Church of England in Virginia, for example, made the presence of Quakers in the state illegal; the assembly punished heretics with burning; and those who denied or struggled with their faith could, among other things, be sentenced to three years in prison (Jefferson 1999, 392–393). Jefferson wrote passionately for toleration and freedom of conscience, arguing that people's rights did not depend on their religious beliefs. He observed wryly: "I doubt whether the people of this country would suffer an execution for heresy, or a three years imprisonment for not comprehending the mysteries of the trinity" (Jefferson 1999, 396). Jefferson and Tocqueville show that instituting religious freedom in the new nation was vital to the success of the American experiment. It can be inferred that religious liberty remains integral to the well-being of a diverse population, as well as the pursuit of happiness.

Christianity fortified the pursuit of happiness with a proper orientation and a fixed moral foundation, where happiness was seen primarily as loving God and one's neighbor. From the standpoint of the 1700s, the question remained whether the religious spirit and the principle of self-interest rightly understood would continue in the future to help people rein in their passions, cultivate healthy desires, and serve one another, or whether, as many great thinkers of the day feared, pursuing happiness would devolve into singular concern for personal interests. Tocqueville was reasonably optimistic, but also troubled by the prospect. Once people take their eyes off God and their neighbor, he thought, they turn inward, finding the pull of their own prosperity and pleasures irresistible (McMahon 2006, 341). Tocqueville observed presciently:

> When the taste for physical gratifications among them has grown more rapidly than their education…the time will come when men are carried away and lose all self-restraint at the sight of the new possessions they are about to obtain. In their intense and exclusive anxiety to make a fortune they lose sight of the close connection that exists between the private fortune of each and the prosperity of all. It is not necessary to do violence to such a people in order to strip them of the rights they enjoy; they themselves willingly loosen their hold.
>
> (Tocqueville 1997)

Jefferson likewise surmised that the spirit of the times would change. In arguing for establishing religious liberty while the country was still united on principle after the Revolutionary War, he wrote:

> [People] will forget themselves, but in the sole faculty of making money, and will never think of uniting to effect a due respect for their rights. The shackles, therefore, which shall not be knocked off at the conclusion of this war, will remain on us long, will be made heavier and heavier, till our rights shall revive or expire in a convulsion.
>
> (Jefferson 1999, 396)

Unfortunately for future generations, the meaning of the right to pursue happiness was not fixed during this time as were other rights.

The right of pursuing happiness expires in a convulsion

After the 18th century, Lockean liberalism began to evolve beyond Locke's initial ideas and was gradually set free from the constraints of classical republicanism, Enlightenment moral sense, and Christianity to embody the pursuit of personal pleasure however people see fit. In the second *World Happiness Report* (Sachs 2013, 81), economist Jeffrey Sachs explains that the quest for happiness shifted from virtue ethics to consumerism after the turn of the 18th century. Whereas the pursuit once signified people developing their character, devoting time and attention to others, and striving to live virtuously, during the 18th and 19th centuries the quest for happiness deteriorated into the singular pursuit of personal pleasures and economic interests. As economics took over the pursuit, it was discovered that people's greed could be utilized to fuel growth, so loosening self-restraint was encouraged; then the idea that greed could be regarded as a vice at all was undermined; and finally the idea of vices like greed were dispensed with altogether

(Sachs 2013, 91). Jefferson's prediction that people would forget themselves in the sole faculty of making money seems to have come to pass, as did the demise of the pursuit of happiness as a right or a universal moral norm. A claim to the natural right still exists, but the reality of the right in everyday life has been divested of meaning: happiness is no longer associated with virtue, ethics and duties, but rather with vice, egoism, materialism and hedonism. As I will argue in the next section, happiness as a right "expired in a convulsion" (to borrow Jefferson's words), the extent of which people are barely cognizant of today, although it represents a catastrophic loss of values.

Over time, virtue was replaced as the foundation of happiness by the economic doctrine of utility and a corresponding ethos of consumerism. Prior to this transition, John Stuart Mill, along with Tocqueville, noted that even in the midst of abundance there was a restlessness to the American pursuit (a feature common to the human endeavor in general, but particularly acute in America), which Mill attributed to rising commercialism. Even though Mill was a "prophet" of the free market (Galbraith 1978, xii–xiv) and a "defender of classical liberalism" (McMahon 2006, 345), he warned that "the most serious danger to the future prospects of mankind is in the unbalanced influence of the commercial spirit" (Mill 1977, 198; McMahon 2006, 345). Nevertheless, commentators note that times changed to embrace that exact danger.

With the rising prosperity of society, philosophers took a worldlier stance, where the economic view of "material goods as the very key to happiness" came to supplant all other approaches to happiness, including the social, psychological and ethical, at which Jeffrey Sachs notes "we have to marvel, and with considerable dismay" (Sachs 2013, 85–86). The reason for dismay lies in the way in which the commercial spirit began to replace the spirit of religion (or concern for morality generally) and enlist the ego to serve the principle of self-interest, but not rightly understood (i.e., as the pursuit of individuals' own interests without restraint). The serious danger into which this places humankind, as Mill noted earlier, is that people can forget the meaning of virtues and vices, as well as the moral significance of their choices. While everyday choices usually do not seem morally potent, evil or extreme, it is worth pointing out that their effects can be. For example – this is critical for human rights – as the United States Holocaust Memorial Museum observes, "the Holocaust was not an accident in history; it occurred because individuals, organizations, and governments made choices that not only legalized discrimination but also allowed prejudice, hatred, and ultimately mass murder to occur" (Ushmm.org n.d.). This essay questions the view that many in modern society appear to uphold, namely, that ethics and self-restraint are unimportant and the takeover of commercialism is morally neutral rather than sinister.

A closer examination of the takeover of commercialism is in order, and I will attempt to make one here, if only in brief. First, Jeffrey Sachs explains that economic utility theory stepped in to define happiness so that well-being (an individual's utility) is "determined by the possession and consumption of material goods, mainly through market purchases" (Sachs 2013, 85). Well-being would thus no longer be determined by virtue, character or achieving a state of tranquility. Sachs (2013, 86) elaborates that, for modern economists, happiness is signified by a "utility function," which shows how individuals indicate their preferences for certain "baskets of goods" by purchasing, within their means, those baskets that they believe will result in their greatest happiness. He identifies four features of this function:

> The utility function is *egoistic*, meaning that it focuses on the individual's relationship to commodities, rather than to other individuals and their well-being. It is *materialistic*, in that it focuses on goods and services purchased in the market, rather than on ideas, values, or behavior. It is *hedonistic*, in that it assumes that the market commodities give pain or pleasure to the consumer, varying according to the basket of commodities consumed. And it is *stable*, either unchanging over time or changing in a wholly predictable way anticipated by the individual.
>
> (Sachs 2013, 86)

Economics, then, not only redefines happiness, it also ensures, as a result of these features, that the pursuit of happiness becomes unconcerned with the education or ethical shaping of people's preferences as to the rightness and wrongness of actions.

Utility, and thus happiness, have taken on these meanings – egoism, materialism and hedonism – over the last few centuries, with different philosophers contributing different aspects of each, and I will outline them briefly below. Sachs argues that egoism derived from Thomas Hobbes, materialism from Bernard Mandeville and Adam Smith, and hedonism from Jeremy Bentham (Sachs 2013, 86–88). While Bentham's philosophy inspired concern for happiness in public policy and brought about many social reforms, in setting aside virtue and focusing on self-interested pleasure hedonism also had a negative impact on people's perceptions and behaviors. Prior to Bentham, though, Bernard Mandeville promoted the idea of private vices and public benefits, wherein humankind's greed and immorality could be harnessed to produce greater levels of material wealth (Sachs 2013, 86–87). The effect of these new approaches to "happiness" was to tinker with humanity's moral compass. By neglecting to remedy and even capitalize on vice, they would eventually hamstring our ability to discern virtue from vice and destroy our willingness to entertain ethics in the pursuit of happiness.

Central assumptions of utility theory: Happiness deprived of virtue

By the 19th and 20th centuries, a number of assumptions characterized both the theory and daily marketplace practice of utility. Jeffrey Sachs lists four of these:

1 The egoistic and materialist assumptions that utility is a function of the individual's consumption of market commodities rather than of social relations, virtues, state of mind, well-being of others, and other non-market conditions;

2 The stability assumption that the utility function is unaffected by experience, education, social norms or moral instruction;
3 The moral presumption that individual tastes should be taken as a given, in both a moral and descriptive sense. As Stigler and Becker famously put it, quoting a Latin saying, "*De Gustibus Est Non Disputandem*," tastes are not subject to dispute, and certainly not subject to improvement through ethical training; and
4 The loss of interest in happiness per se, as utility theory is reinterpreted not as a theory of well-being (as with Bentham, for example), but as a theory of consumer behavior. (Sachs 2013, 89–90)

Although economics purported to offer a new take on happiness, the field's true interest was consumer behavior, including individuals' static tastes and responses to market commodities. Happiness, character development, virtuous behavior, and respect for others and their rights were not on the agenda. This dismissal of the moral dimensions of happiness is especially problematic if people's "tastes" involve harming others, rather than helping them.

Further, Sachs observes: "Such was the growing influence of the economics profession that no other profession, such as moral philosophy or psychology, succeeded until the past quarter century in counteracting the economists' retreat from the study of happiness" (Sachs 2013, 89–90). Although there were moral philosophers such as Philippa Foot writing on the moral dimensions of happiness from the late 1950s, it seems they were overshadowed by the rising prominence of economists in public life. Measuring the nation's welfare in terms of its gross domestic product (GDP), or economic production, became increasingly popular after World War II. Into the 21st century, the GDP has served around the globe as the measurement of a nation's level of well-being, with the notable exception of Bhutan, which in 1972 began measuring welfare in broader terms, labeling its formula Gross National Happiness (GNH) (Burns 2011). Elsewhere, however, courtesy of economic utility theory, the study of happiness was actually divested of happiness.

The utility function brought radical change from earlier views on happiness, such as those of Thomas Jefferson, who argued that virtue is the foundation of happiness and that virtue consists of prudence, temperance, fortitude and justice. According to these earlier views, a happy life is to be achieved by living virtuously: making wise, informed decisions; practicing self-restraint; remaining steadfast in the face of adversity or temptation; adhering to a moral code; developing character; and treating others with dignity and respect. Not only were commitments to these virtues weakened, but so was the individual's sense of responsibility for contributing to the well-being of others and of society. Success seems now no longer measured in terms of doing justice to the welfare of others or of achieving happiness virtuously, as Tocqueville once observed of Americans, but of the achievement of scientific measurements for happiness, where happiness is studied particularly through brain scans and then applied to people's behaviors (Sachs 2012, 7–9). Jeffrey Sachs explains that, with the advent of utility, tragically "[i]ndividuals are no longer seen to derive their happiness from altruism, compassion, social connections or virtue. Their happiness comes from their relations to objects of pain and pleasure, rather than their relations to people" (Sachs 2013, 89).

Sachs admits that, while many economists have acknowledged the importance of sympathy and altruism, as well as "interdependent utility functions," where a person's happiness is interrelated with that of other people, "[t]hese refinements, while real, have not fundamentally shaken the Benthamite edifice of individualism and object-based utility" (Sachs 2013, 89). In fact, the perspective of economics has crossed over into happiness research, which is conducted mostly according to modern liberalism and the "standard economic view of modernity," according to Daniel M. Haybron (2008, 20–21), where "well-being [happiness] consists roughly in people getting whatever they happen to want." Haybron declares:

> Inspired by Enlightenment optimism about the individual's powers of reason and self-government, modern liberals tend to believe in one or another form of *sovereignty* of the individual in matters of personal welfare: By and large, people know what's best for them and tend to act rationally in the promotion of their interests. We all make mistakes, of course, but not so much that we urgently need enlightenment about our own well-being. What people need more than anything, on this view, is *freedom*. In particular, they need the liberty and resources to pursue their various goals however they see fit.
>
> (Haybron 2008, 20–21)

Modernity takes liberalism to the extreme, something which John Locke did not intend to happen. Further, John Stuart Mill, Thomas Jefferson, Alexis de Tocqueville and others, including everyday 18th-century Americans, thought liberalism dangerous without influences that would moderate people's pursuits, such as classical republicanism, Enlightenment moral sense, and Christianity.

This can be seen in how many 18th-century Americans, in keeping with the principle of self-interest rightly understood, according to Tocqueville, would "show with complacency how an enlightened regard for themselves constantly prompts them to assist each other, and inclines them willingly to sacrifice a portion of their time and property to the welfare of the State" (Tocqueville 1952, 393). But today, as Haybron explains above, "enlightened" self-regard prompts people to fixate on the liberty and resources needed to pursue individual goals however people see fit. Unbeknownst to us, then, we are living among the ruins of Enlightenment philosophy and Jefferson's (and the other founders') intentions for the pursuit of happiness.

An ethos of unfettered hyper-commercialism: Abolishing self-governance, virtue and restraint

The problem with researching and living according to the standard economic view of modernity is that the economic view of modernity has actually eliminated self-governance and restraint in order to rise to new, outrageous heights, which is contrary to the picture painted by Haybron. By the 20th century, Jeffrey Sachs elaborates, the "social ethos" of America, "the world's richest and most commercialized society, evolved into a full-throated consumerism and hedonism, exemplified by the 'Roaring Twenties'" (Sachs 2013, 91). Personal wealth came to signify happiness, and making a virtue out of the vice of greed no longer sufficed to garner more wealth. Thus to fuel modern consumerism, "the notion of private vice was dropped" (Sachs 2013, 91). Advertisers and public relations specialists became the "leading applied psychologists of the day," stimulating the unconscious mind to desire even greater levels of consumption; thus, "America slid into hyper-commercialism, untethered by ethical, religious, or philosophical constraints" (Sachs 2013, 91).

Whereas the social or cultural ethos of 18th-century America was based on virtue and altruism, the pursuit of happiness can now be seen as being centered on unfettered egoism, hedonism and materialism. In his book *A Humane Economy* (1960), Wilhelm Röpke, for example, explains what unfettered commercialism looks like, identifying the times we live in as the "age of advertising":

> To assert oneself all the time by ubiquitous advertising, day and night, in town and country, on the air and on every free square foot of wall space, in prose and in verse, in word and picture, by open assault or by the subtler means of "public relations," until every gesture of courtesy, kindness, and neighborliness is degraded into a move behind which we suspect ulterior motives; to fashion all imaginable relations and performances on the principle of supply and demand and so to commercialize them, not excluding art and science and religion; forever to compare one's own position with that of others; always to try out something new, to shift from one profession and from one place to the next; to look with constant jealousy and envy upon others – such extreme commercialization, restlessness, and rivalry are an infallible way of destroying the free economy by morally blind exaggeration of its principle. This is bound to end up in an unhealthy state of which the worst must be feared.
>
> (Röpke 1960, 128)

Jeffrey Sachs observes among the consequences of this principle in our society today that "private ethical responsibility has seriously atrophied" (Sachs 2013, 92). There are many facets to the atrophying of private ethical responsibility.

In addition to the general climate of suspicion, jealousy, restlessness and rivalry that Röpke describes, another of these facets is the heavy toll that this atrophy takes on one's personal life. Sachs elaborates: "Consumer addictions of all sorts (compulsive shopping, compulsive gambling, heavy TV watching, fast-food addictions, eating disorders, tobacco addiction, excessive borrowing and more) seem to be soaring" (Sachs 2013, 92). Recall that one of the central assumptions of utility theory, upon which this ethos operates, is the so-called 'moral' idea that a person's tastes are a given and not open to debate, correction or improvement through moral training. Thus, our taste for physical gratification has finally outstripped our education even beyond Tocqueville's predictions, since we now deny the need for ethical education and have built the modern pursuit of happiness on the rejection of self-restraint. For this, Tocqueville supplies one of the best critiques: "These people think they are following the principle of self-interest, but the idea they entertain of that principle is a very crude one; and the better to look after what they call their own business, they neglect their chief business, which is to remain their own masters" (Tocqueville 1997).

Conclusion: Restoring ethics to the pursuit of happiness

In this essay, two radically different ways of pursuing happiness have been presented: first, the 18th-century version, where people sought to virtuously achieve not only their own happiness, but the success and happiness of their fellow citizens; and second, the 20th-century version, where people define and seek their own happiness for themselves, mainly in terms of acquiring material goods and pleasures. Although I have focused here on America, the same ethical concerns about the pursuit of happiness apply to the world at large; wherever people are interested in being happy, they will have to consider the implications of their efforts. So the question now facing humankind, especially given what the pursuit of happiness has become with the commercialized spirit, is this: how *ought* or *should* we pursue happiness? Does having the right to seek happiness mean that people are excused from private ethical responsibility, from being their own masters? Or does it mean that each person has a responsibility to use freedom wisely, both in conducting their personal lives and in pursuing happiness in such a way as to also give tangible regard and assistance to others?

The common sense of the 18th century held that the ethical pursuit was the more worthy. The idea that happiness was intimately related to moral virtue, character development, one's behavior toward others, altruism, and the quality of society was clear to many elites and everyday people alike in keeping with traditions of thought that extended all the way back to ancient Greece and Rome. Today, however, the connection between happiness, virtue and society has been severely impaired. Humanity has ended up with an entitlement view of happiness, wherein it is thought that the right to happiness principally consists of self-centered, hedonistic, materialistic pursuits. As I have argued, this amounts to an expiry of the right in terms of being a real or active right, where people understand that the right to happiness also involves responsibilities and are, moreover, able to undertake them.

In its place is an emaciated form of rights and an ethos that is in fact inimical to the practice of human rights, since the ethos of unfettered hyper-commercialism results in the deterioration of private ethical responsibility and the creation of an environment that opposes, denies and distorts moral values and responsibility. Human rights, as moral norms, require a healthy understanding of ethical responsibility, as well as a robust practice of it, much like the 18th-century pursuit of happiness. The evidence suggests that the modern pursuit of happiness should be transferred back to a morally sound understanding of rights, wherein people are still free to choose what makes them happy, but are guided in their pursuits by a clear apprehension of personal responsibility, a restored ethos of virtue and self-restraint, and an active practice of contributing to the welfare of others and society. This is the legacy that Thomas Jefferson and the founding generation – for good reason – wished to leave humanity.

Notes

1 This essay is part of a larger chapter in the author's doctoral dissertation. Thanks to Paul Copan and Sandra Lynch for providing comments on earlier drafts.
2 Throughout Western history, happiness has been primarily discussed in philosophical, religious and moral terms, until after the Enlightenment when liberalism, economics and science took over. For a start on this topic, see McMahon (2006), Annas (1993), and Cahn and Vitrano (2007). For more on the definition of human rights, see Nickel (2007) and Griffin (2008).
3 From his investigation of Jefferson's copy of Aristotle's *Nicomachean Ethics* housed in the Library of Congress, O'Toole concludes: "It turns out we know exactly what Jefferson meant [by the right to pursue happiness] because he was an Aristotelian through and through, so, as they say, 'you could look it up'" (O'Toole 2005, 28). I differ with O'Toole on this point.
4 Jefferson's understanding of Epicurus differs somewhat from that of DeWitt (1947), especially on the greatest good (*summum bonum*) for human beings, which Jefferson saw as not being pained in body or mind, while DeWitt maintains that it is life.
5 The other two accomplishments Jefferson wanted to be remembered for were authoring the Declaration of Independence and fathering the University of Virginia. Among his other accomplishments were United States Minister to France, Secretary of State, Vice-President and President.

Bibliography

Annas, Julia. 1993. *The Morality of Happiness*. New York: Oxford University Press.

Aristotle. 2009. *Nicomachean Ethics*, trans. David Ross, ed. Lesley Brown. Oxford: Oxford University Press.

Burns, George W. 2011. "Gross National Happiness: A Gift from Bhutan to the World." In *Positive Psychology as Social Change*, ed. Robert Biswas-Diener. Dordrecht: Springer Netherlands, 73–87.

Cahn, Steven M., and Christine Vitrano. 2007. *Happiness: Classic and Contemporary Readings in Philosophy*. Oxford: Oxford University Press.

Derrida, Jacques. 1986. "Declarations of Independence." *New Political Science* 7(1): 7–15. Accessed March 15, 2016. http://dx.doi.org/10.1080/07393148608429608.

DeWitt, Norman W. 1947. "Epicurus: Philosophy for the Millions." *The Classical Journal* 42(4): 195–201.

Diener, Ed. 2009. "Introduction–the Science of Well-Being: Reviews and Theoretical Articles by Ed Diener." In *The Science of Well-Being, Social Indicators Research Series 37*, ed. Ed Diener. Dordrecht: Springer Netherlands, 1–10.

Eid, Michael, and Randy J. Larsen. 2008. "Ed Diener and the Science of Subjective Well-Being." In *The Science of Subjective Well-Being*, ed. Michael Eid and Randy J. Larsen. New York: Guildford, 1–13.

Galbraith, John Kenneth. 1978. *The Affluent Society*. New York: Mentor.
Griffin, James. 2008. *On Human Rights*. Oxford: Oxford University Press.
Haybron, Daniel M. 2008. "Philosophy and the Science of Subjective Well-being." In *The Science of Subjective Well-Being*, ed. Michael Eid and Randy J. Larsen. New York: Guildford, 17–43.
Jefferson, Thomas. 1950. "To Henry Lee." In *The Basic Writings of Thomas Jefferson*, ed. Philip S. Foner. New York: Halcyon House, 802.
Jefferson, Thomas. 1975. "To William Short." In *The Portable Thomas Jefferson*, ed. Merrill D. Peterson. New York: Penguin, 564–567.
Jefferson, Thomas. 1999. "Notes on Virginia: Query XVII." In *Political Writings*, ed. Joyce Appleby and Terence Ball. New York: Cambridge University Press, 392–396.
Jefferson, Thomas. 2004. "To John Page." In *Light and Liberty: Reflections on the Pursuit of Happiness*, ed. Eric S. Petersen. New York: Modern Library, 7.
"Jefferson's Gravestone." *Thomas Jefferson Encyclopedia*. Monticello. Accessed September 18, 2015. https://www.monticello.org/site/research-and-collections/jeffersons-gravestone.
King, Laura A. 2008. "Interventions for Enhancing Subjective Well-Being: Can We Make People Happier, and Should We?" In *The Science of Subjective Well-Being*, ed. Michael Eid and Randy J. Larsen. New York: Guildford, 431–448.
Locke, John. 1970. *Two Treatises of Government*, ed. Peter Laslett. 2nd ed. Cambridge: Cambridge University Press.
Locke, John. 1975. *An Essay Concerning Human Understanding*, ed. Peter H. Nidditch. Oxford: Clarendon Press.
McMahon, Darrin M. 2006. *The Pursuit of Happiness: A History from the Greeks to the Present*. London: Penguin.
McMahon, Darrin M. 2008. "The Pursuit of Happiness in History." In *The Science of Subjective Well-Being*, ed. Michael Eid and Randy J. Larsen. New York: Guildford, 80–93.
Mill, John Stuart. 1977. "De Tocqueville on Democracy in America (II)." In *The Collected Works of John Stuart Mill*, Vol. 18: *Essays on Politics and Society Part I*, ed. John M. Robson. Toronto: University of Toronto Press, 153–204.
Myers, David G. 1992. *The Pursuit of Happiness*. New York: William Morrow.
Nickel, James W. 2007. *Making Sense of Human Rights*, 2nd ed. Malden, MA: Blackwell.
O'Toole, James. 2005. *Creating the Good Life: Applying Aristotle's Wisdom to Find Meaning and Happiness*. New York: Rodale.
Röpke, Wilhelm. 1960. *A Humane Economy: The Social Framework of the Free Market*. Wilmington, DE: ISI.
Rorty, Richard. 1989. *Contingency, Irony, and Solidarity*. Cambridge: Cambridge University Press.
Sachs, Jeffrey D. 2012. "Introduction." In *World Happiness Report* (United Nations), ed. John Helliwell, Richard Layard and Jeffrey D. Sachs, 2–9. Accessed September 21, 2015. http://worldhappiness.report/.
Sachs, Jeffrey D. 2013. "Restoring Virtue Ethics in the Quest for Happiness." In *World Happiness Report*, (United Nations), ed. John Helliwell, Richard Layard and Jeffrey D. Sachs, 80–97. Accessed September 21, 2015. http://worldhappiness.report/.
Smith, Adam. 1853. *The Theory of Moral Sentiments*, ed. Dugald Stewart. London: H. G. Bohn.
Tocqueville, Alexis de. 1997. "Chapter XIV: How the Taste for Physical Gratifications is United in America to Love of Freedom and Attention to Public Affairs." In *Democracy*

in America. American Studies Program, University of Virginia, ed. Henry Reeve. Accessed July 13, 2015. http://xroads.virginia.edu/~hyper/DETOC/ch2_14.htm.

Tocqueville, Alexis de. 1952. *Democracy in America*, trans. Henry Reeve and ed. Henry Steele Commager. London: Oxford University Press.

Un.org. 2015a. "UN Connects Well-Being and the Pursuit of Happiness." UN DESA | United Nations Department of Economic and Social Affairs. Accessed August 29, 2015. http://www.un.org/en/development/desa/news/social/intl-day-happiness.html.

Un.org. 2015b. "The Foundation of International Human Rights Law." In *The Universal Declaration of Human Rights*, United Nations. Accessed September 5, 2015. http://www.un.org/en/documents/udhr/hr_law.shtml.

Ushmm.org. n.d. "Why Teach about the Holocaust?" In *Resources for Educators*. United States Holocaust Memorial Museum. Accessed September 21, 2015. http://www.ushmm.org/educators/teaching-about-the-holocaust/why-teach-about-the-holocaust.

Wood, Gordon S. 1991. *The Radicalism of the American Revolution*. New York: Alfred A. Knopf.

Wood, Gordon S. 2009. "The Purpose of the Past: Reflections on the Uses of History." *Historically Speaking* 10(1): 2–6.

3 How to make room for God – in man

Tracing Epictetus' totality of religious freedom

Hendrik Kaptein

1. Introduction

A visit to the great city of Cologne, about 10 years ago now, brought something totally unexpected. Next to the grandiose gothic cathedral, a Christian shop had on offer something special in more than one sense. In a corner of the late-afternoon sunlit church square a book both small and great lay in wait: Epictetus' *Enchiridion*, the famous little handbook, for sale for a handful of euros.

What to do with it? Was Epictetus not mainly reputed as a rather morbid thinker, advising his readers to accept all things in life as if they are as inevitable as death itself and preaching total loneliness of man both as an inevitable fact and as a basic norm? No wonder that a Christian bookshop had the booklet on prominent display, probably to be taken along for a pious read in the nowadays no longer so silent semi-darkness of the cathedral. Indeed, buying such a fatalistic booklet dating to the time of the general decline of the Roman Empire did not really fit in with jolly expectations of one or more cold *Kölsch* (beers) and a wholesome dinner, all in most comforting company.

But then what is a handful of euros in the grand scheme of things? So I went ahead and bought the booklet. And my strong Christian background commanded me not to waste this opportunity to get hold of such solemn preaching. Of course, having such a background also meant that it was likely that I may have bought the very same booklet long ago, only for it to remain hidden away in a bookcase full of silent or even just dusty wisdom waiting to be perused.

Upon returning home, the little tome was duly stored away and more or less forgotten about (again?), until a well-reputed literary weekly from the United Kingdom published fragments of another scathing criticism of Epictetus as the pet philosopher of the weak and the cowardly refusing to live their lives. His everlasting popularity in such depraved spheres of doom may have been an ominous sign indeed. But then how is it that that thinkers as different as Pascal and Nietzsche thought so highly of him? Was their reading of these antique fragments different from Epictetus' well-nigh general reception?

So the next and long overdue step was to get hold of Oldfather's edition of the *Diatribai* (*Discourses*), which, apart from a few scattered fragments, was the only work of Epictetus still extant. Or rather, they were the only words probably spoken by him, as the *Diatribai* are in fact Arrianus' transcriptions of Epictetus' speeches and sermons. Insofar as they were originally complete, half of them are likely gone forever: only four out of eight original books are still available.

Reading through this work was and is a transformative experience. In fact, the well-known and much-praised *Enchiridion*, supposedly a (or even the) summary of Epictetus' essential wisdom, is more of a mockery of it than anything like a faithful representation of Arrianus' records of Epictetus' real philosophy. Suffice it to say that the *Enchiridion* is one more conclusive demonstration of how to distort or even destroy a grand vision by badly biased "cutting and pasting." This simplistic and rather repetitive selection from the *Diatribai* leaves out the best parts, in order to create a false impression of saddening fatalism.

Hard to follow as the *Diatribai* surely are at times, reading through them anew not only radically improves one's understanding of Epictetus' philosophy against so much wrongheaded received opinion, but also changes human existence itself. The inexplicably transcendental joy of life is what Epictetus tried to bring to light, or better what he still conveys after almost 2,000 years.

Epictetus advises that our life is a feast and should be lived like one, no matter the circumstances, and that we should live as guests of honor at God's own table. By such metaphors, and so much more, Epictetus tries to convey what life is, however antiquated his language may seem at times. (So the booklet I picked up near the cathedral still relates more to the beers and dinner than it does to the church.)

Here, there will be no attempt to once more reinterpret Epictetus in Christian terms, or to reinterpret Christian belief and theology in terms of Epictetus. Instead, this contribution is aimed at a radical reinterpretation of religious freedom as not just one freedom but as a wrongly disregarded core concept and reality in religious and secular life.

In fact, I will explain here that freedom, whatever its so many conceptual and other guises, cannot be explained at all without essential reference to religion and theology. Freedom is nothing without God. And I will elaborate on this point by attempting to explain Epictetus as positively as he admonished us to explain and accept reality in the best possible light.

Section 2 offers a brief overview of some of Epictetus' core concepts and conceptions – also making clear that there is no substitute for reading Epictetus himself. Section 3 briefly outlines relationships with later thought developed by Kant, Wittgenstein and others (leaving Pascal and Nietzsche out of account this time). Though Epictetus' thought is deeply religious and indeed was and is popular in Christian circles, some more than marginal differences between Epictetus' theology and Christianity need to be briefly explained (Section 4). Institutionalized religion is not easily made compatible with Epictetus' philosophy of life, as will be explained in Section 5. Still, our Christian or sometimes not so Christian culture may profit from Epictetus' identification of man with God (Section 6). Section 7 concludes with a plea both for religious tolerance and a war cry against any violence, wrong as it is in itself and wrongly related to religion as it may be – however much any war cries may have been anathema to Epictetus himself.

2. Man is God: Theology, teleology and the totality of religious freedom

Here, no more than a rather free, fragmentary and probably slightly frivolous interpretation and explanation of some main lines in the *Diatribai* is to be found. It will stress differences with received stoicism and focus on issues of outer and inner freedom.

Logos in a broad sense is central for Epictetus. Unique among both inanimate and living beings, man is able to not just comprehend reality to certain extents, including himself, but also to judge reality, including his own being, judgment, rationality and conduct. Also, man is uniquely able to do something with it. This ability for more or less effective reflection is what makes man human in the first place. Thus, while some higher animals may display seemingly rational behavior, man alone is able to rationally determine whether such behavior is rationally apposite in specific circumstances and to act upon it.

Indeed, man may reflect not just on outer reality, on his living world, but on his "inner world" as well. The outer world, constituted in part by other people's conduct good and bad, may give rise or even cause all kinds of positive and negative feelings, emotions and other states of mind. Happiness and joy may follow, but more often sadness and depression result.

These positive and negative states of mind – or better, of man – are results of immediate, unthought, and thus unreformed reactions to what happens to man. So many palatial, sexual and other physical pleasures may be highly enjoyable, just as being hurt and/or falling ill may lead to sometimes well-nigh unbearable pain. Still, more complex mechanisms may be at work. Thus, praise by peers and superiors may lead to temporary joy, just as perceived injustice may lead to resentment, hatred and revenge.

More often than not, such varying experiences sooner or later lead to frustration, sadness and other negative emotions and feelings. Epictetus noted that man more or less automatically chooses against himself by obsessively dealing with a world he cannot change at will, apart from marginal room for constructive conduct, instead of trying to reform his reactions to the world.

Thus, a man falling ill, feeling the pain of it and worrying about possibly diminished life prospects, may ask himself torturing questions like, "Why me?" "Why do I deserve this pain?" "Why ought I to go before my time?" and "What is to happen to my kin?" (normally in this very order). Or, people may seriously suffer from a lack of self-respect caused, among many other factors, by perceived injustice in some or other social order. Somebody may resent being passed over in a promotion and having to work and live "under" other people who do not deserve their higher rank and standing at all – at least in the eyes of the person left behind.

So many negative emotions are senselessly spent on what befalls man not just as a result of other people's conduct, accident or unacceptable fate, but also as a result of man's own conduct. Hurtful and counterproductive feelings of regret, remorse, guilt and shame are all consequences of both a refusal to accept the world as it is and a lack of attention to the powers of consciousness and self-consciousness.

Thus, man expends enormous and enormously saddening amounts of negative energy on reactions to the world and (mostly) futile attempts to change it. What ought to come first is the insight that, although the world may not be changed at will, man's unlimited resources of reaction to the very same world is a matter of reason, and thus of freedom.

All feeling and emotion is judgment is something Epictetus stresses time and again. "I feel pain" means "more or less unconsciously, I do not do anything against this mere feeling." Even such a basic feeling ought to be rationally transformed to a sensation to be handled in the best possible fashion, however inevitable it is *qua* sensation.

One way to realize at least part of this transformation is Epictetus' original application of the Golden Rule – important to him anyway as amply illustrated in the story of the father fleeing from his sick child (*Diatribai* Bk. 1, Ch. 11, Section 1,V; henceforth 1.11.1.v.). People may deeply worry about serious illnesses and other harm befalling them, aggravating their adverse effects. But then what would be the same people's judgments about and emotions concerning the same illnesses befalling strangers? Probably nothing more serious than something like, "unlucky things like this do happen." So, Epictetus puts it, you should have the same basic attitude toward your own mishaps. (In fact, the *Diatribai* are full of such fruitful heuristics or rules of thumb toward a better life.)

This, indeed, is the archetypical *Umwertung aller Werte* ("transvaluation of all values"), to use Nietzsche's phrase. Normally man sometimes enjoys reality; is oftentimes hindered by it; and sometimes vainly tries to control or even change it while entertaining all kinds of more or less free-flowing negative states of mind about it. Thus, man forgets his omnipotence, his unlimited ability to reinterpret the world, his own reactions to it, and his inner life or consciousness and self-consciousness as well. This is the essence of man as God, of man as the real master of his own universe, however bleak and saddening it may seem at first sight.

Omnipotence is the obvious bridging principle here. This is the new light, which is illustrated by Epictetus' stolen brass lamp (1.18.15.v.). A normal negative reaction to this situation would be to resent the theft and to deplore the loss, and to then become sad and upset about having to spend money on a similar lamp. Epictetus radically reinterpreted this kind of event: for him, the lamp was passed on to a new station, so that it could shine a still more beautiful light. And why not be satisfied with a cheap lamp offering the same illumination? And then, of course, nothing is forever, and every moment is a new beginning.

This omnipotence, however rarely experienced and realized to the full, also ought to counter any lack of respect and self-respect. Every fellow human being is God himself, however often poor humans are oblivious to this fact. So don't feel small at all; remember that everybody ought to be treated like God. There is no need for anybody to prove herself or himself in whatever sense and by whatever means against others anyway. Pride ought to be just as radically reinterpreted as modesty ought to. All false comparison or in fact all comparison of human beings in terms of value or worth ought to be done away with.

This notion again relates to the idea of every human being as a *civis mundi* ("citizen of the world)" (2.10.3.v.). Everybody being God implies everybody being of equally high or in fact incomparable standing. Still, this does not imply social equality, in any sense of the term, at least not so for Epictetus, who stresses the need to optimally realize one's given and proper role in society (see, for example, 1.29.39). In fact, Epictetus equates the world with God as well. Thus, the world or in fact the universe is absolutely perfect as it is. Hard to understand as this equation may be anyway, it at least leads to the question of how both man and the world can be God. Man is part of the world, of course, but how can there be two masters here?

The answer may be found in Epictetus' dream or sometimes even reality of man simply being there – without undue reflection, self-reflection, worrying and worse. Then man is in harmony with his world, "is" his world in a totally unencumbered and harmonious sense. Man ought not to be "in himself," but ought to enjoy life, be life, be the world – however metaphorical this may sound or even be. This relates to Epictetus' conception of body and soul. It is firmly dualistic: on the one hand, the human body is no more than a flimsy and ephemeral part of the universe; on the other hand, the soul, or man as a rational being, is everything and thus may not even be called small, ephemeral or even large for that matter at all (see 1.12.26.v). It is God itself, just as the universe, man's universe, is.

That same world is regarded by Epictetus not only as perfect, but also as totally harmonious in itself. And it is not just with the benefit of hindsight that this concept may be one of the strangest in his philosophy, dating as it does from prescientific times and before man started to radically change his living world (not always for the better). In line with this, however, is the weaker but still most important idea that the world ought to be interpreted as if it is the best possible and a totally harmonious world.

In real life, man's godlike omnipotence is more or less a dream of course. This totally detached ideal of insensitivity to any of so many worldly evils or better, the unlimited power to radically reinterpret anything for the better, may not always be practicable in the real world; still, it is an ideal to be striven for in hard times at least. It is good hard work, like life itself is. In fact, Epictetus seemed well aware of this, sometimes leaving his ideal role himself in getting angry with his students or even with criminals (see, for example, 2.4, and compare it with 2.2.9).

But the situation is not hopeless: man can do something about it. Though Epictetus is generally interpreted as a teleological determinist denying free will, he emphasizes freedom of choice in at least two respects. First, man enjoys total freedom of choice concerning his reactions to what happens in the world, however hard it may be to realize this freedom. Second, Epictetus repeatedly admonishes man not to forget his freedom of choice in changing the real world for the better, however marginal possibilities for this may be.

In one moving passage about boarding a ship – one of his favorite metaphors – Epictetus urges the potential passenger to choose the right captain, helmsman and crew, just as he ought to be wary about the weather when he tries to determine the time for taking his leave (see *Enchiridion*, Ch. 7).

In fact, Epictetus' ethical admonitions would not make any sense without such freedom of action, however minimal. Man is totally free in his interpretations of the universe around him, but he is also free to act on behalf of his fellow human beings – being God(s) as well. Anybody's freedom to see everything in the best possible light does not preclude the need to do good to everybody concerned, thus adding to the harmony of the universe.

How to reconcile this freedom of action with Epictetus' idea that the universe is totally perfect as it is, seemingly logically precluding any possibility of changing the world for the better, is another matter. It may be best to interpret the universe as identical to God as a regulative idea: "as if" the universe is perfect indeed.

In reference to the distinction between positive and negative freedom as defined by Berlin in 1958 (Berlin 1969), Epictetus' philosophy of life is rather different from Berlin's stoic variety of positive freedom as total insensitivity or "the retreat to the inner citadel." Epictetus wants man to be way beyond negative sensitivity; he wants man to be the master of his sensitivities in the first place. Thus, Seneca and others, in famously not deploring death but being born, would be anathema to him.

However often wrongly interpreted in quietist and fatalistic terms – and indeed such an interpretation is at least suggested by a tendentious reading of the *Enchiridion* – such a "standard stoic" reading of Epictetus is a total mistake. In fact, Epictetus tries to merge negative and positive liberty. For him, "freedom from" does not imply giving up all goals and even hope; rather, it implies the positive reform of our goals, desires, wishes, penchants and so on in the light of the world. This reform is to lead to positive freedom as complete autonomy, to independence from any inner forces, to "simply" being there. Really free human beings cannot be hindered by anybody or anything, not even by their own inner life.

This is fully compatible with Epictetus' conception of life as a party, a feast (4.1.108.v). The metaphor of being seated at the dinner table of the gods is not meant to convey the need to feel good or something like that, but to express both deep gratitude for being there in this perfect and thus beautiful world and the indescribable feeling of "forgetting oneself" by simply being there, together, unencumbered by any unnecessary thoughts and sorrows about oneself, about others, and about the world.

Thus, the dinner table of the gods also serves to express the importance of being harmoniously together. Though Epictetus is no enemy of solitude at all: he does stress sociability, friendship and love for one's kin as essential in and for life. This is one important aspect of every human being as an essential part of the universe that would not be perfect without everybody being there in the full sense.

So, and to conclude this all too brief but hopefully still helpful summary of Epictetus' message, what is religious liberty? In essence, it is not liberty to believe in the first place. Religious freedom is nothing else but total independence from any negativity in man and in the world, by reinterpretation and acceptance of everything, driven by the insight that man as God is omnipotent in and over the universe – this universe in a sense being himself. A grandiose vision maybe, but not otherworldly at all for anybody giving it a serious try. See everybody, yourself and everything in the best and most beautiful possible light. (This is no disinterested relativism at all.)

3. Fragments of related visions: Philosophy (and some psychology)

Other major thinkers developed ideas closely comparable to Epictetus' conception of man and the world. Does this add to the plausibility of this conception? Maybe not per se, as such plausibility ought not to depend on sources as such, however seemingly authoritative. Still, some comparison with other philosophies may shed some more light on the lessons contained in the *Diatribai.*

Plato may be skipped here, though it is rather obvious that Epictetus tries to "merge" the two worlds of appearances and ideas. Socrates' influence is obvious: Epictetus tries to "wake up" his fellow human beings by bringing to light what they already knew and what they already were. Aristotelian anti-dualism may not be compatible with Epictetus' mind-body distinction at first sight. Still, the idea of man as a rational animal is important for Epictetus too.

Spinoza can only be briefly mentioned here as well. His pantheism, probably still more "hermetic" than Epictetus' version of it, was and is highly regarded by Christians and others. Like Epictetus, Spinoza equates real freedom with real happiness, as "beyond" the mere satisfaction of desires. Kant and Kantianism are still more interesting here. For one thing, the distinction between *homo phenomenon* and *homo noumenon* forcefully reminds us of Epictetus' idea of the body as a physically limited phenomenon in space and time, in contrast to the mind as "unlimited" or even "un-dimensional": "Your body is nothing, your mind is everything" (*Diatribai* 1.12.26). Related to this is Kant's notion of man as an end in himself. This echoes Epictetus' conceptions of every human being as God and of everybody as a *civis mundi.* (Though Epictetus was still less egalitarian than Kant was, given his emphasis on the need to fulfill "one's proper role in society.") Another interesting similarity to be explored further is to be found in Kant's final formulation of the categorical imperative: "Act according to the rules of the Kingdom of Ends" (Kant 2012). Or, even though man finds himself in an imperfect world, he ought to act according to the rules of a perfect world of equally well-respected human beings as ends in themselves, thus contributing however marginally to some or other approximation of such a perfect world. Epictetus' more or less implicit conception of freedom of action echoes in Kant's "theory of aspects" of freedom and choice. From an empirical perspective, the world must be understood and explained in terms of determinism: *natura non facit saltum*, or "everything happens according to laws."[1] From a rational perspective, "man acts according to the representation (*Vorstellung*) of laws" and indeed may violate them in acting irrationally. This again points to Hume/Mill/Schlick-like compatibilitist theories of determinism and freedom (see also Strawson 1973, though his notions of freedom and resentment may not evidently be compatible with Epictetus' teachings).

Nietzsche's thought may seem far away from Epictetus' emphasis on total acceptance. Still, Nietzsche held Epictetus in high regard and not for nothing. Epictetus' totally autonomous human being embodying God is in fact an *Übermensch* in a totally positive sense.

Lastly for now, and skipping more than a few interesting intermittent thoughts and visions, a brief comparison with Wittgenstein's earlier philosophy may be apposite. "I am my world" is a central theme of the *Tractatus* (Wittgenstein 1921, 1922), just as "life is everything" is a metaphor intended to convey the same meaning. Death is not an event in life, so death is nothing, as it was for Epictetus. Like Wittgenstein but probably still more practically oriented, Epictetus stressed the importance of living in the here and now. Wittgenstein equated eternity in life not with endless duration of time but with the timelessness of the moment. This relates to Epictetus' admonition to live life to the fullest, as it is here and now. This is not escapism, but acceptance of life as it is without saddening counterfactual conditionals like "if x would have happened / if only I had done x, then life would be better."

Another highly interesting parallel is to be found in ultimate denial of the very possibility of ethics. Wittgenstein famously denied the very possibility of ethics: "Any book that would be really about ethics would destroy all other books in the world" (Wittgenstein 1965, 7). The world is what it is. This goes way beyond any is/ought distinction and indeed provokes thoughts on Epictetus' implicit merging of the real and the ideal world.

Today, Epictetus plays only a minor role in academic philosophy – maybe all the worse for such philosophy. Contemporary rigor in philosophical argumentation kills off many if not all of Epictetus' teachings. Sure his logic is primitive at times, but then metaphors need not be logical in order to still impress or even change life for the better. Indeed modern psychology explicitly refers to his teaching, not just in rational emotive therapy but in cognitive behavioral therapy as well. Even though Epictetus' teleological vision of the universe may no longer be acceptable to modern minds, or if it even seems to be incomprehensible, the ancient philosopher's adages for everyday life are still of major importance: "give it a try," one may say to any skeptic. The issue of religious liberty is a practical issue in the first place, and thus it may still be informed by at least some of Epictetus' recommendations.

4. Fragments of related (?) visions: Theology – mainly Christian

Religion is another well-nigh endless field of fruitful comparison regarding Epictetus' teachings, expressing essential wisdom in so many different ways. I will mention just a few of them here.

"He who saves a man saves a world": though not to be found literally in the *Diatribai*, this old Jewish (or even wider) wisdom aptly expresses the unity of man and world, however metaphorical, as one of Epictetus' main points.

Christianity, probably unknown to Epictetus apart from one passing reference to a possibly Christian but still rather small sect in Asia Minor, always held

Epictetus' teachings in high esteem (*Diatribai* 4.7.6). Thus, Pascal famously valued Epictetus' philosophy even higher than Plato's. Generations of Christians were influenced by Epictetus' teachings. In fatalistic interpretations of the *Enchiridion*, this popularity may be understandable enough.

But then the *Diatribai* seems to be at odds with Christian theology and teaching at more than a few main points. First and foremost, and still simplifying varieties of Christian belief and theology more than a bit, God, his Son and his Holy Family are conceived of in some ways as distinct entities with definite relationships. Though Epictetus mentions gods and the need to worship them according to the rules, in fact his philosophy culminates in the well-nigh ineffable unity of everything, the perfect harmony of man, men and the universe. Distinctness, then, is rather less important than striving for harmony and unity.

Also, Epictetus urges man first to believe in himself and the world, in order that he not "escape" from himself and the world. This is at odds with belief in any "outside," transcendent God or gods residing in heaven. Thus, Epictetus would probably have at least criticized certain varieties of Christianity as escapist.

"My kingdom is not of this world" (John 18:36) is a central tenet of Christianity of course. Epictetus would disagree, in one sense at least. The world is the kingdom of man, oblivious of his omnipotence in reinterpreting and recreating the perfect universe. But Epictetus' kingdom is still not of this world in another sense. This appears from his staunch denial, derision in fact, of the importance of any material goods beyond the needs of physical subsistence. Respect and self-respect ought to be completely independent from any material position in this world, just as social rank ought to play no role at all. In fact, Epictetus reads as a scathing criticism of individual and collective narcissism *avant la lettre*.

Still, Epictetus is no Christian. This is also apparent from his basic attitude toward guilt and sin. For Christianity, these are essential elements of man and the world. One or even the central role of Jesus Christ was his suffering and death in order to transfer immeasurable human guilt, in order to liberate man. Jesus Christ as the subject of ultimate punishment and the symbol of total forgiveness indeed presupposes the existence and importance of sin. This is totally at odds with Epictetus' teachings. Epictetus repeatedly emphasized that there ought to be no guilt at all. The wise man does not indict others, nor does he indict fate or himself. Of course, for Epictetus this is no license to do whatever one wants to do at all, vehemently critical as he is against all evil disturbing the harmony of man and world. But this elimination of guilty feelings and guilt itself is one more confirmation of man as God, who is not to be debased by himself and others in any way. For Epictetus, sin is not sin but lack of knowledge, which is dramatically illustrated in his version of the infanticide committed by Medea (1.28.7.v).[2] In fact, and this is rather different from most major religions, Epictetus does not prescribe and proscribe specific conduct, religious or otherwise. His implicit ethics goes no further than the admonition to respect the harmony of the world and to add to it by acting according to the demands of one's station and its duties.

A deeply related and no less stark contrast to Christianity and other religions is to be found in rather different ideas of the afterlife. Though Epictetus indeed

conceives of life as "a brief presence as a guest of honor at the dinner table of the gods" (4.1.108.v), and thus imagines necessarily temporary human existence as something like entering life and leaving it again, any afterlife as such plays no role in his published thoughts. In Christianity and in other religions, this is rather different, of course, deeply related as conceptions of the afterlife are to sin, guilt, punishment and repentance but also to merit and reward.

Distinctions between life and afterlife relate to the imperfection of the living world compared to heaven. Hell may be the other extreme. In fact, Epictetus makes no such distinctions at all in his basic assumption that the world is perfect as it is, or at least that the world ought to be interpreted as if it is perfect. The timelessness of the here and now is central for him, in contrast to the "living unto death and the afterlife" (or even the dream of eternal life) as found in Christianity and in other major religions for that matter.

One more related difference between Epictetus' teachings and Christianity appears in the value of life. Epictetus repeatedly stresses that life as such is of no value at all (see, for example, 2.6.1.v). All that matters is value in life. This contrasts with the sanctity of life as a gift of God to be taken away by him alone, according to the tenets of Christianity. Thus, Epictetus suggests suicide to people who don't like life: "Shut up complaining or just step out of it; remember that the door is open" (1.24.20). This, of course, is not easily compatible with Roman Catholicism and with Christianity in general.

Getting back to the "gods' own dinner table", this is one more reference to Epictetus' sound advice to enjoy life as a feast. Indeed, God is not looking for people who do not like life, who keep on thinking and worrying, while forgetting to simply live and make the best out of it. Christians and others picked this up in the meantime. Not all of them have, however, even though the present Pope recently and rightly referred to this joyful wisdom against some of his all too serious and stern-looking dignitaries.

5. The problem of institutionalized religion – against God?

Indeed, religion is well-nigh inextricably bound to institutionalization. Religious rituals and other practices are determined by intricate sets of constitutive and regulative rules designed to make religion visible and tangible for believers and non-believers alike. Temples, churches and other sacred places are theaters for the worship of God and gods, however remote such a practice may seem, at least to outsiders, from modesties prescribed by major Holy Scriptures.

What would Epictetus think of this, that is, in circumstances allowing for some kind of freedom of speech? He would probably remark that religious institutes and practices are part of the world as it is and thus are to be regarded as God's own work. Remember that the world is perfect as it is or at least ought to be interpreted as if it is perfect.

But such "as if" perfectionism is no fatalism. There is still room for criticism. Indeed, Epictetus would wonder why man being God himself is in any need for any consolation and certainty outside himself in the first place. If man is God, he ought to be able to be totally autonomous in principle, without any need for a consoling father figure more or less "outside" his living world. Thus regarded, religious rituals are only ornamental in the end.

The one and only real Church is reality itself. Churches and other religious organizations are superfluous "duplications" of the perfect universe being God itself, then. This is not just an issue of "Occam's razor." Religious organizations are expressions of drastic underestimation of reality itself, as if the universe is in need of anything superior to it. This at least is Epictetus' teaching, which urges man not to flee from reality by entering a church, however consoling such a maneuver may be.

Anyway, Epictetus would not condone religious institutions and practices clearly not respecting the fact that every human being is God. But then one problem of institutionalized religion is ecclesiastical hierarchy. Whatever its religious significance, one side or not-so-side-effect of such hierarchy is status and status anxiety. So there are priests, bishops, cardinals and popes, and rather much more common believers, or simply commons. (How to reconcile this with Christian condemnation of vanity may be another matter.)

Epictetus would have been rather critical of this, and probably rightly so. Anybody deriving self-respect from social and specifically hierarchical status, ecclesiastically or otherwise, is a mentally poor and pitiful human being, just as anyone feeling himself less than others as a consequence of being "lower" in any social and/or institutional ranking wrongly judges himself not as being God but as dependent on the "respect" of others.

Adding to the negative aspects of institutionalization is greater "visibility" and thus greater offense against non-believers. Such negative visibility may be still enhanced by deep-seated "preacher and flock" effects. The flock is still more wrong, at least according to Epictetus. Not only does it debase itself in submission to "leaders," it also forgets the basic truth that man is God himself and so does not need any guidance in terms of higher truths, or in terms of "truths" at all.

False inequalities, however, are not just issues within churches and congregations. In fact, almost all religion condones inequalities of human beings *qua* human beings by implicitly or sometimes explicitly and even violently declaring the superiority of believers in the one right religion over too many varieties of wrong- or simply non-believers. Then some people are deemed to be more God or godlike than others. Vehemently denied as this may be at least in varieties of contemporary Christianity – and rightly so of course – even a brief look at its history amply confirms this.

A next and fatal step – nowadays practiced by Islamist organizations and individuals – is using violence against non-believers and even fellow-believers, in order to assimilate or simply eliminate them. This ranges from genital mutilation to mass killing, all in the name of some or other god. But then would all this happen without institutionalized religion? This is a good question, though some Islamic and other forms of radicalism might still make one think otherwise.

What is to be learned from this? Modesty. Any real religious belief, however differently this may be experienced, ought not to need over-institutionalized and other ostentatious preaching and practice. Fewer religious utterances or at least less religious offense may make the problem of religious freedom less pressing. Real belief ought to be totally self-evident. Real truth "forces itself upon us" without any need for teaching, let alone violence.

6. The quest for total religious freedom

It may be sufficiently clear by now that for Epictetus religious freedom, or any freedom for that matter, is no problem at all in principle. Man is God in his omnipotence, and so he is totally free in principle. Thus regarded, there is no need for further reflection on the theme of freedom, religious or otherwise. All that needs to be done is to realize this insight by living one's life to the fullest, again, as if one is God himself. This is not hubris. It is the discovery and development of man's privileged position in the universe as it is.

Still, some more practical recommendations may be in order. Even less-converted followers of Epictetus may try to obviate or at least reinterpret semblances of opposition to their religion and its practices in the best possible light. Real belief cannot really be hindered by any more or less official resistance to it.

Next, respect others, not least because this is or at least ought to be one of the central tenets of your own religious belief. Such respect may imply you have to limit attempts to "save souls" by trying to convert them to your own one and true belief. Be modest, at least, in the knowledge that you are man and not God in the sense of governor of the whole world. (Try first and foremost to be the wise governor of your own life.)

Such respect for others may imply being less ostentatious when it comes to religious practices, from the presence of crucifixes in classrooms to the staging of religious and sometimes violent public demonstrations (and even the committing of acts of terror) against so-called "enemies" of true belief. So many conflicts over religion and ensuing issues of religious freedom originate from enthusiasm or even violent fanaticism in communication of the (supposed) one and only true belief. But then the problem is that there is nothing like the one and only true belief, at least not in a descriptive sense. And even if there were to be, not everybody would necessarily agree. Preaching or even enforcing one's own conviction, driven by whatever motives, is not always a good substitute for living life to the fullest.

This given fact of a multitude of fundamental convictions implies leaving as much room for different religions as is practically feasible within any civilized jurisdiction. It leaves no room in principle for attempts to thwart the beliefs and practices of others (e.g., Islamic expressions of religious belief, as has been done in Switzerland and elsewhere) – that is, as long as there is no evidence that such beliefs and practices wrongfully harm citizens of other denominations. Indeed, some so-called "humanistic" liberals further see measures against Islam and Islamic institutions as expressions of intolerance and of non-liberal ideology in general. Such measures are wrongheaded, not least because they are deeply at odds with humanist ideals. What we need to do is effectively limit really wrongful harm, however difficult it may be to determine what relevant harm is and to develop responsible measures against it. Not all Muslims are criminals and terrorists, just as not all terrorists are Muslims, even if some of them call themselves by that name. What counts is religious freedom, or just freedom, for everybody.

How to practically implement this state of affairs is quite another matter, of course. Epictetus' teachings may be of rather limited value in this respect at least. Still, *laïcité* may be the best solution in principle. A religiously neutral state, fully respecting different religions as long as no wrongful harm is done may be the best expression of respect for every human being, whatever his or her fundamental convictions, as being God.

Again, this is not disinterested relativism. Rather, it is respect for different human realities, including religious persuasions, from a humane and thus non-relative standpoint. In fact, Epictetus himself, however much he explicitly eschewed ethical discourse, was deeply anti-relativist and subjectivist, for an obvious reason: God is no relativist, so man does matter as well. Everybody, whatever his or her persuasions in religion and otherwise, is to be enabled to be a god, or God, insofar as it is possible. This is "freedom from" undue interference, in warding off any hindrance not demonstrably necessary in order to prevent wrongful harm. This ought to create room for everybody to believe what ought to be believed. But it ought also to create room for a fundamental question: is belief really necessary for gods themselves? Religion may not be reduced to psychology, but then inner freedom may still profit from some insight into man's sometimes irrational need for certainty or at least a foothold beyond man and world. This would be "freedom to" live life to the fullest.

7. Agenda: A war cry against any violence against man and God

There can be no agenda for religious freedom without an understanding of religious freedom's essence. This is man's unlimited power, in principle, to reinterpret the world for the better, even to change it for the better however marginally. It is also man's essence of being there, here and now, unhindered by anything. And the very essence of religious freedom, however often forgotten or even explicitly acted against, is man being God.

However metaphorical this identification of man as God may be, at least it ought to imply respect for human beings as infinitely valuable per se, whatever their persuasions, religious or otherwise. Thus, respecting religious freedom is respecting man. The same point may be made the other way around. As man is God, respect for man is respect for God as well. This version of the same core idea holds good in Christianity and other major religions as well, even without outright identification of man with God. Live and act in accordance with this idea, however hard this may be at times. Do not offend with religious practices that are not unconditionally essential for living any religion. But one must also respect religion, as such respect for religion is nothing else than respect for man.

Such total freedom of religion is not always very practicable of course. Wrongful harm and offense against non-believers may stand in the way of this. But then religious practices are never to be curtailed *qua* religious practices. This would amount to trying to curtail God himself indeed. On the other hand, religious or quasi-religious activities of whatever kind that do not respect God in any human being concerned ought to be treated as godless in themselves. This holds true for missionary and other violence against "non-believers."

Indeed, it is unclear what Epictetus would have thought about the need to fight terrorism and other crimes. Activism against such evils is not easily compatible with his basic idea of freedom from evil in reinterpreting and accepting everything as it comes in the best possible light. True as this may be in principle, doing nothing about terrorism and so many other evils threatening so many infinitely valuable human beings would be unacceptable as well. So even with Epictetus' wisdom, it may be difficult to strike a good balance here.

So whatever religious liberty may mean, on paper and in practice, it can be neither understood nor enjoyed at all without prior understanding of the essentially religious nature of liberty itself. If man is God, however metaphorically so, real life starts with the insight that human freedom rightly understood has no limits at all. Religious liberty or just liberty in the end is the grandiose idea that this is *your* world, *our* world, however small and threatened one may feel at times. Remember that life is sitting as a guest of honor at the dinner table of the gods.

To conclude: if this contribution awakens any motivation to read and re-read the *Diatribai*, it has more than sufficiently served its purpose. There is no substitute for reading the *Diatribai* yourself. It is and remains the wake up call to start living – not as if man is God, but because man is God.

Notes

1 Literally, "nature makes no jumps." This saying is commonplace among early modern philosophers.
2 For a discussion of this literary episode in the play by Greek playwright Euripides, see Easterling (1991).

Bibliography

Berlin, Isaiah. 1969. "Two Concepts of Liberty." In *Four Essays on Liberty*. Oxford: Oxford University Press, 118–172.

Easterling, P. E. 1977. "The Infanticide in Euripides' *Medea*." In *Yale Classical Studies*, Vol. 25: *Greek Tragedy*, ed. T. F. Gould and C. J. Herington. London: Cambridge University Press, 177–191.

Epictetus. 1925. *The Discourses: Books I and II*, ed. and trans. William A. Oldfather. Cambridge: Harvard University Press.

Epictetus. 1928. *The Discourses: Books III and IV, Fragments* and *The Enchiridion*, ed. and trans. William A. Oldfather. Cambridge: Harvard University Press.

Kant, Immanuel. 2012 [1785]. *Groundwork to the Metaphysics of Morals*, ed. Mary Gregor and Jens Timmerman. Cambridge: Cambridge University Press.

Strawson, Peter F. 1973. "Freedom and Resentment." In *Freedom and Resentment, and Other Essays*. London: Methuen, 1–28.

Wittgenstein, Ludwig. 1921. "Logisch-Philosophische Abhandlung." *Annalen der Naturphilosophie* 44: 185–262.

Wittgenstein, Ludwig. 1922. *Tractatus Logico-Philosophicus*, trans. Charles K. Ogden. New York: Harcourt Brace and Company.

Wittgenstein, Ludwig. 1965. "A Lecture on Ethics." *Philosophical Review* 74(1): 3–12.

4 The right to religious freedom: A judicial approach

Dallas K. Miller

1. Introduction – A case study

In 2014, the Honorable Michael Kirby delivered a report of the Commission of Inquiry on Human Rights in the Democratic People's Republic of Korea (North Korea). Few nations surpass North Korea in terms of widespread human rights abuses in such a systematic fashion over the past 70 years. Mandated by the United Nations Human Rights Council, the commission of inquiry was to investigate the systematic, widespread and grave violation of human rights in the following nine specific and substantive areas (Kirby, Biserko and Darusman 2014, 3):

- Violations of the right to food;
- Violations associated with prison camps;
- Torture and inhumane treatment;
- Arbitrary arrest and detention;
- Discrimination, in particular, the systemic denial and violation of basic human rights and fundamental freedoms;
- Violations of the freedom of expression;
- Violations of the right to life;
- Violations of the freedom of movement; and
- Enforced disappearances, including in the form of abductions of nationals of other states.

The framework utilized by the commission of inquiry was the binding legal obligations created by North Korea when it voluntarily signed the Covenant on Civil and Political Rights; the Covenant on Economic, Social and Cultural Rights; the Convention on the Rights of the Child; and the Convention on the Elimination of All Forms of Discrimination against Women. The commission of inquiry used a standard of proof known as "reasonable grounds" and took a balanced and even-handed approach when reaching its conclusions.

In terms of human rights abuses, the commission of inquiry's findings are wide-ranging, detailed and disturbing. However, leading the list of egregious human rights abuses are the violations of the freedom of thought, expression and religion. The other areas of discrimination, state-sponsored repressions and arbitrary detention, executions and prison camps all relate to the denial of freedom of religion and its related fundamental freedoms (Kirby, Biserko and Darusman 2014, 6).

Some have described North Korea as a "seculocratic" state, where government has an identity and legitimacy that is rooted in a secular political philosophy. Described as a communist or Marxist state with a one-man dictatorship, North Korea allows for no religious freedom (Shah, Franck and Farr 2012, 71).

The findings of Judge Kirby's commission of inquiry in this area are telling:

> The commission finds that there is an almost complete denial of the right of freedom of thought, conscience and religion, as well as of the rights to freedom of opinion, expression, information and association.
>
> The State operates an all-encompassing indoctrination machine that takes root from childhood to propagate an official personality cult and to manufacture absolute obedience to the Supreme Leader (*Suryond*), effectively to the exclusion of any thought independent of official ideology and State propaganda.
>
> The State considers the spread of Christianity a particularly serious threat, since it challenges ideologically the official personality cult and provides a platform for social and political organization and interaction outside the realm of the State....Christians are prohibited from practising their religion and are persecuted. People caught practising Christianity are subject to severe punishments in violation of the right to freedom of religion and the prohibition of religious discrimination.
>
> (Kirby, Biserko and Darusman 2014, 7)

Judge Kirby's report has spawned significant reaction from religious freedom advocates. Within weeks of the report's release, the Religious Liberty Partnership issued the "Ottawa Statement" expressing concern over North Korea's systemic and egregious religious persecution and consequential gender violence, forced separation of citizens from China, and state-sponsored suffering and starvation through its vast concentration camp system. The "Ottawa Statement" calls on the international community to circulate the findings of Judge Kirby's report, act on its recommendations and bring the North Korean leadership to justice for having perpetrated crimes against humanity (Religious Liberty Partnership 2014).

The case of North Korea's blatant and purposeful denial of religious freedom has significant ramifications for all human rights on a broader scale. The interconnectedness of basic human rights and fundamental freedoms are made obvious in the case of North Korea. By denying its citizens the right to communally practice their religion, the North Korean regime denies its people the right to assemble freely, the right to speak freely, and the right to organize and discuss an alternative way of being governed. By denying its people the right to express their religious faith, the regime ensures that there are no advocates for the persecuted, the wrongly accused or the victims of concentration camps. The restriction on religious expression prevents individuals in North Korea from acting charitably to their fellow citizens in the form of distributing food, providing humanitarian assistance, and preventing gender-based violence.

If the right to religious freedom affects other human rights and if its outright denial and repression adversely affect other human rights, as the case of North Korea seems to indicate, what can be done to maximize religious freedom and other basic human rights and fundamental freedoms? The answer to this question can be found in a recent work by researcher Brian Grim, who has correlated religious freedom with other freedoms and aspects of social well-being:

> Religious freedom is embedded within a much larger bundle of civil liberties. At the core of religious expression is the freedom of speech and at the core of freedom to worship is the freedom to assemble. To claim freedom of speech without allowing for a freedom to express religious beliefs quickly erodes freedom of speech in other areas. Likewise, allowing for restrictions on the assembly of religious groups opens the door for curtailing the activities of other groups as well. The denial of religious freedom is inevitably intertwined with the denial of other freedoms.
>
> (Cited in Shah, Franck and Farr 2012, 21)

2. The international legal standard for religious freedom

A. The history of the UDHR

The basis on which modern human rights are protected and advanced internationally is the same for religious freedom as it is for other fundamental rights.

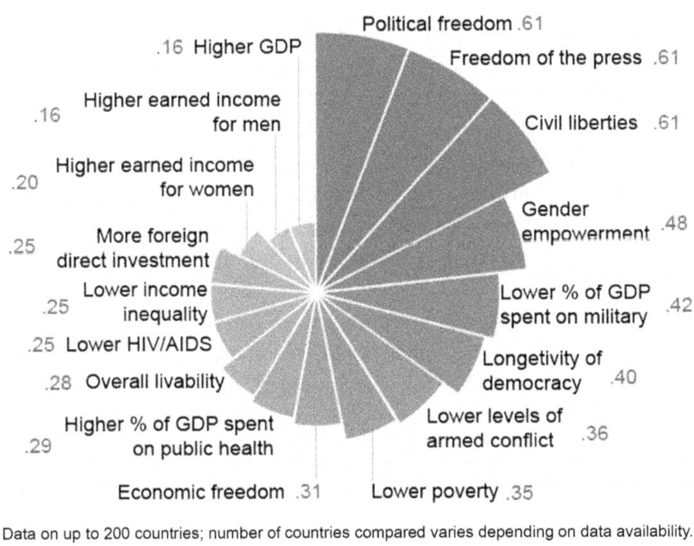

Figure 4.1 Correlation of religious freedom with other freedoms and well-being within countries

Source: (Grim and Finke 2011, 206).

The UDHR was adopted by the United Nations General Assembly (UNGA) on December 10, 1948, without an opposing vote. The UDHR is not a Western document, but a *universal* one authored by four individuals from around the globe. Eleanor Roosevelt, the Chairperson of the Human Rights Commission of the newly founded United Nations, had the prestige and gravitas to both represent and influence the United States in supporting the UDHR. René Cassin, the skilled legal adviser to Charles de Gaulle and the Free French, was instrumental in creating the UDHR as an integrated whole rather than as an enumerated "bill" of rights. P. C. Chang, a Chinese philosopher and diplomat, played an important role in facilitating consensus by ensuring that the principles in the UDHR were translatable from one culture to another. It is widely acknowledged that the most influential drafter of the UDHR was Charles Malik, a Lebanese philosopher and diplomat, who made sure that the terms in the UDHR and specifically the rights that were protected therein were truly universal. He was also instrumental in moving the final draft through to its adoption by the UNGA during the tense times of the emergence of the Cold War in 1948 (Glendon 2002, xv–xxi; Malik 2000, 100–101).

It is important to note that the UDHR revived basic human rights as part of "natural law," not as part of positive law. Language in the UDHR includes words like *recognition, inherent, inalienable, born* and *endowed*. All these words denote a natural law origin, a recognition that nature or something pre-dating the state or government is the origin of human rights.

B. Article 18 – Protecting religious liberty

While the preamble to the UDHR specifically identifies freedom of "belief" and articulates that the enumerated rights be "protected by the rule of law," freedom of religion is specifically protected in Article 18 of the UDHR:

> Everyone has the right to freedom of thought, conscience and religion; this right includes freedom to change his religion or belief, and freedom, either alone or in community with others and in public or private, to manifest his religion or belief in teaching, practice, worship and observance.

What is unique about this article is the inclusion of the phrase "this right includes the freedom to change his religion or belief." In drafting the UDHR to articulate how humans are free, Charles Malik was opposed by those who denied this particular freedom. There are some (who ironically are supported by their religious faith) who are of the view that religion is "not a question of free choice but of birth and tradition." According to Malik, the importance of freedom was lost, if it did not include the freedom of the intellect, the freedom of the will, and man's ultimate freedom with respect to the worship of God (Malik 2000, 101).

The importance of religion, according to Malik, was not restricted to Article 18. He saw that in order for all human rights to be properly sustained and protected there needed to be more than just man and the state. He articulated and advocated a philosophy that analyzed the nature of the human person, the place of the individual in society, and a person's relation to the state. In analyzing the individual's relation to the state, Malik allowed for mediating institutions – what Catholics call "subsidiarity" and Protestants refer to as "sphere sovereignty" or "orders of creation." Malik's rhetorical questions help us to see the value of mediating institutions as spheres of liberty independent of states:

> Is his loyalty to the state all-embracing, absolute, unconditional, intolerant of every other loyalty and attachment? Or, is he allowed to develop loyalties at least side by side with his loyalty to the state? Is it in harmony with his natural rights as a man to allow the state to determine for him all his beliefs and ideas and even hopes, all the material basis of his existence, all the patterns of his life?
>
> What about the family, church, intimate circle of friends, independent pursuit of science and truth, sustaining folk songs and folkways that are utterly independent in their origin of any government and any state? What about this whole plenum of intermediate institutions that span the chasm between the individual and the state?
>
> Do we not rather enjoy our deepest and truest freedom and humanity in our family, in the church, in our intimate circle of friends, when we are immersed in the joyful ways of life of our own people, when we seek, find, see, and acknowledge the truth?
>
> But unless the proposed Bill of Rights can create conditions that will allow man to develop ultimate loyalties with respect to these intermediate sources of freedom, over and above his loyalty to the state, we shall have legislated not for man's freedom but for his virtual enslavement.
>
> (Malik 2000, 110)

In allowing for the freedom to believe and to practice religion in the enumerated rights in the UDHR and in allowing for religion to be part of the mediating structures of society, Malik was indeed prescient. One of the reasons Malik saw the enduring importance of religion in nations, as well as its importance in undergirding human rights, was that he soundly rejected the aspect of Enlightenment thinking that rejected religion. In advocating for the UDHR, he would regularly make reference to 19th- and early-20th-century thinkers who ridiculed what he called "the classical ages of faith." Many of these Enlightenment thinkers now found themselves in the middle of the 20th century, a most barbarous time after World War II, without a foundation for human rights. The concept of the proper worth and dignity of humanity was vanishing because of this loss of faith from the 18th- and 19th-century Enlightenment secularists. It was Charles Malik's goal to restore the dignity and worth of mankind through the UDHR and the natural law embedded in the document, as well as to ensure that man was free to pursue a life unhindered by the state and with the full participation of intermediate institutions like the home, the community and the church (Malik 2000, 115–116).

In his speeches and writings that led up to the drafting of the UDHR, Malik articulated a clear worldview justifying its acceptance. He undertook what could perhaps best be described as producing the equivalent of the *Federalist Papers* to support the UDHR. He never ceased to advocate why, after the horrors of two World Wars, the international community needed to focus on the foundation of peace and security in the United Nations Charter. And the foundations of the Charter were the human rights that were clearly articulated in the UDHR, which protected religious freedom in its fullest sense. It cannot be lost in this analysis that the United Nations Charter and the UDHR came about within three years of the world realizing the horrors of the Holocaust. It is important to be mindful that the Holocaust had its genesis in the so-called "final solution," which was based on eliminating an entire race of people because of its religious identity (Roseman 2002).

While there is no explicit mention of a deity as the source of human rights in the preamble or the articles of the UDHR, it is clear where Charles Malik stood on this issue. Article 1 includes the phrase "endowed by reason and conscience," and Malik later acknowledged that he had included this phrase as a clear reference to Christian natural law theory (Morsink 1999, 284).

Today, there are those who argue that protecting religious freedom as part of the overall human rights framework should not be made a priority. Brian Leiter, a University of Chicago law professor and prominent legal academic, argues that there is nothing inherent in religion that justifies its having a special place in legal or constitutional protection. Leiter takes a Rawlsian approach in arguing that, in order to be purely neutral in a liberal democracy and to encourage public reasoning, we must be careful to rid the public square of religious arguments. This approach only provides the right to liberty of conscience, a more encompassing religious liberty. Leiter uses the utilitarian approach of John Stuart Mill, who argued for the maximum good for the greatest number of people. Mill restricts the advancement of religious freedom beyond mere protection of liberty of conscience. These two thinkers – Rawls and Mill – are used by Leiter to identify grounds for protecting liberty of conscience, but he argues that they do not justify advancing a special category for the protection of religion or religious belief, practice and worship. In a sense, Leiter collapses all arguments for the protection of religious liberty into an argument for the protection of liberty of conscience. He is of the view that in today's world special protection for religion is an anachronism:

> There may be compelling principled reasons for the state to respect liberty of conscience – the conclusion established by the Rawlsian and Millian arguments of chapter 1 – but there is no apparent moral reason why states should carve out special protections that encourage individuals to structure their lives around categorical demands that are insulated from the standards of evidence and reasoning we everywhere else expect to constitute constraints on judgment and action, even allowing that those demands may figure in systems of belief that have some utility-maximizing effects (e.g., existential consolation). Singling out religion for toleration is tantamount to thinking we ought to encourage precisely this conjunction of categorical fervor and its basis in

> epistemic indifference, and that we should simply bite the speculative bullet. If matters of religious conscience deserves [sic] toleration – as they surely do given the arguments of chapter 1 – then they do so because they involve matters of *conscience*, not matters of religion.
>
> (Leiter 2012, 63–64)

It is interesting that Leiter does not mention religious freedom or the protection of religious liberty on an international level. He certainly does not interact with the recent data that shows the widespread international problem of persecution and restriction of religious people and groups. This infringement upon religious believers comes about from governments themselves or by hostile acts of private individuals or social groups not properly sanctioned by government. In a recent study, it was reported that one third of the nations in the world "have high to very high restriction on religion." This translates, in terms of population, to "nearly 70 percent of the world's 6–8 billion people" living "in countries with high restrictions on religion" (Pew Forum on Religious and Public Life 2009, 1).

If there is validity to the research on the vast amount of religious persecution taking place around the world, it would seem that the approach of failing to protect religious belief and practice legally on an international scale, as espoused by Leiter within the United States and other liberal democracies, is the wrong direction to take. It seems as though Charles Malik would also be opposed to this public policy approach both domestically and internationally. Malik strongly argued that a form of natural law theory ran through the UDHR and that because it espoused a higher standard from which to judge a nation's laws and actions it had authority to protect human rights. He argued that a legal positivist approach to human rights was a failure. What the world needed was a declaration on human rights like the UDHR at this very vulnerable time in history similar to the natural law of John Locke, which undergirded the Constitution of the United States. When positive law grounds one's conception of human rights, they are extremely vulnerable. The absurdity of a positive law grounding of human rights was clear to John Locke, and it was even more obvious in the post-World-War II era. Malik's disdain for positive law thinkers is obvious in the immediate shadow of the Holocaust (Malik 2000, 143–191).

3. From Article 18 to Declaration

Article 18 of the UDHR was, like other enumerated rights, the genesis of further international law for specific human rights protections in the modern era. The United Nations Charter created the Commission on Human Rights, and the Commission saw as its mandate the drafting and adoption of three key instruments: the UDHR, the Covenant on Economic, Social and Cultural Rights (CESCR) and the Covenant on Civil and Political Rights (CCPR). The Covenants were adopted by the UNGA in 1966 and had the requisite number of signatory nations sign and ratify them by 1976 (Buergenthal, Shelton and Stewart 2007, 29–76). Combined, these three instruments have been described as the International Bill of Human Rights. Article 18 of the CCPR protects religious freedom:

> 1 Everyone shall have the right to freedom of thought, conscience and religion. This right shall include freedom to have or to adopt a religion or belief of his choice, and freedom, either individually or in community with others and in public or private, to manifest his religion or belief in worship, observance, practice and teaching.
> 2 No one shall be subject to coercion which would impair his freedom to have or to adopt a religion or belief of his choice.
> 3 Freedom to manifest one's religion or beliefs may be subject only to such limitations as are prescribed by law and are necessary to protect public safety, order, health, or morals or the fundamental rights and freedoms of others.
> 4 The State Parties to the present Covenant undertake to have respect for the liberty of parents and, when applicable, legal guardians to ensure the religious and moral education of their children in conformity with their own convictions.

While the CCPR does not go as far as Article 18 of the UDHR in terms of the freedom to change one's religion, it was certainly not the intention of those who valued religious freedom in the international sphere to end at the covenant stage. Much more work was to be done to advance religious freedom.

As was the case with other fundamental human rights, such as racial equality and gender equality, it was the goal of the UNGA to ultimately have a treaty specifically dedicated to religious freedom. This can be seen in General Assembly Resolution 1781 in 1962:

> *Desiring* to put into effect the principle of the equality of all men and all peoples without distinction as to race, colour or religion, as stated in the Charter of the United Nations,
>
> *Deeply disturbed* by the manifestations of discrimination based on differences of race, colour and religion still in evidence throughout the world,
>
> *Considering* the necessity of taking all possible steps conducive to the final and total elimination of all such manifestations, which violate the Charter of the United Nations and the Universal Declaration of Human Rights,
>
> *Emphasizing* that each State ought to take all the necessary action to put an end to these violations, which infringe human dignity,
>
> *Noting* that the Commission on Human Rights is preparing draft principles on freedom and non-discrimination in the matter of religious rights and practices,
>
> 1 *Requests* the Economic and Social Council to ask the Commission on Human Rights, bearing in mind the views of the Sub-Commission on Prevention of Discrimination and the Protection of Minorities, the

debates at the seventeenth session of the General Assembly, any proposals on this matter that may be submitted by Governments and any international instruments already adopted in this field by the specialized agencies, to prepare:

2 A draft declaration on the elimination of all forms of religious intolerance, to be submitted to the Assembly for consideration at its eighteenth session;

3 A draft international convention on the elimination of all forms of religious intolerance, to be submitted to the Assembly if possible at its nineteenth session and, in any case, not later than at its twentieth session;

4 *Invites* Member States to submit their comments and proposals concerning the draft convention by 15 January 1964.

The Declaration on the Elimination of all Forms of Intolerance and of Discrimination Based on Religion or Belief was adopted by the General Assembly on November 25, 1981. The legal import of a "declaration" is certainly limited. A declaration is a written instrument of expression of general principles by the United Nations, and these principles are intended to have considerable moral and political authority. Over the course of time, the principles may become binding as a matter of customary international law when consistent state practice or usage arises. A declaration is not a binding legal document, unless it becomes customary law by evidence of state practice. Part of the problem of international religious persecution or discrimination is that it is so widespread and systemic in many nations so that the likelihood of a declaration in this area becoming customary state practice is remote.

The intention of the UNGA after the adoption of the Declaration was that it would be followed by a treaty or convention. A convention creates binding international legal obligations between states that ratify the convention. The convention establishes norms for the conduct of states, and conventional law or treaty law is distinct from customary law. It is clear from the historical record that a declaration was only an intermediate step. The ultimate goal was the adoption of a convention that created binding legal obligations on nation states to prevent discriminatory treatment by governments, to provide for members of religious faiths to practice their religion without state interference, and to create an obligation on states to suppress intolerance of religious expression and belief (Sullivan 1988; Tahzib-Lie 1996).

The Declaration on the Elimination of all Forms of Intolerance and of Discrimination Based on Religion or Belief consists of eight articles, and can be summarized as follows:

Article 1 articulates the principle of the freedom to have a religion or hold the beliefs of one's choice, and this freedom extends to theistic, non-theistic and atheistic beliefs. It is also clear that freedom to hold religious beliefs includes the right to "manifest" one's religious beliefs; in other words, there is a right to act out the tenets of one's belief alone and in community with others. Also, no one should be subject to coercion that would impair his freedom to hold a belief or religion of his choice.

Article 2 prohibits states, institutions, or groups of persons from discriminating on the basis of religion. It protects many aspects of an individual's life, which are encompassed in the "recognition, enjoyment or exercise of human rights."

Article 3 has a general description of how religious discrimination is an affront to human beings and offends the human rights principles in the UDHR and those rights detailed in the Covenants on human rights (i.e., the CESCR and the CCPR). While some may argue that this is an aspirational statement better suited for the preamble, it could also be argued that the all-important Article 18 of the UDHR and Article 18 of the CCPR are hereby incorporated by reference in the body of the Declaration.

Article 4 obligates states to review legislation and take positive steps to ensure that the rights guaranteed in the previous articles can be exercised without legislative obstacle, and there is an obligation to fill any legislative gaps that may prevent such exercise.

Article 5 perhaps has the most substantive provision. It integrates the full panoply of religious freedom rights with that of parental rights and education. It is clear that there is a strong presumption that parental wishes in terms of a child's education must be respected, with the "best interest of the child being the guiding principle."

Article 6 contains a list of the various manifestations of religion or belief that are protected. It includes the right to worship and assembly and the right to establish and maintain places of worship as well as maintain an organized structure. The right to make and acquire articles and materials for rites or customs and the right to write and disseminate publications are included in this article, as are the rights to teach, solicit funds and train and designate leaders. The freedom to observe days of rest and celebrate holidays and to establish and maintain communication with individuals and communities in matters of religion at the national and international level are protected. While not exhaustive of all actions that could be described in manifesting one's religious beliefs, this list is nonetheless remarkably detailed for an international instrument, and it is most helpful to victims of religious discrimination and persecution.

Article 7 stipulates that states are obligated to enshrine the protections spelled out in the Declaration as national legislation, so that the protections are universally available.

Article 8 says that one cannot use the terminology of the Declaration to restrict or derogate from any right in the UDHR and the Covenants. This is important because it cannot be denied, with the inclusion of Article 8, that the Declaration is in fact a progressive step forward in protecting religious freedom. Notwithstanding this, however, the Arab states have succeeded in removing from the final Declaration any reference to the right to change one's religion. This right is clearly set out in Article 18 of the UDHR, and, as we have just seen, Article 8 does not allow the diminution of that right (Clark 1983).

4. From Declaration to Convention

Throughout the lengthy history of the drafting process of the Declaration, it was clear that it was only the first step in international efforts needed to protect religious freedom. Discrimination on religious grounds is not necessarily universally condemned; in fact, there may "be little genuine consensus" (Claydon 1972, 412) to combat this problem at the international level. Therefore, early in this process it was the consensus that the proper legal development of establishing an international standard of protection required an international declaration. This would help lay the groundwork for an eventual convention or treaty. This was a practice that the United Nations had developed concerning other instruments dealing with other human rights issues, such as racial discrimination and children's rights. Furthermore, these were the precise instructions, in terms of progression, from the General Assembly in Resolution 1781 (Claydon 1972, 412–423).

A. Interrelationship of rights

When advocating for the protection of one of the fundamental rights, such as freedom of religion and belief under Article 18 of the UDHR, it is important to remember the very interconnectedness of all fundamental rights. For example, the rights in Article 18 are supported in Article 19 and Article 20 of the UDHR:

> ARTICLE 19. Everyone has the right to freedom of opinion and expression; this right includes freedom to hold opinions without interference and to seek, receive and impart information and ideas through any media regardless of frontiers.
>
> ARTICLE 20. (1) Everyone has the right to freedom of peaceful assembly and association. (2) No one may be compelled to belong to an association.

The parallel between these two articles and Article 18 clearly supports a person making a claim to the freedom to disseminate religious materials and peacefully associate and assemble and vice versa. If only the people in North Korea could practice their religion by gathering together to worship, they could also peacefully assemble and associate. Exercise of one of these rights causes a cross pollination of freedom in society and the advancement of all fundamental human rights.

The interconnectedness of rights can be seen more clearly when one looks at the Convention on the Elimination of All Forms of Racial Discrimination (CERD 1969). The preamble and Article 5 make reference to freedom of religion:

> Preamble:
>
> Considering that the Charter of the United Nations is based on the principles of the dignity and equality inherent in all human beings, and that all Member States have pledged themselves to take joint and separate action, in co-operation with the Organization, for the achievement of one of the purposes of the United Nations which is to promote and encourage universal respect for and

> observance of human rights and fundamental freedoms for all, without distinction as to race, sex, language or religion.
>
> Article 5:
>
> In compliance with the fundamental obligations laid down in Article 2 of this Convention, States Parties undertake to prohibit and to eliminate racial discrimination in all its forms and to guarantee the right of everyone, without distinction as to race, colour, or national or ethnic origin, to equality before the law, notably in the enjoyment of the following rights:
>
> (a) The right to equal treatment before the tribunals and all other organs administering justice;
> (b) The right to security of person and protection by the State against violence or bodily harm, whether inflicted by government officials or by any individual group or institution…;
> (c) Other civil rights, in particular…;
>   (vii) The right to freedom of thought, conscience and religion;
>   (viii) The right to freedom of opinion and expression; [and]
>   (ix) The right to freedom of peaceful assembly and association.

The CERD, specifically Article 5, which itemizes many religious practices, can be seen as protecting individual rights that are not only religious in nature. The freedom of thought that is affirmed in both Article 18 of the UDHR and the CERD can also be claimed to protect political and social thought (Sullivan 1988).

B. *The danger of a lack of international will*

The UDHR is clearly the starting point of the modern human rights movement. It is the first comprehensive human rights instrument that can claim international recognition. In the years since its acceptance, it has gained a moral status and a political and legal importance to rank with the Magna Carta, the American Declaration of Independence, and the French Declaration of the Rights of Man and of the Citizen. It is truly a milestone in the history of humanity's struggle for human rights and justice. Its purpose is to establish a "common understanding" of human rights and fundamental freedoms that are referenced in the United Nations Charter. These human rights are to be "protected by the rule of law" (Buergenthal, Shelton and Stewart 2007, 38).

The UDHR spawned various regional human rights protection systems and several international covenants or treaties targeting certain human rights problems. Specifically, language similar to that contained in Article 18 of the UDHR can be found in the American Convention on Human Rights (1978) and the European Convention on the Protection of Human Rights and Fundamental Freedoms (1953).

One human rights scholar has described the influence of Article 18 of the UDHR as follows:

> The authoritative nature of Article 18 is evident in the replication of its provisions in national constitutions of states and the consistent references to Article 18 within various constitutional and legislative documents. As an integral part of the UDHR, Article 18 has been translated into more languages and dialects than any other international document in the world. National and international tribunals have also relied upon provisions stemming from Article 18, treating such provisions with considerable authority and weight.
>
> (Evans et al. 2013, 11)

Some would argue, however, that the clear meaning and intention of Article 18 has lost some of its textual power. For example, the clear right of a person "to change his religion or belief" was not included in Article 18 of the CCPR, nor was it specified in the Declaration on the Elimination of all Forms of Intolerance and of Discrimination Based on Religion or Belief. Donna Sullivan, in her detailed analysis of the Declaration, has this to say about the omission of the clear right to change one's religion or belief:

> The right of individuals to maintain their own beliefs is central to the concerns that motivated the drafting of the Declaration itself. This principle necessarily entails not only the right to retain a belief, but also the freedom to choose a belief without coercion, including the right to reject one's current belief and accept another. Although explicit reference to the right to change beliefs was dropped from the Declaration, that right remains implicit in the right to have a religion or belief. Moreover, Article 8, the savings clause of the Declaration, preserves the standards set forth in the Universal Declaration of Human Rights (the Universal Declaration) and the International Covenants on Human Rights by stating that "[n]othing in the present Declaration shall be construed as restricting or derogating from any right defined in the Universal Declaration of Human Rights and the International Covenants on Human Rights." The Universal Declaration affirms the freedom to change beliefs and the Political Covenant refers to the freedom to adopt a religion or belief.
>
> (Sullivan 1988, 495)

Some have argued that, notwithstanding the clear omission of the right to change one's religion in the Declaration, Article 8 states that nothing in the Declaration can be construed as restricting or derogating from any right defined in the UDHR and the CCPR. The history of the drafting process is enlightening in this regard. Arab nations opposed the inclusion of the right to change one's religion in the Declaration. The drafting committee actually faced a double-edged pressure because the atheist Soviet bloc countries opposed the examples of manifesting one's religion as listed in Article 6. A compromise was reached by the inclusion of Article 8. The rationale for the ultimate wording of the Declaration is found in the words of the Chairman of the Third Committee responsible for the Declaration:

> I understand from Islamic delegates that in Arabic, the words "or to adopt" have a clearer meaning than in English and precisely because of that clearer meaning, their deletion was requested from the Draft Declaration. In my own view, although I could see advantage in having words "or to adopt" retained as from the Covenant, I did not see them as essential to the question of the rights to change religion. It is true, however, that the removal of the specific mention of the right to change religion in discussions subsequent to the Universal Declaration was a concession by Western states which they felt obliged to make in order to advance the subject of religious belief.
>
> (Clark 1983: 28, 38)

While the importance of Article 18 of the UDHR is not questioned by anyone, its full impact and duplication in international instruments has not been as successful and as fulsome as predicted, nor has there been a complete international convention or treaty dedicated to religious freedom. A comparison with other basic or fundamental human rights itemized in the UDHR is worth noting.

When one reviews the various core international treaties adopted by the United Nations, it is interesting that the Convention on the Rights of the Child (CRC) came into force some 30 years after the related declaration. This is the largest gap between a declaration and a convention thus far. Virtually all of the core treaties that have been adopted and that have come into effect since the founding of the United Nations have found the source of the human right that is to be protected by the convention in the UDHR.

Table 4.1 Human rights and their sources

PARTICULAR HUMAN RIGHT	UDHR SOURCE	DECLARATION	CONVENTION
Children's rights	Article 25(2)	UNGA-1959	CRC 1989
Women's rights	Articles 2, 16, 25	UNGA-1967	CEDAW 1979
Racial discrimination	Article 2	UNGA-1963	CERD 1969
Slavery	Article 4	Various international covenants through the ILA	Supplementary Convention on the Abolition of Slavery 1957
Torture	Article 5	UNGA-1975	Torture Convention 1987
Migrant workers	Articles 13, 23, 25	Various ILO Conventions	Convention on the Protection of All Migrant Workers 2003
Freedom of religion	Article 18	UNGA-1981	?

5. Conclusion

It has now been over 30 years since the Declaration on the Elimination of all Forms of Intolerance and of Discrimination Based on Religion or Belief was adopted by the UNGA. Rather than the fundamental human right of freedom of religion gaining strength in international instruments such as the CCPR and the Declaration, it could be argued that a key aspect of the right, namely, the freedom to change one's religion, has lost some of its strength since the UDHR.

In the almost 70 years since the UDHR, religious freedom is the only fundamental human right that has not received protection by way of a convention. This is in spite of the clear direction of the UNGA in Resolution 1781 issued in 1962 that a draft convention on the elimination of all forms of religious intolerance be submitted or adopted by 1968. There is no current effort to draft a convention, despite the fact that much of the world's population is living in countries with "high restrictions on religion." Furthermore, the evidence of direct state denial of religious freedom and the failure of states to prevent or deal with cultural and social hostilities and actions of non-state actors is manifold (Leiter 2012).

My proposal moving forward is the following. The international community, both from a civil society and government leadership perspective, must reactivate the process outlined in Resolution 1781 and begin negotiating a legally binding Convention on the Freedom of Religion or Belief. This convention must reflect the fulsome nature of the right that is contained in Article 18 of the UDHR. Drafters must be mindful of the forces that have tried to diminish the right in the CCPR and in the Declaration on the Elimination of all Forms of Intolerance and of Discrimination Based on Religion or Belief. The Convention must be preventative and contain mandatory periodic reviews that publicly expose violators and commend those state parties that honor and live up to the Convention's standards. The task will not be easy, but neither was the drafting and ultimate adoption of the UDHR. If we are to finish the task of protecting human rights "by the rule of law," as articulated by the UDHR, those leaders who want to see religious freedoms protected internationally must take up the cause for a convention that was directed over 50 years ago.

The lack of a current effort to adopt a mandatory treaty in the area of freedom of religion or belief is not due to a paucity of legal scholarship in the area. It appears to be a matter of will. In this regard, the words of a pioneering academic in this area are worth hearing:

> None of the several suggestions and proposals to that effect adequately answer why this essential manifestation of human liberty has received less attention than other fundamental rights. Indeed, religion profoundly impacts the state of the world. Tragic events that demonstrate the powerful influence of ethnicity and religion, and in some cases require the intervention of massive international force, are but additional proof that religion plays a weighty role in xenophobia, racism, group hatred, and even territorial changes. Furthermore, religious persecution and conflicts between believers and non-believers;

> between different churches in multireligious countries; between dominating protected, or preferred religions and religious minorities; and between newly established religions are all common phenomena. Some even argue that a shift from violence between sovereign states to conflicts between ethnic and religious groups is taking place. In fact, the problem is so pervasive that the United States, the major political force in the world, considered it necessary to go through the complicated legislative process (legally and otherwise) to enact domestic legislation to protect endangered religious groups abroad. These problems, and the United States' response, suggest the time is ripe for the international community to give equal attention to freedom of religion or belief.
>
> (Lerner 2004, 64)

Aside from creating international legally binding obligations on signatory states, what would a Convention on the Freedom of Religion or Belief accomplish? It would solidify in international law the work begun in Article 18 of the UDHR. It would also give an opportunity to solidify and clearly enumerate the basic right to change one's religion and clear up any ambiguity on this issue. As well, it would require nations to regularly report their progress to an international committee in the area of protecting religious freedom similar to a nation's obligation to report on the advancement of women's rights and children's rights, and on torture.

Finally, it will round out and complete the protection of core or fundamental human rights by way of treaty or convention as planned in the aftermath of the UDHR. To those who may find this project pointless, or a wasted effort, I would like to remind the reader of the case of the British House of Lords in its decision involving Augusto Pinochet, the former President of Chile (Bartle and the Commissioner of Police and Others Ex parte Pinochet 1998, 4 All ER 897). Victims of torture in Chile had alleged breaches of the Torture Convention of 1984, a convention to which Chile, Spain and the United Kingdom were parties. The House of Lords had found that acts of torture, being against international law and domestic law, were sufficient to override head of state immunity, a long-held international doctrine. The Torture Convention prevailed and only because it was a convention. The case was one of the most important human rights cases in the 20th century. Perhaps in the 21st century, the development of a convention protecting religious freedom will see a case where leaders such as the President of North Korea, who continuously breaches North Koreans' rights to religious freedom with all of the negative consequences to society, will see true national and international sanctions against such egregious behavior. But this will only happen if a convention protecting religious freedom as a fundamental, core human right is drafted and adopted, and becomes a binding treaty obligation among nation states.

Bibliography

Bartle and the Commissioner of Police and Others Ex parte Pinochet. 1998. House of Lords. Accessed July 24, 2015. http://www.publications.parliament.uk/pa/ld199899/ldjudgmt/jd981125/pino01.htm.

Buergenthal, T., Shelton, D. and Stewart, D. 2007. *International Human Rights in a Nutshell*, 4th ed. St. Paul, MN: West Publishing.

Clark, Roger S. 1983. "The United Nations Declaration on the Elimination of All Forms of Intolerance and of Discrimination Based on Religion or Belief." *Chitty's Law Journal* 31: 23–39.

Claydon, John. 1972. "The Treaty Protection of Religious Rights: U.N. Draft Convention on the Elimination of All Forms of Intolerance and of Discrimination Based On Religion or Belief." *Santa Clara Law Review* 12(2): 403–423.

Evans, Malcolm. 1997. *Religious Liberty and International Law in Europe*. Cambridge: Cambridge University Press.

Evans, Malcolm, Javaid Rehman, Ziya Meral, Nazila Ghanea-Hercock, Katherine Cash and Sean Oliver-Dee. 2013. *Article 18: An Orphaned Right*. Report for the All Party Parliamentary Group for International Freedom of Religion or Belief. Accessed May 17, 2015. https://freedomdeclared.org/media/Article-18-An-Orphaned-Right.pdf.

Glendon, Mary Ann. 2002. *A World Made New*. New York: Random House.

Grim, Brian J., and Roger Finke. 2011. *The Price of Freedom Denied: Religious Persecution and Conflict in the 21st Century*. New York: Cambridge University Press.

Kirby, Michael, Sonja Biserko and Marzuki Darusman. 2014. *Report of the Commission of Inquiry on Human Rights in the Democratic People's Republic of Korea. A/HRC/25/63*. United Nations Human Rights, Office of the High Commissioner for Human Rights. Accessed May 16, 2015. http://www.ohchr.org/EN/HRBodies/HRC/CoIDPRK/Pages/ReportoftheCommissionofInquiryDPRK.aspx.

Leiter, Brian. 2012. *Why Tolerate Religion?* Princeton: Princeton University Press.

Lerner, Natan. 2000. *Religion, Beliefs and International Human Rights*. Maryknoll, NY: Orbis.

Lerner, Natan. 2004. "The Nature and Minimum Standards of Freedom of Religion or Belief." In *Facilitating Freedom of Religion or Belief: A Deskbook*, ed. Tore Lindholm, W. ColeDurham, Jr. and Bahia G. Tahzib-Lie. Boston: Martinus Nijhoff, 63–84.

Malik, Habib C. ed. 2000. *The Challenge of Human Rights: Charles Malik and the Universal Declaration*. Oxford: Charles Malik Foundation.

Montgomery, John W. 1975. *The Law above the Law*. Minneapolis: Bethany Fellowship.

Montgomery, John W. 1986. *Human Rights and Human Dignity*. Grand Rapids: Zondervan.

Morsink, Johannes. 1999. *The Universal Declaration of Human Rights: Origins, Drafting, and Intent*. Philadelphia: University of Pennsylvania Press.

Pew Forum on Religious and Public Life. 2009. *Global Restrictions on Religion*. Pew Research Center. Accessed May 16, 2015. http://www.pewforum.org/2009/12/17/global-restrictions-on-religion/.

Religious Liberty Partnership. 2014. *Ottawa Statement on the Report of the Commission of Inquiry on Human Rights in the Democratic People's Republic of Korea (North Korea)*. Accessed May 17, 2015. http://www.iirf.eu/fileadmin/user_upload/PDFs/Statement_on_North_Korea_-_RLP_2014.pdf.

Roseman, Mark. 2002. *The Villa, The Lake, The Meeting: Wannsee and the Final Solution*. London: Penguin.

Shah, Timothy S., Matthew J. Franck and Thomas F. Farr. 2012. *Religious Freedom: Why Now? Defending an Embattled Human Right*. Princeton: Witherspoon Institute.

Stahnke, Tad, and J. Paul Martin. eds. 1998. *Religion and Human Rights: Basic Documents*. New York: Columbia University Press.

Sullivan, Donna. 1988. "Advancing the Freedom of Religion or Belief through the UN Declaration on the Elimination of Religious Intolerance and Discrimination." *American Journal of International Law* 82(3): 487–520.

Tahzib-Lie, Bahia G. 1996. *Freedom of Religion or Belief: Ensuring Effective International Legal Protection*. Cambridge: Kluwer Law International.

United Nations General Assembly. 1965. *International Convention on the Elimination of All Forms of Racial Discrimination*. United Nations Human Rights, Office of the High Commissioner for Human Rights. Accessed May 16, 2015. http://www.ohchr.org/EN/ProfessionalInterest/Pages/CERD.aspx.

United Nations General Assembly. 1979. *Convention on the Elimination of All Forms of Discrimination Against Women*. United Nations Human Rights, Office of the High Commissioner for Human Rights. Accessed May 16, 2015. http://www.ohchr.org/Documents/ProfessionalInterest/cedaw.pdf.

United Nations General Assembly. 1981. *Declaration on the Elimination of All Forms of Intolerance and of Discrimination Based on Religion or Belief*. United Nations. Accessed May 16, 2015. http://www.un.org/documents/ga/res/36/a36r055.htm.

Van der Vyver, Johan D., and JohnWitte, Jr). eds. 1996. *Religious Human Rights in Global Perspective: Legal Perspective*. Boston: Martinus Nijhoff.

Part II

The scope and limits of religious liberty

5 The secular state's interest in religious liberty[1]

Angus J. L. Menuge

Introduction: The secular state and religious neutrality

An important ideal of the secular state is (or should be) religious neutrality. In the First Amendment to the United States Constitution, this is understood to mean that the state is neither to endorse any religion (the "non-establishment clause") nor to abridge religious freedom (the "free exercise" clause). However, in 1791, when the First Amendment was adopted, "religion" generally referred to various Christian denominations, and since that time the United States and other Western countries have seen significant changes in the general character of their religiosity (Pew Research Center 2015). On the one hand, there is increasing religious indifferentism, usually taking the forms either of secularism (Berger, Davie and Fokas 2008; Grossman 2014) or of an unfocused and anonymous spirituality divorced from institutional religion (Smith and Denton 2005; Bass 2012). On the other hand, there is a vocal minority of New Atheists and other militant secularists who argue that historic, theistic religions are harmful to personal and social well-being. For example, Richard Dawkins complains that the religious indoctrination of children is "a grievous wrong" (Dawkins 2006, 308). These attitudes of indifference or hostility may explain why some politicians and lawmakers support increasing limitations on religious liberty. Some would argue that historic, theistic religions can expect a certain degree of toleration, but no encouragement. Others would insist on the privatization of religion: faith and its expression must be confined to personal conscience and houses of worship, but should not be evident in contributions to public decision-making (a view critiqued by Neuhaus 1996). And there are increasing calls to go further still by imposing secularist preferences that run counter to the dictates of religious conscience, two examples of this being efforts to require religious organizations to provide health insurance coverage for abortifacient drugs (George 2013, 106–107) and to prohibit pastors from expounding on scriptural texts deemed to be "hate speech" (Wachtler 2014).

I believe that there are many good arguments against this trend and in favor of a robust form of religious liberty. Not least of these is that, contrary to a simplistic dichotomy between "religious" and "secular" people, *all* human beings are inherently religious if religion is understood in a broad sense that includes both theistic and non-theistic beliefs about ultimate reality and the meaning of life

(Calvert 2013). As Roy Clouser argues, "a religious belief is a belief in something as…having unconditionally non-dependent reality" (Clouser 2005, 23). For secularists, nature is that "unconditionally non-dependent reality." This leads the secularist to a very different understanding than the theist's of another obviously religious issue – the meaning of life. The idea of a completely non-religious, "neutral" position on the nature of reality and the meaning of life is a myth.

In this essay, however, I will argue that it is in the secular state's interest to *encourage* religious liberty whenever secular reason can discern that it clearly contributes to social welfare. True, the state has the right to curb religious liberty that demonstrably promotes harms to its citizens (Montgomery 2013). But the Christian church offers several clear examples of religious liberty benefiting social welfare by providing (1) a place for independent thought and expression; (2) care for the poor; and (3) resources for community-building. I will focus on benefits that the church provides for which it is unlikely or impossible that the state could provide an equally effective substitute.

There are a couple of natural objections to such a project. First, it might be charged that the argument unfairly privileges the Christian faith. My response is that the social contributions of the Christian church are merely an illustration of how *a* religion may contribute to the good of a secular state. Second, it could be urged that there is something oddly cynical about arguing that a religion ought to be taken seriously by the secular state merely because it is good for society. Since there is no logical connection between being useful and being true, it may seem odd to defend religion merely for its salutary influence on society. My response to this objection is that the purpose of this paper is not apologetics: it is not an attempt to show that the secular state should recognize the truth of a religion such as Christianity. Rather, my argument assumes that competent governing authorities need not subscribe to a particular religion in order to see that the religion makes valuable contributions to the state. Certain religions deserve free exercise, not because the state knows them to be true, but because they support social goods that can be recognized using secular reason.

1. A place for independent thought and expression

Why should a secular state encourage religious thought and expression? One reason is rooted in the value of freedom of thought and expression in general: there is a *general benefit* in giving a fair hearing to a plurality of voices. Another reason depends on the specific character of religions like Christianity that subscribe to a transcendent God: there is a *particular benefit* to the state in hearing perspectives that go beyond the pragmatic consideration of the best means to preconceived social ends to a serious evaluation of the ends themselves.

The general benefit of freedom of thought and expression

John Stuart Mill ably argued for the great value deriving from liberty of thought and discussion (Mill 1978). Mill emphasized that this liberty should extend to minority opinions that the majority finds obnoxious, impious, immoral or obviously false, so long as those holding the opinions do not advocate harm to others. This is because the opinions bear on questions of the purpose of life that are vitally important to a well-functioning state, but which cannot be settled with absolute certainty. It is in the state's interest that its citizens have the chance to get as close to the truth as possible in their search for answers to these questions, and the state is not competent to foreclose the discussion by declaring some answers correct and outlawing the others. For "[a]ll silencing of discussion is an assumption of infallibility," and history shows that this assumption is indefensible, for it is not only individuals but whole ages that are fallible, "every age having held many opinions which subsequent ages have deemed not only false but absurd" (Mill 1978, 17).

Since a whole age can be wrong, minority or unpopular opinions must be allowed expression in case they are true, or contain a portion of the truth otherwise neglected. But Mill argues that even if the opinions are false, they should still be discussed, because sound doctrines become mere prejudices if they are not defended against erroneous alternatives (Mill 1978, 50). In that case, we soon find that even those who (perhaps) have the truth can give no articulate explanation or defense of it:

> But when it has come to be an hereditary creed, and to be received passively, not actively...there is a progressive tendency to forget all of the belief except the formularies, or to give it dull and torpid assent, as if accepting it on trust dispensed with the necessity of realizing it in consciousness, or testing it by personal experience, until it almost ceases to connect itself at all with the inner life of the human being.
>
> (Mill 1978, 38–39)

There are some important implications of this for Christians. When their views are culturally ascendant, they must not silence apparently obnoxious opinions with anti-blasphemy laws or the harsh treatment of heretics, not only because these opinions may sometimes be (partially or wholly) true, but also so that they better understand the grounds of their own beliefs by comparing and contrasting them with alternatives. By the same token, however, if some form of secularism or non-specific spirituality becomes culturally dominant, it should allow traditional religious opinions to be aired. For example, there are many contributions to civilization which appear to have resulted from Christian conviction (Schmidt 2001), and while others contend that Enlightenment rationalism (Pinker 2011) or New Age spirituality (Robinson 2015) could do the same or better, this is certainly controversial (D'Souza 2007). If society is best served by allowing an open search for the truth, it must allow this discussion to take place. More generally, even if some Christian opinions are viewed by some as outdated or obnoxious, still their expression should be encouraged in case our age falls into widespread error (a new dark ages) or in case that age's beliefs, even where they are true, become dead relics in the minds of a sleepwalking populace.

The particular benefit of transcendent religious perspectives

Another of Mill's important themes is the danger of oppressive or totalitarian societies. These easily arise if autocratic leaders impose their vision of humanity on everyone, but they can also arise in representative democracies: "'The tyranny of the majority' is now included among the evils against which society requires to be on its guard" (Mill 1978, 4). In practice, a great danger is that the *Zeitgeist* creates enthusiasm for a social order that is not in the long-term best interest of society. If those in power are infected, they are the least likely to understand the danger signs, as their ideological commitments will lead them to reinterpret these signs as necessary growing pains or even as social goods, such as national unity. Using the techniques of propaganda and a compliant media, many ordinary citizens can also be deceived into acquiescence. Who, then, will bring people to their senses and prevent (or mitigate) an orgy of self-destructive behavior?

What humanity most needs when those in power are in the grip of a persuasive, immersive, but ultimately inhumane and socially harmful ideology is a place of refuge, a secure place for at least some people to stand that is not conditioned by that ideology. The fisherman wading in a strong current can avoid being swept away so long as his feet are on rock. But what would that rock look like if the currents were statist ideologies like fascism or communism? It is often argued that the church offers no answer, because so many churches accommodated to these ideologies. While many churches did capitulate to Nazism (Eriksen 2012), for example, further investigation reveals that there was a marked difference *between* churches and that some of them did provide a rock of refuge where protest and resistance were possible and sometimes successful.

During the Nazi regime, the so-called "German Christians" (*Deutsche Christen*) took the view that even under a dictatorship God required obedience to His earthly representatives, and many of its members were in any case strongly pro-Nazi (Thielicke 1984). This posture precluded any effective protest against Nazi abuses, including the child Euthanasia program, the Aktion T4 program (which extended the killing to mentally and physically defective adults), the burning of synagogues, the exile of Jews and other "undesirable" peoples to labor camps, and the Holocaust (Lifton 1986). This was a failure not only of courage, but of theology. The German Christians were not able or willing to see that when the Nazis demanded absolute allegiance to the Third Reich, this was a violation of the First Commandment – "You shall have no other gods before me" (Exodus 20:3; Deuteronomy 5:7) – and that their criminal acts had to be resisted because they were in direct opposition to the "Law of God" (Acts 5: 29).

But, as Uwe Siemon-Netto argues, it is a *cliché*, an oversimplification, to suggest that all Christian churches in Germany capitulated to Nazism (Siemon-Netto 2007). In fact, "as far back as 1933 some 6,000 pastors, one-third of Germany's entire Protestant clergy, had joined the anti-Nazi *Pfarrernotbund* (Pastors Emergency League)" and "thousands of clergyman critical of Hitler…were jailed, forbidden to preach, or drafted and often sent to the Russian front, from whence most did not return" (Siemon-Netto 2007, 147). Several thousand clergy, as well as bold members of their congregations, belonged to the Confessing Church (*Bekennende Kirche*), in which Dietrich Bonhoeffer was a prominent voice (McElroy 2013). Early on, the Confessing Church returned to historic Christian teaching to affirm a place to stand against the Nazis. In 1934, the Synod of Barmen adopted the Barmen Declaration drafted by Karl Barth (1934), which consists of six articles, each including an affirmation and a repudiation.

Particularly telling is the second article. The affirmation upholds the First Commandment and explains why a biblical Christian recognizes an authority that transcends any man-made ideology:

> As Jesus Christ is God's assurance of the forgiveness of all our sins, so, in the same way and with the same seriousness he is also God's mighty claim upon our whole life.

The repudiation rejects the German Christian idea that one can divide the Christian life into two compartments, one focused on spiritual life and worship, dedicated to God, the other focused on worldly living, dedicated to the state:

> We reject the false doctrine, as though there were areas of our life in which we would not belong to Jesus Christ, but to other lords – areas in which we would not need justification and sanctification through him.

At a practical level, the strength of this confession is that it offers a foundation for morality that is independent of prevailing ideology. It reminds everyone in society – Christian or not – of the importance of permanent values, values that transcend the particular socio-political interests of the time, which easily devolve to a utilitarianism that promotes inhumane means to allegedly noble ends.

A good illustration of this point is Carl Friedrich Goerdeler (1884–1945). Goerdeler resigned as the mayor of Leipzig in 1937 after the Nazis removed and destroyed a monument to composer Felix Mendelssohn in front of Leipzig's famous concert hall. From then on, Goerdeler plotted to overthrow the Nazi authorities by any legal means possible, hoping to bring Hitler to trial and to replace him as Chancellor and appealing to the authorities in the United States and Great Britain to stand against Hitler's expansionist agenda in the late 1930s (Young 1974). Although Goerdeler ultimately failed, it is important to see *why* he failed and why he might have succeeded had more people shared his perspective. When Goerdeler brought his concerns about the Nazi regime to Neville Chamberlain and Franklin Roosevelt, arguing that the Nazis were lawless gangsters intent on removing the Judeo-Christian foundations of civilization, he did so because he had "internalized…Lutheran attitudes" (Siemon-Netto 2007, 107) that allowed him to recognize "the eternal moral code" (Siemon-Netto 2007, 120). His entreaties were dismissed because Chamberlain was deceived by appearances – thinking Hitler a man of honor seeking restitution for the losses incurred after the highly punitive Treaty of Versailles – and because many suspected that Goerdeler was a self-interested traitor who simply wanted power for himself. Perhaps only the British industrialist Arthur Young, who met with Goerdeler on many occasions, saw that "Goerdeler's moral outrage was motivated by his Christianity" and realized that Goerdeler's loyalty to the state was conditioned by a higher loyalty to transcendent moral values (Siemon-Netto 2007, 123).

Despite all his efforts, Goerdeler and his partners in the resistance failed to convince the West to stand against Nazism in the late 1930s, which might have averted a ghastly war and other atrocities it helped to conceal, precisely because of the inability of most people at the time to think beyond the prevailing currents of ideology:

> The German opposition's endeavors were frustrated by cliché thinking and its sibling, the *Zeitgeist*. The spirit of the time, being finite, was no place for theological insights such as [Helmut Thielicke's]: "We have all too often observed how an alien spirit has taken hold of people who had perhaps been quite nice and reasonable before...how it made them commit acts of cruelty and [drove them into an] ecstasy of power and madness of which they had thought themselves incapable."
>
> (Siemon-Netto 2007, 143, quoting his translation of Thielicke 1964, 140)

To recognize such an alien spirit for what it is requires one not to be so intoxicated by it that one has no effective counter-perspective. One needs a standard of objective goodness that is independent of the prevailing stream of socio-political ideology.

If enough people had found this transcendent perspective, could the Nazis have been overthrown earlier? Some evidence they could have was provided by subsequent developments in the German Democratic Republic (GDR). In 1968, Walter Ulbricht, the leader of the Communist Party, destroyed the University Church in Leipzig (including Bach's favorite pipe organ), because it symbolized the traditional, bourgeois Christian values that communism sought to efface. This moral and cultural outrage led to an international Bach music festival a mere 20 days later, forming the nucleus of a protest movement. Easy to overlook is the fact that Bach's music was both a priceless cultural treasure and a repository of transcendent reflection on God and the nature of man (Parton 2015). Many people would have realized that communism was attempting to erase reminders that some of German culture's most distinguished representatives, like Bach, recognized a higher authority than the communist state.

Like the German Christian churches of Nazi Germany, the churches in the GDR that accommodated by adopting a modernist and anthropocentric theology offered no refuge for those alienated by communism. But to traditional churches with orthodox preaching and historic liturgy, organ concerts and cantatas, young people flocked in large numbers "in search of an alternative to a system they clearly perceived as wrong" (Siemon-Netto 2007, 158). Significantly, the church was a magnet not only for the faithful: many non-Christians came to churches and associated prayer groups because only there did they feel comfortable in sharing their concerns and misgivings. The churches offered "pastoral care to opponents of the regime" while "congregations allowed their parish houses to be used by all kinds of *Gesprächskreise* (discussion groups) debating political, economic, and cultural questions they would not have been able to discuss elsewhere" (Siemon-Netto 2007, 154). And when people were increasingly forced to live in unpopular government housing,

> Christians were the ones willing to listen to people in those horrible tenements....And it was precisely this trust that enabled the church to persuade them to act nonviolently. Without this nonviolence, the October revolution of 1989 would never have succeeded.
>
> (Siemon-Netto 2007, 163)

One of the key leaders of the protest movement was Christian Führer, a Lutheran pastor at St. Nicholas Church in Leipzig. In 1988, he invited to the church 50 people who believed citizens had the right to leave the GDR, but 600 showed up. Subsequent prayer meetings and vigils attracted more people, and when the authorities closed the church on October 7, 1989, the gatherings continued to grow in size. The police attempted to intervene with dogs, batons and water cannons, but this led to an even larger gathering of 70,000 people. At Führer's urging, the crowd remained peaceful, bearing only candles and flowers, and the police felt unable to act. Soon, there were vigils of 120,000, then 320,000, and, finally, on November 9, 1989, the Berlin Wall came down (Obituary for Christian Führer 2014).

Not everyone who was inspired by the various Christian gatherings was, or became, a Christian. But those dissatisfied with communism all benefited from the church because, in its recognition of an ultimate authority beyond this world (John 18:36), it will not put its final trust in any temporal authority (Psalm 146:3). For its own health, so that it is not blinded by some self-destructive ideology that raises up amoral liars and thugs as leaders while it imprisons, enslaves, tortures and murders the law-abiding people who should be in their care, the state needs to defend the freedom of thought and expression of those who subscribe to a transcendent foundation for human welfare.

Without this independent perspective, society is liable to be deceived by ideologies which present a utopian vision but mask the ruthless measures of forced integration that will be employed in its implementation, such as compulsory "re-education," imprisonment for dissidents, blacklisting for employment, the intrusive regulation and monitoring of citizens and their associations, torture, and execution. The utopian vision is often so intoxicating that it anesthetizes its proponents to the harm and suffering they are causing. One reason a secular state ought to encourage freedom of Christian thought and expression is that it helps to protect the rights and liberties of *all* its citizens.

2. Care for the poor

Steven Pinker contends that the modern support for human welfare derives from the humanitarian revolution of the 17th-century Age of Reason. He claims that "Enlightenment humanism" can ground a good society, while the religious contribution must simply be discarded: "Faith, tradition, dogma, authority, the ecstatic glow of subjective certainty – all are recipes for error" (Pinker 2011, 180). Pinker affirms that "the universality of reason...defines a place for morality" (Pinker 2011, 182). In particular, it is the rational planning of enlightened secularist governments that is most likely to alleviate poverty. This attitude has fueled the widespread conviction among the predominantly secularist American Left that they are more compassionate than conservatives because of their support for government aid programs (Brooks 2006, 15–30).

However, this conviction overlooks the strong historical and contemporary connections between the Christian church and care for the poor. Concern for human welfare certainly did not begin in the 17th century, and in fact the assumptions of Enlightenment humanism, including its concern for the universal rights of man, are highly derivative from much earlier Christian sources. One way to see this is to consider how Christian teaching transformed the moral thinking of the ancient Greco-Roman world.

Study of that world reveals a shocking absence of compassion, which can be traced to a fundamentally different assumption about the nature and purpose of giving. Pagan thinking about charity was modeled on *liberalitas*, not *caritas*:

> *Caritas* meant giving to relieve the recipient's economic or physical distress without expecting anything in return, whereas *liberalitas* meant giving to please the recipient, who later would bestow a favor on the giver. For centuries the Roman pagans practiced *liberalitas*, not *caritas*.
>
> (Schmidt 2001, 126)

Liberalitas is eminently rational from the perspective of self-serving prudence, but it is more of a wise investment strategy than an example of what we now recognize as an act of charity. Charity in the sense everyone (including secularists) recognizes today – *caritas* – was almost non-existent in the ancient world. William Lecky concluded:

> There can...be no question that neither in practice nor in theory, neither in the institutions that were founded nor in the place that was assigned to it in the scale of duties, did charity in antiquity occupy a position at all comparable to that which it has obtained by Christianity. Nearly all relief was a State measure, dictated much more by policy than by benevolence; and the habit of selling young children, the innumerable expositions, the readiness of the poor to enrol[l] themselves as gladiators, and the frequent famines, show how large was the measure of unrelieved distress....[T]he active, habitual, and detailed charity of private persons, which is so conspicuous a feature in all Christian societies, was scarcely known in antiquity, and there are not more than two or three moralists who have even noticed it.
>
> (Lecky 1890, 78–79)

Pagans had modeled their giving on their gods, self-interested deities who would help one's family, business or crops to prosper if one offered a sacrifice. The idea that giving to the gods was a prudent investment was transferred to the interpersonal realm, so that it was normal to offer gifts to the wealthy and powerful, since they could provide the most help in return. As a result, it was mostly people who did not really need any help who received special gifts (Schmidt 2001: 126). It would seem pointless and irrational to give to the genuinely needy, since they were usually in no position to offer anything in return, and their plight did not provoke compassion anyway, since they were judged accursed by the gods.

By contrast, Christ announced that he came into the world not – like the pagan gods – in order to be served, but so that *he* could serve and give his life as a ransom for ours (Matthew 20:28). Christ came to those whose sins made them powerless to be right with God (Romans 5:6–8), and he sacrificed himself for those who could give him nothing in return. As a free response of gratitude, Christ then called his disciples to pursue lives of self-sacrifice, showing love to the "least of these" (Matthew 25:40), including those who could not repay (Luke 14:12–14).

The change in the culture was apparent:

> [T]he early Christians had a common fund to which they gave voluntarily, without any compulsion…[which] supported widows, the physically disabled, needy orphans, the sick, prisoners incarcerated for their Christian faith, and teachers requiring help; it provided burials for poor people and sometimes funds for the release of slaves….[E]very Christian was expected to give one-tenth of his income to charity.
>
> (Schmidt 2001, 125–126)

This giving was not simply a matter of Christians helping each other out: as Christ's sacrifice was for all people, so Christians extended their charity to everyone. Indeed, in the fourth century, Emperor Julian the Apostate lamented that, while pagans left their sick to die, Christians helped them as well as fellow Christians (Schmidt 2001, 129).

So there is considerable evidence that the modern idea of voluntary charitable giving to aid the poor is a Christian innovation. And still today, in countries like the United States, Arthur Brooks has shown that religious conservatives are the most generous in their charitable giving, followed by religious liberals, secular liberals and secular conservatives (Brooks 2006, 46–50). But some secular liberals would defend their lack of charity by arguing that tax-supported government programs are a more effective means of combatting poverty (Wielenberg 2014, 61–66).

This raises an important question: would society be just as well (or better) off without private charity, leaving care for the poor to the government? There are several reasons to answer in the negative. First, there is considerable evidence that long-term dependence on government welfare is not beneficial for recipients. Receiving payment in exchange for no service rendered easily becomes addictive, inducing much longer-term dependence than was intended and exacerbating the problems it was meant to solve:

> Unemployed people received support, lost job skills (or never acquired them), and became unable to gain stable employment, making them chronically reliant on state aid. During the 1990s, welfare support in America extended beyond a year for about half of recipients....Furthermore, nearly half of all the people who left welfare were back on the rolls within a year. Millions of people found themselves permanently on the dole.
>
> (Brooks 2006, 85)

Second, the existence of such an open-ended welfare system also seems to encourage people who could find a job not to do so, and the results of welfare reform beginning in 1996 provide strong evidence for this:

> In the first seven years after the enactment of welfare reform in 1996, the poverty rate fell from 13.7 percent of the U.S. population to 12.5 percent – and this period covered an economic recession. Furthermore, according to the U.S. government, welfare reform helped to move 4.7 million Americans from welfare dependency to self-sufficiency within three years of enactment, and the welfare caseload declined by 54 percent from 1996 to 2004.
>
> (Brooks 2006, 89)

Third, at a deeper level, humans are social beings that need to feel that they are making a worthwhile contribution to society. Work is not just about making money. It is also an important way individuals experience a sense of meaning and self-worth and can have their hearts and minds diverted from their own problems to consider the needs of others. Christian theology understands this dimension of work: it is not merely an economic activity, but a vocation: through the abilities God has granted to us and the needs of our neighbor, God is calling us to be an avenue of His loving care of His creatures. We receive a sense of dignity when we are able to assist others, but merely receiving financial aid does not create that sense. In fact, George Gilder seems right that it often demoralizes its recipients, as it creates a sense of futility: if I am rewarded no matter what I do, what is the point of doing anything (Gilder 2012, 39)? Sadly, this sort of existential *angst* about the meaning of life seems to make people more self-preoccupied and lacking in concern for others, so that, even with all of the additional available time, volunteer service is low among welfare recipients. One way to show this is to compare the working poor to those on welfare. Although the wealthiest give away the largest amount of money, in terms of the *percentage* of income donated to charity, the working poor are the most generous segment of American society (Brooks 2006, 80), and even when income is held constant,

> the working poor family gives more than three times as much to charity as the welfare family. It is more than twice as likely to give, and also almost twice as likely to volunteer. The working poor family is more likely to give to every

> type of charity than the welfare family, including religion, charities serving the poor, youth-related causes, international aid, and the environment.
>
> (Brooks 2006, 83)

This strongly suggests that dependence on welfare tends to turn people in on themselves, making them less social and less generous to others; and it may also be linked to increased crime (Brooks 2006, 95), whereas work, even if it produces no more money, tends to do the opposite. A Christian explanation of this is that work crucifies the selfish, sinful, old man in us with the demand to serve: for non-Christians, they find that the demands of their office compel them to serve, while for Christians the new man in Christ appears, who forgets himself and serves others willingly. But secularists can also see that playing a meaningful role in the community by making a worthwhile contribution will tend to produce better citizens.

Further, when people do require assistance because of job loss, health problems or inadequate income, there are several reasons to prefer private charity. For one thing, a culture of charity encourages people to be concerned about their own communities, and can create a meaningful bond between giver and recipient. Welfare checks are issued by law through an anonymous bureaucracy of salaried civil servants, and this creates a sense of entitlement without gratitude and does not engender the desire to give back. One knows of no one who has (voluntarily) made a sacrifice to help out. By contrast, church-based charity, which depends on local gifts and volunteers, is clearly motivated by concern and generosity, and those helped by the sacrifice of others often feel a stronger calling to give back to their community as soon as they get a chance. For example, it is a commonplace to find that previous (or ongoing) beneficiaries of a food pantry also serve among its volunteers. Here is a typical story from "Claudia" in California:

> I first visited my local food pantry five years ago. I am a single mother and although I work almost every day, it's just not enough. I needed some extra help – so I decided to ask for it. Visiting the pantry changed my life. Not only has it helped me feed my growing girls, but it also has given me a community and a purpose beyond what I could have imagined.
>
> I began volunteering at the pantry a few months after my first visit.... Volunteering for us is a family affair. Each one of my daughters has a different role....Through our time at the pantry, I have been able to teach my children the value of giving back and helping people in need – a lesson I hope they carry with them all of their lives.
>
> The pantry has also taught us the value of community. Through volunteering I have built invaluable relationships with my neighbors – who are both the people we serve and my fellow volunteers. People around town recognize me now; they say hi and share their stories. They tell me how much the food pantry is helping them – and it feels good to know I am making a difference in their lives.
>
> (FeedingAmerica.org 2015)

Claudia's story suggests three other benefits of private charity: it helps people connect with their community and place a higher value on it; it is an opportunity to teach children about the importance of caring for others; and it can give people a sense of dignity and happiness because they know they are doing something to help those in need. An estimated 70 percent of food pantries are operated by faith-based organizations (Siddons 2009). But arguably, even those that are based in secular organizations would not exist were it not for the internalization of a notion of charity that Christ brought into the world.

Private charity is not only of greater benefit than government aid to the recipient, it is also good for the giver. When other relevant factors are held fixed, "the volunteer will enjoy greater happiness and better health than the nonvolunteer" (Brooks 2006, 150), and even when both are healthy and able to give blood, "the donor will be 9 percentage points more likely to say that he or she is very happy than the nondonor" (Brooks 2006, 151). That this is a real effect has been corroborated by several studies of the effects of giving behavior, which found that it increases confidence, reduces depression, and generally improves mental health (Brooks 2006, 152).

Finally, charity is also good for society as a whole. This is because charity and volunteer work participate in various social structures that mediate government and the people (Berger and Neuhaus 1977). This participation makes one a more active citizen, more involved in building the community, and better informed about its real needs. Because these mediating institutions draw on unpaid work and local knowledge, they are more efficient and more effective than the "one-size-fits-all" edicts of central government. They are more efficient because governmental regulations require staff to be paid and regulated by expensive layers of bureaucracy, human resource departments, and so on. And they are more effective because local conditions are highly variable, so concerned citizens within a particular context who know the specific factors and the sort of people who need assistance have the best chance of crafting solutions that precisely target a community's needs. Though not the only possible sources of aid, churches are ideally situated to identify those in need, to call for charitable donations, and to recruit highly motivated volunteers.

Christianity teaches that each person is precious to God because that person is made in His image, redeemed by Christ, and called into the world to make a unique and valuable contribution. Christians who understand this, therefore, do not look at a person in need as a statistic or a social problem but as a fellow child of God. What matters is not just a temporary need for assistance, but the whole person, including the integration of that person into the human community and their spiritual life. By their nature, anonymous government aid programs are unable to address these holistic concerns.

3. Community-building

The church also serves an important pedagogical function that helps build society (Bach-Golecka 2013). First, when faithful to its mission, the church is a place where all sorts of people, from all walks of life, male or female, rich or poor, and regardless of race, are welcome (Galatians 3:28). The only condition the church has for needing Christ is that one is a sinner, and, since this includes everyone, no one is excluded from its central message. Sin and grace are great levelers: they help people see that, whatever distinctions exist within society, we are all equal before God, and this creates an important sense of unity that the world cannot take away. More than that, participation in church-related activities has the salutary effect of bringing diverse people together to serve a common cause. Whether in worship or in volunteer work, one is constantly caused to recognize the humanity of particular individuals in social groups with which one might otherwise never have a meaningful association.

Second, the church models a *via media* between collectivism and individualism. A collectivist society tends to follow a utilitarian ethic which elevates general outcomes over the individual, and, as a result, individuals who do not "get with the program" are mere inefficiencies. In practice, collectivist societies mean that the will of some – the party – is imposed on everyone else. At the other extreme, an individualist society so exalts personal autonomy, that it has no resources to promote the common good. Since individuals have a variety of conflicting goals, society quickly balkanizes into warring interest groups which see no reason to compromise for the sake of a stable and coherent community. And individualism is bad for individuals themselves. As Plato long ago observed, even a single person's desires are at war with each other. Plato compared our appetites to a "multifarious beast" and argued that the man who thinks he should allow this beast to feast while starving his wisdom and virtue (which might restrain his desires for the sake of some good higher than the individual, such as the good of family or community) will find himself dragged around in an erratic, uncontrolled path by those desires (Plato's *Republic*, Book IX, 588e-589a). If Plato is right, although it exalts personal autonomy, individualism denies any meaningful personal freedom: capitulating to our desires enslaves us to the arbitrary and dissonant voices of warring masters. We are therefore less free than ever when we can do just as we please: *license* does not yield personal *liberty* (George 2012, 149–160).

There is also a connection between discord in the individual and discord in society. What is destructive at a personal level also creates conflict and discord in wider society. There is ample evidence to support St. James's question: "What causes quarrels and what causes fights among you? Is it not this, that your passions are at war within you?" (James 4:1). We see this in the clamoring for special rights to protect an increasing number of passionate desires even when it results in societal conflict because the alleged rights are incompatible.[2] If we do not give a place to wisdom and virtue, which call us to make sacrifices for the common good, then society will be torn apart by factions competing to impose their desires on everyone else. By contrast with both collectivism and individualism, the church values both the individual and the common good. Unlike collectivism, Christian teaching holds up the value of each individual:

> Are not two sparrows sold for a penny? And not one of them will fall to the ground apart from your Father. But even the hairs of your head are all numbered. Fear not, therefore; you are of more value than many sparrows.
>
> (Matthew 10:29–31)

This includes those the world ignores and despises (criminals, tax collectors and prostitutes), and it affirms the precious value not only of every individual made in the image of God and for whom Christ died, but also of their specific individuality. The unique personal abilities and circumstances of a person matter to God because they are His gifts. But unlike the modern doctrine of individualistic autonomy, God does not provide these gifts as a *license* to "float our own boat" with no concern for the community (see George 2012, 112). *Au contraire*, our gifts are a trust intended to equip us to love and serve our neighbor. This is the doctrine of vocation emphasized by the Reformers (Veith 2011).

Vocation finds the right balance between recognizing and valuing individual differences and promoting the common good because the differences exist as complementary tributaries to that good. St. Paul compared the church to a body with many members, each of which performs a distinct and invaluable function and all of which collectively support the body's health (Romans 12; 1 Corinthians 12). Extended to secular society, vocation teaches us that whatever our abilities or circumstances, there is someone we can use those resources to help, thereby contributing to social welfare.

One reason why this simple, yet powerful idea is unpopular is because it involves a cost: seeing our gifts as a means of helping others requires us to sacrifice our egotistical cravings. Our tendency is to use our gifts in the pursuit of self-interest. Combined with the toxic idea that self-realization is attained by the maximum satisfaction of desires, this leads (for a contemporary example) to the dangerous mindset of some members of the millennial or so-called "Me Me Me" generation (Stein 2013), who exhibit a high incidence of narcissism, over-confidence, entitlement and laziness and a lack of empathy and understanding of viewpoints contrary to their own (Siemon-Netto 2015, 150). Part of the problem is that technological interaction does not present us with the true otherness of other people, something that draws us out of ourselves and leads us to see how the world looks to them.

This is not a recipe for social health, as it enables indifference, or even hostility, toward the needs of others. But it is also not good for the individual. Plato was right about our warring desires, and we cannot be happy by simply "doing what we want." For example, many of us would like a quiet life *and* recognition; to lose weight *and* enjoy fine dining; to be smart *but not* to read; a big house *and* no debt; more time *and* not to be bored; and the culture of town *and* the beauty of the countryside. At a practical (if not always strictly logical) level, our desires are not mutually consistent, and so we can expect nothing but unhappiness and frustration from the quixotic attempt to satisfy them all.

More than that, we will also miss out on higher forms of happiness that can only be attained through self-sacrifice. As Louis Pojman (2014) points out, the exclusive pursuit of self-interest faces a paradox: it entails that we can never enjoy that kind of deep, authentic relationship (friendship, camaraderie, or love) which depends on genuinely self-forgetful self-giving that does not calculate a personal benefit because it is focused on the other, not the self. And this entails, paradoxically, that it is not in our self-interest always to act out of self-interest; rather, it is in our best interest to sometimes forget about our best interest! The same can be said about the satisfaction that comes from knowing that you have genuinely helped another human being or that you have made your community a better place for everyone. Millennial students at my school who have volunteered to build homes for the poor regularly report that such community-building behavior is also a source of personal satisfaction (this is a discovery, and not their initial motivation).

So the church's gift to secular society is the tried and trusted truth that personal fulfillment and a healthy community are *not* at odds with one another. To be sure, the ancient Greek philosophers also emphasized that an individual can only flourish in community. But what was missing from their philosophy was a realistic assessment of human nature – especially what Christians call sin – and so helpful though it is to train people in virtue, it is not sufficient to produce the kind of *sacrificial* living that is best both for individuals and for society. At any rate, the secular state should be able to recognize that the church makes an important and distinctive contribution to community-building, one that cannot be replicated by government programs. And this certainly helps to counteract the polarizing and divisive rhetoric of our news media, which benefits by creating highly emotional, sensational clashes over politically charged issues.

Conclusion

Using the teaching and action of the Christian church as an example, I have argued that religious liberty can be highly beneficial to the secular state, and that this can be recognized by employing secular reason. Liberty of Christian thought and speech is important because society is harmed by a truncated search for truth and because a transcendent perspective on permanent human values can help people resist dangerous, totalitarian ideologies that undermine the social fabric in search of a utopian dream. Both historically and today, the church also offers a better means of helping the disadvantaged, one that brings individuals together and encourages recipients to help others. And in many ways, the Christian church provides a compelling model of a unified community that values both individual differences and the common good. An important corollary in the US context is that it would be a disastrous mistake for the government to limit religious expression, or to limit religious action by withdrawing the tax exemptions of churches and church-related organizations, or to attempt to replace faith-based social services with government agencies.

Notes

1 Thanks to the participants of the IVR World Congress 2015 special workshop on religious liberty, Washington DC, July 27 – August 1, 2015, for their comments on an earlier draft of this paper.

2 For example, it is hard to see how the right of children to grow up free of sexual abuse can be harmonized with those who demand a "right" to inter-generational sex. And the only way the Freedom From Religion Foundation could achieve its "right" to live without encountering religious messages would be if the right to free exercise of religion was denied to others.

Bibliography

Bach-Golecka, Dobrochna. 2013. "Why is Man the Primary and Functional Way for the Church? The Involvement of Christian Teaching in Contemporary Human Rights Discourse." In *Legitimizing Human Rights: Secular and Religious Perspectives*, ed. Angus J. L. Menuge. Farnham, UK: Ashgate, 199–212.

Barth, Karl. 1934. "The Barmen Declaration." Accessed August 28, 2015. http://www.academia.edu/10743325/THE_BARMEN_DECLARATION_May_1934_THE_SIX_ARTICLES.

Bass, Diana. 2012. *Christianity after Religion: The End of Church and the Birth of a New Spiritual Awakening*. New York: HarperOne.

Berger, Peter, Grace Davie and Effie Fokas. 2008. *Religious America, Secular Europe? A Theme and Variations*. Aldershot, UK: Ashgate.

Berger, Peter and Richard John Neuhaus. 1977. *To Empower People: The Role of Mediating Structures in Public Policy*. Washington, DC: American Enterprise Institute for Public Policy Research.

Brooks, Arthur. 2006. *Who Really Cares: The Surprising Truth about Compassionate Conservatism*. New York: Basic.

Calvert, John. 2013. "Human Rights in a Secular State Will Depend on its Legal Definition of Religion." In *Legitimizing Human Rights: Secular and Religious Perspectives*, ed. Angus J. L. Menuge. Farnham, UK: Ashgate, 103–125.

Clouser, Roy. 2005. *The Myth of Religious Neutrality: An Essay on the Hidden Role of Religious Belief in Theories*, revised ed. Notre Dame, IN: University of Notre Dame Press.

D'Souza, Dinesh. 2007. *What's So Great about Christianity*. Washington, DC: Regnery.

Dawkins, Richard. 2006. *The God Delusion*. New York: Houghton Mifflin.

Eriksen, Robert. 2012. *Complicity in the Holocaust: Churches and Universities in Nazi Germany*. New York: Cambridge University Press.

FeedingAmerica.org. 2015. "Your Story: Claudia." Accessed August 29, 2015. http://www.feedingamerica.org/hunger-in-america/hunger-in-your-community/your-stories/your-story-claudia.html.

George, Robert P. 2013. *Conscience and its Enemies: Confronting the Dogmas of Secular Liberalism*. Wilmington, DE: ISI.

Gilder, George. 2012. *Wealth and Poverty: A New Edition for the Twenty-First Century*. Washington, DC: Regnery.

Grossman, Cathy. 2014. "Secularism Grows as more U.S. Christians Turn 'Churchless.'" *Religionnews.com*. Accessed August 29, 2015. http://www.religionnews.com/2014/10/24/secularism-is-on-the-rise-as-more-u-s-christians-turn-churchless/.

Lecky, William. 1890. *History of European Morals: From Augustus to Charlemagne*, Vol. 2. London: Longmans, Green, and Company.

Lifton, Robert Jay. 1986. *The Nazi Doctors: Medical Killing and the Psychology of Genocide*. New York: Basic.

McElroy, Wendy. 2013. "Dietrich Bonhoeffer and the Confessing Church." *Laissez Faire*. Accessed August 28, 2015. https://lfb.org/dietrich-bonhoeffer-and-the-confessing-church/.

Mill, John Stuart. *On Liberty.* 1978. Ed. Elizabeth Rapaport. Indianapolis: Hackett.

Montgomery, John Warwick. 2013. "Restrictions on Religious Freedom: When and How Justified?" In *Legitimizing Human Rights: Secular and Religious Perspectives*, ed. Angus J. L. Menuge. Farnham, UK: Ashgate, 143–156.

Neuhaus, Richard J. 1996. *The Naked Public Square.* Grand Rapids: Eerdmans.

"Obituary for Christian Führer." 2014. *The Daily Telegraph*, July 1. Accessed August 29, 2015. http://www.telegraph.co.uk/news/obituaries/10938435/Christian-Fuhrer-obituary.html.

Parton, Craig. 2015. "Christian Liberty, the Arts, and J. S. Bach." In *Where Christ is Present: A Theology for All Seasons on the 500th Anniversary of the Reformation*, ed. John Warwick Montgomery and Gene Edward Veith. Corona, CA: New Reformation, 165–192.

Pew Research Center. 2015. "America's Changing Religious Landscape." Accessed August 29, 2015. http://www.pewforum.org/2015/05/12/americas-changing-religious-landscape/.

Pinker, Steven. 2011. *The Better Angels of Our Nature: Why Violence Has Declined.* New York: Viking Penguin.

Pojman, Louis. 2014. "Egoism and Altruism: A Critique of Ayn Rand." In *Philosophy: The Quest for Truth*, 9th ed. Ed. Louis P. Pojman and Lewis Vaughn. New York: Oxford University Press, 482–487.

Robinson, Bruce. 2015. "New Age Spirituality." Accessed August 28, 2015. http://www.religioustolerance.org/newage.htm.

Schmidt, Alvin. 2001. *Under the Influence: How Christianity Transformed Civilization.* Grand Rapids: Zondervan.

Siddons, Sarah. 2009. "How Faith-Based Organizations Work." *Howstuffworks.com.* Accessed August 29, 2015. http://money.howstuffworks.com/economics/volunteer/organizations/faith-based-organizations.htm.

Siemon-Netto, Uwe. 2007. *The Fabricated Luther: Refuting Nazi Connections and Other Modern Myths*, 2nd ed. St. Louis: Concordia.

Siemon-Netto, Uwe. 2015. "Vocation versus Narcissus." In *Where Christ is Present: A Theology for All Seasons on the 500th Anniversary of the Reformation*, ed. John Warwick Montgomery and Gene Edward Veith. Corona, CA: New Reformation Press, 149–164.

Smith, Christian, and Melinda Denton. 2005. *Soul Searching: The Religious and Spiritual Lives of American Teenagers.* New York: Oxford University Press.

Stein, Joel. 2013. "Millennials: The Me Me Me Generation." *Time*, May 20: 28–36.

Thielicke, Helmut. 1964. *Das Gebet das die Welt umspannt.* Stuttgart: Quell.

Thielicke, Helmut. 1984. *Being Human...Becoming Human: An Essay in Christian Anthropology*, trans. Geoffrey W. Bromley. Garden City, NY: Doubleday.

Veith, Gene Edward. 2011. *God at Work: Your Christian Vocation in All of Life*, 2nd ed. Wheaton, IL: Crossway.

Wachtler, Mark. 2014. "Houston Subpoenas Church Sermons for Hate Speech." *Whiteout Press.* Accessed August 8, 2015. http://www.whiteoutpress.com/articles/2014/q4/houston-subpoenas-church-sermons-hate-speech/.

Wielenberg, Erik. 2014. *Robust Ethics: The Metaphysics and Epistemology of Godless Normative Realism.* New York: Oxford University Press.

Young, Arthur P. 1974. *The "X" Documents*, ed. Sidney Aster. London: Deutsch.

6 Developments in law and secularism in Canada

Mary Anne Waldron, James K. A. Smith, Ray Pennings and Christian Vandergeest

Introduction

In his seminal work *A Secular Age*, Charles Taylor (2007) explores the meaning of "secular," arguing that the term is commonly used to refer to (a) the decline of religious belief and practice; and (b) the "secularization" of public spaces, that is, the removal of religion from public spaces. However, he argues that in our modern age "secular" refers more accurately to the "conditions of belief" present in our society, in which all belief is contested and contestable.

Since the creation of the Charter of Rights and Freedoms in 1982, Supreme Court of Canada (SCC) decisions have been developing the fundamental freedom of religion enshrined in Section 2. This formation has coincided with liberal calls for the "secularization" of society (i.e., the removal of religion from public spaces). Schools, city council rooms, degree accreditation programs, and public displays of religion have increasingly been sites of litigation, and the SCC has been forced to define the extent to which religion is present in the public functioning of Canadian society. The result has been that decisions of the SCC reflect a society that is *insufficiently* "secular" in Taylor's third sense ("secular (3)") because they assume a new default belief system – an epistemological confidence in neutrality and "secularity" (in the second sense, "secular (2)") that has been widely questioned.

This essay analyzes SCC decisions concerning religious freedom through the lens of Taylor's philosophy. Section 1 finds that decisions prior to 2012 reflect a more secular ("secular (2)") perspective, in that they reflect a narrowing out of the public aspect of religion in Canadian public life. Section 2 suggests that a *more* "secular" court (in Taylor's *third* sense) would recognize that the belief and value system it takes for granted is itself contestable and contested, and that in that sense a "secular (3)" court would foster a genuine pluralism. Section 3 analyzes more recent SCC decisions, from 2012 onward, arguing that they show a divergence from prior decisions and a more encouraging interpretation of religious freedom despite an emerging conflict with equality rights. Finally, Section 4 outlines some possible challenges to religious freedom in Canadian law and provides some perspectives that a court could adopt in dealing with those challenges.

1. A brief history of SCC decisions impacting religious freedom to 2012

The role of religion in society is in flux. Countries and legal systems in the modern Western world accord religion differing roles within the public square and assume varying levels of accommodation for religious freedom.[1] In Canada, the jurisprudence on religious freedom has been developing through SCC decisions since the Charter of Rights and Freedoms[2] was signed into law in 1982. However, these decisions have demonstrated an inconsistent understanding of religious freedom and the role of religion in a secular society.

Many of these decisions have appeared to push religion from the public square. The first major case following the creation of the Charter was *R. v. Big M Drug Mart* ("*Big M*"). Here, the court dealt with a law requiring the closing of businesses on Sunday, ruling it constitutionally invalid. Note that here the Canadian circumstance differs from the American in that the constitution does not include an establishment clause prohibiting the government from supporting a particular religion, and indeed the SCC noted that state support for religion will need to be decided on a case-by-case basis (*R. v. Big M Drug Mart* 1985, para. 109). But while there are good reasons to suggest that support for a *particular* religion should be discouraged, the court instead focused on the purpose of the legislation (to uphold a majority religious practice) as invalid, and ignored any analysis of whether there was actual harm to Sabbath non-observers.[3] This omission raised the question of whether to be unconstitutional a law had to infringe the freedom of religion of others, or whether it was sufficient that its original purpose was offensive to non-believers.

In another pivotal case, *Trinity Western University v. British Columbia College of Teachers* ("*Trinity*"), the SCC majority decision mandated the accreditation of a Teacher's College at a private university with a religiously based code of conduct (*Trinity Western University v. British Columbia College of Teachers* 2001).[4] Here, in an attempt to sidestep the issue of a clash of values, the court separated the freedom to believe and the freedom to practice one's beliefs (*Trinity Western University v. British Columbia College of Teachers* 2001, para. 37). Richard Moon notes that this approach "fits with the contemporary understanding of public secularism as the exclusion of religion from public life or the 'privatization of religious commitment'" (Moon 2012, 330). In practice, this resulted in a ruling that the simple statement of a belief is not discriminatory, but provided no guidance on the question of what *practice* of one's religious beliefs would be discriminatory.

The SCC decisions have thus far failed to work out the tension between religious freedom and equality rights. This tension emerged in *Trinity*, when the court was faced with a conflict between the equality rights of homosexual students taught by graduates of TWU and the religious rights of TWU to enforce a code of conduct based on its religious values. This continued in *Chamberlain v. Surrey School District No. 36* ("*Chamberlain*"), where the court reviewed a schoolboard decision refusing to approve as primary material books representing families with same-sex parents for a Kindergarten–Grade-One classroom.[5] The SCC found that a requirement for "secular" decision-making does not exclude religious considerations from the debate, but requires that decisions by public officials be made in such a way that considers and protects the beliefs of all members of the community (*Chamberlain v. Surrey School District No. 36 2002*, para. 19). However, rather than finding a way to hold an "even hand" between the competing moral and religious views, the court ruled that the board's refusal to approve the books was unreasonable, as it excluded the views of same-sex parents. It is difficult to avoid the conclusion that the court was now simply disregarding the views of religiously conservative trustees and parents.

The court, in the past, was most willing to protect divergence of belief when it could be linked with minority rights. In *Syndicat Northcrest v. Amselem* ("*Amselem*"), the SCC decision (based on the Quebec Charter of Human Rights and Freedoms) ruled that a condominium corporation had the duty to accommodate its Jewish residents by allowing them to build a structure on their balcony to celebrate a religious holiday. In its ruling, the SCC stated that "respect for *religious minorities* is not a stand-alone absolute right; like other rights, freedom of religion exists in a matrix of other correspondingly important rights that attach to individuals [emphasis added]" (*Syndicat Northcrest v. Amselem* 2004, para. 1).

The conflation of religious freedom with minority rights is highly problematic. First, it implies that freedom of religion is a protection only for the minority against a majority rather than a fundamental human right. Thus, for the religious believer, the right to be treated equally and without discrimination may be contingent upon the minority status of a particular group (Waldron 2013, 43). In *Chamberlain*, for example, the court failed to recognize the religiously based majority[6] views espoused by board members as being as legitimate as the minority view of the same-sex teachers. This led to a failure to adopt a solution to protect the rights of both groups, and a decision solely in favor of the rights of the minority. Second, treating freedom of religion merely as a subset of equality rights for cultural minorities seems to produce in the public mind a reaction against minority accommodation, particularly minority religious accommodation, as was illustrated in the Bouchard-Taylor Report.[7]

Finally, SCC decisions have recently limited the state's duty to consider issues of religious accommodation when exercising its legislative function. In *Alberta v. Hutterian Brethren of Wilson Colony* ("*Hutterian*"), the court retreated from its history of requiring governments to consider "reasonable accommodation" that began with *Big M.* [8] Rather, it adopted the position that legislation and regulations do not generally have to be tailored to accommodate the beliefs of religious minorities where the state can frame the purpose of the legislation as excluding such case-by-case exceptions. In this case, the court rejected an obvious accommodation for a well-known religious group that had been accommodated in the past, arguing that "[the government] cannot be expected to tailor a law to every possible future contingency or every sincerely held religious belief" (Alberta v. Hutterian Brethren of Wilson Colony 2009, para. 69). This case appears to privilege the legislative function of government by setting a low bar for justifying legislation that infringes religious freedom.

Thus far, we have outlined a number of problems arising in past SCC decisions: the depiction of religious belief as a private commitment, isolated from its practice; the tension between religious freedom and equality rights; the conflation of religious freedom with minority rights; and the privileging of legislation against a duty to provide reasonable accommodations for religious practices. All of these have a common theme: the narrowing of the scope of freedom of religion and a movement away from the concept of openly lived plurality of belief. In practical terms, the pre-2011 decisions reflect a narrowing of the public aspect of religion in Canadian public life. Rather than encouraging the flourishing of religion, its contribution to public debate, and the open discussion of differences in belief, SCC decisions seem to have failed to engage freedom of religion as a valuable right on the same footing as freedom of expression or freedom of equality. This lack of protection threatens to exclude religion, and religious believers, from our public conversation. We move now to an exploration of how this trend can be viewed through the lens of Charles Taylor's philosophy, particularly as it pertains to his consideration of our secular age.

2. Comparing Canada's experience to Taylor's conception of the secular

In many ways, this trajectory of SCC decisions reflects a court (and society) that has subscribed to the secularization thesis. The problem, however, is that this thesis – and its attendant assumptions about religion and public life – has been subject to thorough criticism over the past 20 years.

In his much-discussed work, *A Secular Age*, Canadian philosopher Charles Taylor has distinguished several different senses of what it means to describe a society as "secular." Even if we grant that Canada is a "secular" society, "it's not so clear in what this secularity consists," he notes (Taylor 2007, 1). In one sense, a "secular" society is one in which our "common institutions and practices" – including, but not limited to, the state – are unhooked from both the institutions and beliefs associated with "religion." A society's "public" spaces are expected to be "secular" spaces insofar as "you can engage fully in politics without encountering God" (Taylor 2007, 1). These public spaces "have been allegedly emptied of God, or of any reference to ultimate reality" (Taylor 2007, 2). In this sense, society is a "secular" *space* of shared institutions in which believers and non-believers alike participate. What religion persists is pushed to "private" spaces in two senses: religious expression is increasingly sequestered to spheres of society that are considered private, but religion is also reduced from being seen as a communal "way of life" to being a set of internal, privately held beliefs or preferences that characterize individuals.[9] Religion, in other words, is reduced to a matter of (individual) conscience.[10]

It is this sense of secularity that generates a normative vision, even "doctrine," that we might describe as secular*ism*: the expectation and requirement that religious beliefs, opinions, views and even expressions must be excluded from shared, public spaces and institutions. Behind this is an often unarticulated *epistemological* assumption that our "public" spaces are *neutral* spaces, and that as actors in the public square we are merely "rational" actors who can operate on the basis of neutral, "objective," unbiased principles (see John Rawls' (1971) influential account of those "rational" actors who inhabit his so-called "original position"). In short, this secularist vision is a bit of an Enlightenment dream that reflects a distinct epistemological confidence in a "neutral" rationality.

This sense of the secular as a "neutral" public space, however, is both distinct from and yet bound up with a second sense in which a society is "secular," namely, when it exists with diminished religious belief and participation. "In this second meaning," Taylor observes, "secularity consists in the falling off of religious belief and practice, in people turning away from God, and no longer going to Church" (Taylor 2007, 613–615). It is usually in this sense that Western European societies are described as "secular": the United Kingdom, for example, retains an "established" church and yet would be described as a "secular" society in comparison with the United States, whose constitution enshrines a key feature of secularism: the distinction between church and state. In other words, things are complicated.

These different senses – secularity as the exclusion of religion from the public square and secularity as the decline in belief and practice (Taylor 2007, 423) – nonetheless overlap in standard versions of "the secularization thesis," a quasi-scientific hypothesis that contends that, as societies go through the advances of modernity (democratization, industrialization, etc.), they will become less and less "religious" and more and more "secular" both in terms of the organization of public space and in terms of the decline of religious belief. In other words, the secularization thesis expects secular societies to become increasingly secular*ist*.

But both the secularization thesis and the epistemology behind secularism have been subject to widespread critique over the past generation. The predictive power of the secularization thesis has been called into question by sociologists who once propounded it.[11] Furthermore, the epistemological assumptions behind secularism have been subjected to withering philosophical critique in Nicholas Wolterstorff's critique of Richard Rorty and Robert Audi (Wolterstorff 2003,129–139; Audi and Wolterstorff 1997), Jeffrey Stout's critique of Rawls (Stout 2004, 64–76), or John Milbank's critique of "secular" social theory (Milbank 1990).[12]

This is why Taylor argues that we need to work out a third sense of "secularity," which is not tied specifically to unbelief or non-belief but which nonetheless recognizes a shift in the "conditions of belief." "The shift to secularity in this sense," he argues, "consists, among other things, of a move from a society where belief in God is unchallenged and indeed, unproblematic, to one in which it is understood to be one option among others, and frequently not the easiest to embrace" (Taylor 2007, 3). In contrast, say, to medieval Christendom, where there was an established or default belief system that was taken for granted, a "secular" society in this third sense is a society in which no belief system is taken to be axiomatic or a "given." This doesn't necessarily tip toward either belief or unbelief (both England and the United States are "secular" in this sense, though they have very different levels of religious belief and participation). Rather, the point is that no one system of belief is given a pass or taken for granted. A "secular age" is one in which all belief is contested and contestable.

The irony, however, is that these decisions of the SCC reflect a society that is *insufficiently* "secular" in this third sense precisely because they assume a new default belief system – "as comprehensive a belief system as any religious faith in its power to shape our visions of the world" (Waldron 2013, 11). In other words, the court's decisions reflect an epistemological confidence in neutrality and "secularity" (in the second sense) that has been widely questioned. Such alleged neutrality instead often masks the ascendency of some particular belief system as unquestioned – in which case we are in a situation that Taylor would describe as *pre*-modern and pre-secular (3). A *more* "secular" court (in Taylor's *third* sense) would have to recognize that the belief and value system it takes for granted is itself contestable and contested. In that sense, a secular (3) court would foster a genuine pluralism.

The court, in that case, would exhibit what Gérard Bouchard and Charles Taylor describe as an "open" (vs. "rigid" or "restrictive") secularism (Bouchard and Taylor 2008). It is "secular" insofar as it grants the neutrality of the state with respect to religious belief (separation or non-establishment). But rather than effectively making the state an agent that quashes or sequesters religion, open secularism encourages a "reciprocal autonomy" between the two. This means that the state (and hence its courts) must "acknowledge the importance for some people of the spiritual dimension of existence and, consequently, the protection of freedom of conscience and religion" (Bouchard and Taylor 2008, 140). "Closed" secularism, in contrast, acts as its own kind of dogmatism that fails to own up to secularity (3). When this happens, Taylor points out elsewhere, "you have to redefine secularism in an indefensible way. Instead of being the regime that defends everyone's freedom of conscience, whether religious or non-religious (what I call 'open' secularism), it becomes a secularism wary of religion, and always ready to set limits to it. Non-religion becomes the common principle.... [T]he common bond is that we are dedicated to something that is incompatible with religion – like 'reason' or 'emancipation' or what have you" (Taylor 2014, 50–55). But such "rigid" secularism would be subject to the epistemological critique outlined above. Therefore, "open" secularism is the better, more viable stance of the state and its courts.

Calls for a court that would reflect this genuine pluralism are not new. The cases discussed above point to a growing diversity of fundamental belief in Canada, a diversity that requires our society and court system to recognize that the differences in our beliefs lead to irreconcilable preferences about the way our lives are lived and governed. As the mechanism by which the freedom to disagree is preserved in our democratic society, the courts should not take sides in conflicts between belief systems, but instead hold an even hand between competing views. When it comes to Charter values, the aim of the courts is not to produce social consensus, but to protect the democratic commitment to live together in peace.

And as we will see, recent SCC decisions may present a fledgling trend in this direction.

3. Recent developments in SCC decisions: From 2012 onward

Recent SCC decisions have provided some positive signs that may indicate a more pluralistic view of freedom of religion and the role of religious groups in society. Most encouraging is the court's apparent recognition that secular "neutrality" often reflects a partisan position, that is, a non-neutral belief and value system.

A glimmer of a new approach may emerge from comments made by the court in *S.L. v. Commission scolaire des Chênes* ("*S.L.*"). In this case, parents requested an exemption from the introduction of a new curriculum in Quebec on the grounds that it infringed their freedom of religion – specifically, their right to educate their children in their religion. They claimed that the "Ethics and Religious Culture Program" (ERC) taught religion in a manner that conflicted with their beliefs. The SCC ruled that the parents were not entitled to an exemption from the program, stating that exposing children to a variety of religious facts does not infringe on religious freedom.

In its decision, the court noted that "from a philosophical standpoint, absolute neutrality does not exist" (*S.L. v. Commission scolaire des Chênes* 2012, para. 31). In support of this argument, it quoted an excerpt from an article by Richard Moon, which is worth quoting in its entirety:

> If secularism or agnosticism constitutes a position, worldview, or cultural identity equivalent to religious adherence, then its proponents may feel excluded or marginalized when the state supports even the most ecumenical religious practices. But by the same token, the complete removal of religion from the public square may be experienced by religious adherents as the exclusion of their worldview and the affirmation of a non-religious or secular perspective.
>
> Ironically, then, as the exclusion of religion from public life, in the name of religious freedom and equality, has become more complete, the secular has begun to appear less neutral and more partisan. With the growth of agnosticism and atheism, religious neutrality in the public sphere may have become impossible. *What for some is the neutral ground on which freedom of religion and conscience depends is for others a partisan anti-spiritual experience* [emphasis added].
>
> (Moon 2008, 217, 231)

This recognition that the removal of religion from the public square is indeed a "partisan experience" is in line with the understanding that excluding religion is insufficiently "secular" in Taylor's third sense. Both conceptions entail recognition that the "neutral" perspective (i.e., neutrality achieved through the removal of religion) is in fact a value-laden perspective on par with the view of religious adherents that their faith should have free exercise.

A further discussion of this concept occurred in *Loyola High School v. Quebec (Attorney General)* ("*Loyola*"). In this case, the SCC ruled again on the new ERC curriculum, this time affirming the right of a Jesuit School to have an exemption from the curriculum in order to teach Catholicism from a Catholic perspective. The decision affirmed the role of the court as a "referee" in a secular state: "The pursuit of secular values means respecting the right to hold and manifest different religious beliefs. A secular state respects religious differences, it does not seek to extinguish them" (*Loyola High School v. Quebec (Attorney General)* 2015, para. 43).

The court also portrayed religion as an aspect of individual and communal identity by once again quoting Richard Moon: "Religious belief lies at the core of the individual's worldview...moreover, religious belief ties the individual to a community of believers and is often the central or defining association in his or her life" (*Loyola High School v. Quebec (Attorney General)* 2015, para. 44). The court stated that "a pluralist, multicultural democracy depends on the capacity of its citizens to engage in thoughtful and inclusive forms of deliberation amidst, and enriched by, different religious worldviews and practices" (*Loyola High School v. Quebec (Attorney General)* 2015, para. 48). All of these statements seemed to affirm religion as a legitimate (or even essential) component of public discourse.

The minority in *Loyola* also understood a point that the court had not seemed to grasp in *S.L.* The main objection to the ERC course in both cases was that its insistence on complete neutrality in presenting all religions as cultural artifacts of equal value, despite their conflicting beliefs, in fact adopts the underlying presumption that all religions are equally false – a stance associated with secularism in senses (1) and (2) discussed above. The majority opinion did not articulate this perspective, despite their affirmation of the principle of state neutrality in dealing with multiple and conflicting beliefs.

A third SCC case that seems to reflect a trend toward Taylor's conception of secular (3) is *Mouvement laïque Québécois v. Saguenay (City)* ("*Saguenay*"). This case dealt with the existence of prayer and religious symbols in the meetings of a municipal council, which were challenged by an atheist who felt excluded from the proceedings. Previous SCC decisions on the use of prayer in public spaces had focused on the "exclusionary" nature of religious practice, noting that including a prayer would cause non-religious attendees to feel excluded. Much of the language in *Saguenay*, however, followed *S.L.* by instead focusing on the concept of state "neutrality" – the idea that the state should stand apart as the neutral referee among competing beliefs.

The decision contained much positive language regarding the role of religion in Canadian society. It noted the importance of promoting and enhancing religious diversity: "[the Charter] requires that the state's duty of neutrality be interpreted not only in a manner consistent with the protective objectives of the Canadian Charter, but also with a view to promoting and enhancing diversity" (*Mouvement laïque Québécois v. Saguenay (City)* 2015, para. 73). It also moved to further protect personal belief, by describing religion as "an integral part of each person's identity" (*Mouvement laïque Québécois v. Saguenay (City)* 2015, para. 74).[13] This reference to religion as "identity" protects religious belief by enshrining it as an inherent trait, rather than as a simple preference. Public perception of religion as a freely adopted and easily altered aspect of one's life seems to have contributed to the understanding of religious freedom as being in opposition to equality rights. Whether a shift to a conception of religious belief as a key part of identity will enhance the court's or the public's willingness to tolerate protection for religious diversity is uncertain.

The decision also contained a discussion of "absolute" vs. "true" neutrality, in which the court repeated the quote from Richard Moon on the impossibility of achieving "absolute" neutrality. The difficulty, the court acknowledged, is that while the removal of religion from city council proceedings is necessary for the state to be neutral toward all religions, that removal gives preferential treatment to non-religious members of society. The court recognized that the legal concepts of "belief" and "religion" encompass non-belief, atheism and agnosticism (*Mouvement laïque Québécois v. Saguenay (City)* 2015, para. 70), a move that accords with Taylor's conception of these belief systems as epistemic alternatives to religion.[14] But the court seemed caught in a supposed paradox: removing religious symbols from state institutions is required for the state to be neutral toward religious practice, but doing so accords with the "religious" beliefs of secularism.

Given the impossibility of resolving this paradox, the court concluded that "a neutrality that is non-absolute is nevertheless true neutrality" (*Mouvement laïque Québécois v. Saguenay (City)* 2015, para. 132). It argued, somewhat dubiously, that the removal of religion from public spaces does not favor an agnostic or atheist belief, suggesting that "a practice according to which a municipality's officials, rather than reciting a prayer, solemnly declared that the council's deliberations were based on a denial of God would be just as unacceptable" (*Mouvement laïque Québécois v. Saguenay (City)* 2015, para. 133).

Here, the court fell short of its earlier recognition that religion forms an integral part of an individual's identity. When the state's "neutral" perspective enshrines the non-religious, it adopts the absence of religion in public spaces as a default position which is not neutral. The court was unable to act on its understanding of the state's neutrality because, despite this emerging principle, the court also relied, as in past cases, on feelings of exclusion created by the prayer for non-believers as a justification for stopping the practice. Unfortunately, neutral solutions cannot be achieved as long as the emotional distress of one group is regarded as a reason to inflict similar emotional distress on another.

Despite these limitations, the *Saguenay* decision may suggest a positive change in the thinking of the SCC about religious freedom. Lower courts may also be engaged in a re-evaluation of the issue. In *Trinity Western University v. Nova Scotia Barristers' Society* ("*TWU v. NSBS*"), the Nova Scotia Supreme Court ruled that the decision of the NSBS to refuse accreditation to TWU's new law school based on a community covenant that requires all students, staff and faculty to abstain from sexual relationships outside religiously defined marriage violated religious freedom.

The ruling noted that the term "secular" is complex and ambiguous, quoting Charles Taylor (*Trinity Western University v. Nova Scotia Barristers' Society* 2015, para. 19). In line with Taylor's philosophy, it stated that "while [Canadian society] may be secular, in the sense that religion has lost its hold on social mores and individual conduct for many people, *the state is not secular in the sense that it promotes the process of secularization* [emphasis added]" (*Trinity Western University v. Nova Scotia Barristers' Society* 2015, para. 19). The court also quoted an article by SCC Chief Justice Beverley McLachlin that declared that "the role of the courts is to reconcile competing cultural values to 'carve out' a space within the rule of law which those religious claims to authority can operate, manifest and flourish" (*Trinity Western University v. Nova Scotia Barristers' Society* 2015, para. 212). This use of the word "flourish" seems to reject the secularization thesis, which posits the inevitable (and desirable) decline of religion. It may signal a transition from Taylor's conception of a secular (2) "fading out of religion" to a *more* secular "secular (3)" conception by suggesting that the role of the courts is not to cut religion from the public square, but instead to protect its ability to contribute to society. This decision is under appeal and will very probably be heard by the SCC and consolidated with similar actions from other provinces.

TWU v. NSBS also highlighted the growing tension between freedom of religion and equality rights. We noted above in Section 1 that in cases such as *Chamberlain* and the earlier *Trinity* decision the court found difficulty in constructing an approach to the clash between equality rights and freedom of religion that could protect both. In *TWU v. NSBS*, the NSBS argued that TWU's community covenant violated the equality rights of homosexuals, effectively denying them admission to the school. The Supreme Court of Nova Scotia ruled that the 2001 *Trinity* case, as binding precedent, protected the right of private religious institutions to adopt such a covenant. But the issue is by no means resolved, with litigation ongoing between TWU and the law societies of other provinces that also refused accreditation to its law school.[15]

In summary, the recent SCC rulings involving religious freedom show signs of moving toward a conception of "secular" more closely in accord with Taylor's secular (3). This can be categorized in two key shifts: (1) A recognition that the "secular," in the sense of the exclusion of religion from public life, is not neutral but is itself a "belief system;" and (2) the development, however imperfectly applied, of the idea of the state as a genuinely neutral referee in a world of conflicting beliefs. There is, however, still much to do in exploring and understanding these principles that the SCC seems to have recently adopted. The clash with equality rights and the widespread development of a morality in conflict with traditional religious belief will provide a stringent test of the court's ability to work out and apply these principles. The next step in preserving religious freedom will need to be a sustained engagement with these ideas as cases such as *TWU v. BSNS* move forward.

4. Projecting forwards: Some concerns, predictions and a conclusion

The Canadian legal framework for religious freedom will continue to evolve as the SCC hears cases that touch on the subject. There are several identifiable locations toward which we might look for new cases to emerge. First, future cases will most likely arise in areas where belief systems come into conflict. Issues will likely continue to arise where we find the growth of religious populations that hold beliefs that conflict with "exclusive humanism" (referring to Taylor's (2007, 19–21) term). Such populations may emerge as a result of a number of factors, such as immigration or the growth of new religious belief. Past examples include the wearing of burkas at citizenship ceremonies (*R v. N.S.* 2012), and the wearing of a kirpan to school (*Multani v. Commission scolaire Marguerite-Bourgeoys* 2006).

Second, we might also expect exclusive humanism to become more tenaciously committed to what Taylor (2007, 159–171) calls "the modern moral order" – the unique concoction of moral obligation forged in the immanent frame that blends expressive individualism with the vestigial aspects of love for neighbor, now expressed primarily in terms of tolerance. An exclusive humanism that is unaware of its own contestability will become increasingly *in*tolerant of those people and communities that it deems intolerant. A court wed to exclusive humanism rather than open secularism runs the risk of the same.

Finally, an objection to robust religious pluralism with many belief systems participating on equal footing in the public square often raises the spectre of how to set a line that marks religious practice that society cannot tolerate from that which it can and should. These questions are difficult and admit no easy answers. In part, we suggest that the solutions may be found in requiring, as a condition of constitutional protection, that belief practices leave space for others to disagree or promote alternative beliefs. A belief system that cannot leave this space has forfeited its right to participate in the democratic conversation by denying to others the protection it would claim for itself. This should apply consistently to the ISIL radical who would force everyone to accept Sharia law, as well as to the secularist who would compel religious believers to confine their religious practice to their private lives. If freedom of religion is, as the SCC recently affirmed, the bulwark of a "pluralist, multicultural democracy," then all the players must acknowledge this mutual respect and accommodation as a necessary qualification to enter the game. And courts must develop a more nuanced sensitivity toward enforcing the rules to allow fair and free play among all, just as a good referee will do.

Notes

1 Laws in the European Union, for example, tend to be much less accommodating of religion than laws in the United States and Canada (Waldron 2013, 78).
2 Henceforth referred to as "the Charter." Freedom of conscience and religion is guaranteed in Section 2.
3 The ruling "completely failed to elucidate how [the purpose] limited or abrogated the freedom of religion of non-Sunday observers (or any other right to which they were entitled) other than to note that, in the opinion of the court, it would cause them offence" (Waldron 2013, 39).
4 Here, the minority dissent disagreed, indicating that the requirement to adhere to a statement of beliefs excluding homosexual practice is discriminatory.
5 The books would still have been available to children in the school library, but they would not be mandated for classroom use.

6 A third problem with the conflation of minority rights with religious freedom arises when one tries to define "majority." In this instance, it very well may be the case that the board members who voted against same-sex material were in the minority when compared to the rest of Canada.
7 See Bouchard and Taylor (2008).
8 *Big M* resulted in a ruling that a law was unconstitutional because it was seen to have the purpose of enforcing a particular religious practice.
9 While we cannot adequately address the issue here, it should be noted that just what constitutes "religion" is itself a matter of debate in ways directly related to our conversation here. Taylor, for example, notes the ways in which "religion" is "excarnated" in modernity, reduced from a communal, embodied way of life to a set of ideas, beliefs and propositions (Taylor 2007, 613–615). This is traced in even more detail in Peter Harrison's Gifford Lectures, now published as Harrison (2015). See also Dubuisson (2007).
10 Cf. the importance, then, of Stanley Carlson-Thies' emphasis on *institutional* religious freedom (Carlson-Thies and Monsma 2015).
11 See Berger (1999) and Martin (2005).
12 See also Smith (2004).
13 Here, the court once again quotes Richard Moon: "If religion is an aspect of the individual's identity, then when the state treats his or her religious practices or beliefs as less important or less true than the practices of others, or when it marginalizes her or his religious community in some way, it is not simply rejecting the individual's views and values, it is denying her or his equal worth" (Moon 2012, 507).
14 Unlike the American Constitution, the Canadian Charter protects both "freedom of religion" and "freedom of conscience" together. Thus, the question of whether any special protection depends upon classifying a belief as "religious" does not arise in Canadian law.
15 For example, in Ontario the Law Society of Upper Canada recently argued before the Divisional Court that TWU's admissions policy discriminates against homosexual applicants and that, as an administrative tribunal empowered by provincial legislation, accrediting the law school would amount to discrimination on the part of a state body. See "*Factum of the Respondent: Law Society of Upper Canada*" TWU and Brayden Volkenant v. Law Society of Upper Canada, Ontario Superior Court of Justice Divisional Court, File 250/14.

Bibliography

Audi, Robert, and Nicholas Wolterstorff. 1997. *Religion in the Public Square: The Place of Religious Convictions in Political Debate.* Lanham, MD: Rowman and Littlefield.

Berger, Peter. 1999. *The Desecularization of the World.* Grand Rapids: Eerdmans.

Bouchard, Gérard, and Charles Taylor. 2008. "Building the Future: A Time for Reconciliation." *Report of the Commission de consultation sur les pratiques d'accommodement reliées aux differences culturelles.* Accessed June 15, 2016. www.mce.gouv.qc.ca/publications/CCPARDC/rapport-final-integral-en.pdf.

Carlson-Thies, Stanley and Stephen Monsma. 2015. *Free to Serve: Protecting the Religious Freedom of Faith-Based Organizations.* Grand Rapids: Brazos.

Dubuisson, Daniel. 2007. *The Western Construction of Religion: Myths, Knowledge, and Ideology.* Baltimore: Johns Hopkins University Press.

Harrison, Peter. 2015. *The Territories of Science and Religion.* Chicago: University of Chicago Press.

Martin, David. 2005. *On Secularization: Toward a Revised General Theory.* Burlington, VT: Ashgate.

Milbank, John. 1990. *Theology and Social Theory: Beyond Secular Reason.* Oxford: Blackwell.

Moon, Richard. 2008. "Government Support for Religious Practice." In *Law and Religious Pluralism in Canada*, ed. Richard Moon. Vancouver: UBC Press, 217–238.

Moon, Richard. 2011. "The Supreme Court of Canada's Attempt to Reconcile Freedom of Religion and Sexual Orientation Equality in the Public Schools." In *Faith, Politics, and Sexual Diversity*, ed. David Rayside and Clyde Wilcox. Vancouver: UBC Press, 321–338.

Moon, Richard. 2012. "Freedom of Religion under the Charter of Rights: The Limits of State Neutrality." *UBC Law Review* 45(2): 497–549.

Rawls, John. 1971. *A Theory of Justice.* Cambridge: Belknap.

Smith, James K. A. 2004. *Introducing Radical Orthodoxy: Mapping a Post-Secular Theology.* Grand Rapids: Baker.

Stout, Jeffrey. 2004. *Democracy and Tradition.* Princeton: Princeton University Press.

Taylor, Charles. 2007. *A Secular Age.* London: Harvard University Press.

Taylor, Charles. 2014. "Imagining an 'Open' Secularism: A Conversation with James K. A. Smith." *Comment* (Fall): 50–55.

Waldron, Mary Anne. 2013. *Free to Believe: Rethinking Freedom of Conscience and Religion in Canada.* Toronto: University of Toronto Press.

Wolterstorff, Nicholas. 2003. "An Engagement with Rorty." *Journal of Religious Ethics* 31(1): 129–139.

Legal decisions cited

Alberta v. Hutterian Brethren of Wilson Colony. SCC 37 (2009).

Chamberlain v. Surrey School District No. 36. 4 SCR 710 (2002).

Loyola High School v. Quebec (Attorney General). SCC 12 (2015).

Mouvement laïque Québécois v. Saguenay (City). SCC 16 (2015).

Multani v. Commission scolaire Marguerite-Bourgeoys. SCC 6 (2006).

*R v. Big M Drug Mart Ltd.*1 SCR 295 (1985).

R. v. N.S. SCC 72 (2012).

S.L. v. Commission scolaire des Chênes. 1 SCR 235 (2012).

Syndicat Northcrest v. Amselem. 2 SCR 551 (2004).

Trinity Western University v. British Columbia College of Teachers. SCC 31 (2001).

Trinity Western University v. Nova Scotia Barristers' Society. NSSC 25 (2015).

7 The challenging parallelism of rights claims based on religious identity and on sexual identity

Dwight Newman[1]

1. Introduction

In this essay, I will examine some of the deeper issues behind the Canadian debate over the proposed opening of a Christian law school, the potential Trinity Western University (TWU) law school. This particular debate is taking place in a historical moment when it serves as an example of a broader debate beginning to be had about issues of religious freedom and sexual orientation. In Canada, this debate has taken on a particular tone in the context of significant movement over the past two decades on sexual orientation equality issues, including the 2005 legalization of same-sex marriage, which has now become the settled Canadian position after a change effected legislatively under a Liberal government (Civil Marriage Act 2005) and a free vote under a later Conservative government not to reopen the question, thus settling the issue for the longer term. As those like Ryan Anderson have noted in the aftermath of the recent United States Supreme Court decision on same-sex marriage in *Obergefell v. Hodges* (Supreme Court of the United States 2015), in addition to those that have already arisen, the United States is almost bound to face analogous religious freedom issues in the years and decades ahead (Anderson 2015).

While I will ground my discussion in a particular debate about a particular issue at a particular historical moment, the broader themes that this debate embodies are actually about a larger, international issue, and one on which I will argue that there may need to be some movement on all sides. After Section 2 sets out the parameters of the debate on Canada's potential Christian law school, Section 3 turns to examine the complex parallelism between claims being put to manifest religious identity and claims being put to manifest sexual identity, trying in the process to show the seriousness of each manifestation of identity through reference to deeper historical roots and pertinent contextual considerations. This history and context is important in light of ongoing challenges to the *bona fides* or seriousness of the respective claims to manifest identity. Section 4 considers whether either side has an easy way out of this parallelism, by which it can claim that its claims should be respected but the other side's should not, ultimately concluding that the established parallelism calls for legal respect for both claims. Section 5 shows the implications that result, which include TWU's legal ability to open a law school but that also involve a middle path different from that which its advocates might prefer, with a resulting suggestion that solutions within the broader debate similarly need to be built upon deeply considered foundations.

2. The debate over TWU's proposed law school

In July 2012, after several years of preparatory work, Trinity Western University (TWU) in Langley, British Columbia (between Vancouver and Seattle), submitted to the pertinent educational and law society authorities its formal proposal to open a law school. This law school would be Canada's first private law school and also Canada's first (current) Christian law school, since TWU itself is a Christian educational community. Throughout Canadian history, many universities have been founded by churches, including some with law schools, but they secularized over time – along with many faith-based high schools and elementary schools (Marsden 1994). And in the United States, many faith-based law schools continue to operate, and new faith-based law schools have opened even in recent years, including some with community covenants very much analogous to that at TWU. Thus TWU's proposed law school stands in high relief in the educational landscape of both Canada and the United States.

Its proposal of a faith-based law school led to TWU's application being subjected to innumerable challenges that are still ongoing and almost surely bound to end up in the Supreme Court of Canada. These challenges were initially put by legal academics (rapidly joined by others) urging Canada's Federation of Law Societies to refrain from recommending TWU's law school for approval (e.g., Craig 2013). When those efforts were unsuccessful and the law school both received curricular approval and was recommended for professional accreditation, opponents of TWU unexpectedly expanded the field on which it needed to fight by seeking to challenge its approval as an accredited law school before each provincial law society, asking the different law societies effectively to break away from a national accreditation process they had adopted in the context of a new wave of law school applications in recent years (Newman 2014).

Some provinces, notably Ontario and Nova Scotia, decided to refuse to accredit TWU for law society admission purposes. Opponents of TWU also launched a court case in British Columbia to challenge the provincial Minister of Education's approval of the educational program to be offered by the law school. And, after the Law Society of British Columbia had, through its duly elected benchers, originally decided to follow the Federation of Law Societies' recommended approval of TWU's law school, opponents mobilized and initiated an unprecedented referendum process to overturn the decision of the benchers. With the Law Society of British Columbia now refusing to accredit the school, British Columbia's Minister of Education suspended curricular approval of the program.

TWU operates as a Christian educational community within a particular Christian tradition. It was originally founded within the tradition of the Evangelical Free Church, but today it embraces various evangelical traditions. Operating as it does within evangelical traditions, TWU has a Community Covenant covering a range of dimensions of conduct within the university. At least ostensibly, the main issue for those challenging TWU's law school proposal is that the university's Community Covenant has discriminatory effects against lesbian, gay, bisexual and transgender (LGBT) individuals, insofar as one provision of that Community Covenant sees students voluntarily agreeing to refrain from "sexual intimacy that violates the sacredness of marriage between a man and a woman" (Newman 2013).

I refer to this issue as the "ostensible" main issue, I would add, because the range of attacks on TWU from legal scholars and others opposed to its law school have expanded at different points in time to include suggestions that the same Covenant provision discriminates against other groups and even suggestions that have gone so far as to assert that scholars working within a Christian university cannot possibly exercise academic freedom (Newman 2016c).

The sometimes rapidly shifting arguments are, to be frank, such as to raise some suspicions. It is difficult to know whether these seemingly malleable arguments simply manifest a variety of rhetorical strategies related to a main issue of discrimination against LGBT individuals or whether they actually manifest an actual anti-TWU or anti-Christian animus. The present paper, though, is focused solely on the issue of the LGBT discrimination argument, which has seemingly been the source of enduring opposition.

Aside from how the arguments have played out in the debates generally, a contest of sorts between religious freedom and sexual-orientation-based discrimination has certainly been the dominant frame within the litigation that the TWU controversy has spawned. That litigation has become complex (Newman 2016c). In a Nova Scotia trial court in early 2015, the trial judge held that the Nova Scotia benchers had acted unreasonably in refusing to accept TWU for accreditation purposes, referring both to this decision being outside their jurisdiction and to the decision infringing on religious freedom. And this ruling was upheld at the Nova Scotia Court of Appeal in 2016. That decision will not be appealed. At trial in Ontario, a three-member panel at the Divisional Court upheld the Ontario benchers' decision not to accredit TWU, citing both a standard of deference to the benchers and an identification of discrimination based on sexual orientation, among other grounds, and this contrasting decision was upheld in Ontario's Court of Appeal in 2016. British Columbia's trial court decided in favor of TWU, and that decision was upheld by its Court of Appeal. The Supreme Court of Canada will hear the appeals from the two contrasting appellate judgments. The underlying philosophical claims related to religious freedom and discrimination are well worth further unpacking.

3. The depth of and complex parallelisms between claims based on religious identity and claims based on sexual identity

TWU surely did not set out to generate controversy in opening a law school and, indeed, did not set out to be subjected to more procedural hurdles around approval than put in the way of any Canadian law school in history. It knew, of course, that its professional programs had previously generated controversy. Its education program, for example, had previously been challenged by the British Columbia College of Teachers (BCCT). This challenge led to a major case in 2001, with the subsequent ruling affirming TWU's program, rejecting any BCCT assumption that TWU teaching graduates would discriminate in the classroom, and upholding TWU's ability to operate a teaching program with an earlier version of the Community Covenant in place (Supreme Court of Canada 2001). As is the case in Christian communities generally, there have been evolving conversations about issues of sexuality and discrimination over the years – even to the point of there being some evangelical voices coming out in support of same-sex marriage or at least of more nuanced and sensitive engagement on LGBT issues (Burk 2015; Sprinkle 2015; Gushee 2015; DeFranza 2015). Unsurprisingly, then, TWU's present Community Covenant reflects ongoing discussions and avoids some language from the version that existed at the time of the 2001 decision that might appear unnecessarily hurtful to those from groups who have faced discrimination over time. Resting on the 2001 precedent, though, TWU presumed that its right to open a program would be based on standard academic and professional criteria and not on concerns about the Community Covenant. A legal opinion from a leading Canadian lawyer and firm obtained by the Federation of Law Societies and annexed to the Federation's report on TWU solidly supported the view that the 2001 precedent determined matters and that religious freedom has not been lessened over the past 15 years of Canadian jurisprudence (Federation of Law Societies 2013).

To the extent that they have discussed the law, however, opponents of TWU have suggested that changes in the legal environment on sexuality-related issues would imply a different legal result today (Craig 2014, 640–643). In doing so, they have drawn particularly on a passage from a hate speech case, *Whatcott v. Saskatchewan Human Rights Commission,* in which Justice Marshall Rothstein wrote as follows:

> I agree that sexual orientation and sexual behaviour can be differentiated for certain purposes. However, in instances where hate speech is directed toward behaviour in an effort to mask the true target, the vulnerable group, this distinction should not serve to avoid s. 14(1) (b). One such instance is where the expression does not denigrate certain sexual conduct in and of itself, but only when it is carried out by same-sex partners. Another is when hate speech is directed at behaviour that is integral to and inseparable from the identity of the group.
>
> (Supreme Court of Canada 2013, para. 122)

The argument some would seek to develop from this passage is that discrimination against same-sex sexual conduct is equivalent to discrimination against LGBT individuals (Craig 2014, 643). Whether this follows as a broad legal interpretation of a passage concerned particularly with hate speech is not particularly clear, especially in light of other passages of the *Whatcott* judgment affirming freedom of expression on issues of sexual morality (Supreme Court of Canada 2013, paras. 169–70, 200). However, those doctrinal issues are not my main focus for present purposes. Rather, what is interesting on a philosophical level is the consequences of the approach that assumes manifestation of an identity to be part of what is protected by fundamental freedoms and/or equality rights.

Manifestation of religious belief through religious practice is of course a long-standing part of what religious freedom protects (Régimbald and Newman 2013, 577). Ironically, the American constitutional context has been relatively less protective of that aspect, insofar as the *Employment Division v. Smith* decision saw the United States Supreme Court refuse constitutional protection to any exemption from general laws that incidentally affected manifestations of religious belief (Supreme Court of the United States 1990). However, what were initially widely supported *Religious Freedom Restoration Acts* reintroduced a balance on that point, one interestingly parallel to that in other jurisdictions like Canada. In principle, in the Canadian jurisprudence, the right to manifest religious belief is part of religious freedom; non-trivial restrictions of manifestations of religious belief are a *prima facie* infringement on religious freedom; and government limits on manifestations of religious belief are thus subject to a proportionality analysis that looks to whether governments have limited religious freedom no more than reasonably necessary to the pursuit of valid state objectives (Régimbald and Newman 2013, 556–565, 578–579).

Building on arguments made by the likes of Grégoire Webber (2012) and Bradley Miller (2014), I have critiqued elsewhere the above-mentioned proportionality analysis for, among other things, the ways in which the results of its application can be altered by the means by which a particular issue is brought before the courts (Newman 2016b). For example, its unreflective application to a context of conflicting rights in the Saskatchewan Marriage Commissioners case (Saskatchewan Court of Appeal 2011) gave significant weight to symbolic or emotional harm to equality for same-sex couples and effectively no scope to religious freedom for marriage commissioners with claims of conscience not to perform same-sex marriages (Biddulph and Newman 2013). However, we can bracket that issue and focus here more simply on the point that the right to manifest a religious identity is an aspect of the fundamental freedom of religion.

Freedom of religion is a multifaceted concept that protects the freedom to live out an identity in both individual and collective ways, an identity with chosen aspects and community aspects, an identity sometimes more closely linked to individual conscience and sometimes more closely linked to a broader cultural identity. Justice Albie Sachs of the South African Supreme Court has described parts of the rich web of relations religion may embody:

> For many believers, their relationship with God or creation is central to all their activities. It concerns their capacity to relate in an intensely meaningful fashion to their sense of themselves, their community and their universe. For millions in all walks of life, religion provides support and nurture and a

> framework for individual and social stability and growth. Religious belief has the capacity to awaken concepts of self-worth and human dignity which form the cornerstone of human rights. Such belief affects the believer's view of society and founds a distinction between right and wrong. It expresses itself in the affirmation and continuity of powerful traditions that frequently have an ancient character transcending historical epochs and national boundaries. For believers, then, what is at stake is not merely a question of convenience or comfort, but an intensely held sense about what constitutes the good and proper life and their place in creation.
>
> Religious bodies play a large and important part in public life, through schools, hospitals and poverty relief programmes. They command ethical behaviour from their members and bear witness to the exercise of power by state and private agencies; they promote music, art and theatre; they provide halls for community activities, and conduct a great variety of social activities for their members and the general public. They are part of the fabric of public life, and constitute active elements of the diverse and pluralistic nation contemplated by the Constitution. Religion is not just a question of belief or doctrine. It is part of a people's temper and culture, and for many believers a significant part of their way of life. Religious organisations constitute important sectors of national life and accordingly have a right to express themselves to government and the courts on the great issues of the day. They are active participants in public affairs fully entitled to have their say with regard to the way law is made and applied.
>
> (Constitutional Court of South Africa 2005, paras. 89–90)

At the same time, in the same-sex marriage case in which Justice Sachs wrote those words, he also went on to hold that "[i]t would be out of order to employ the religious sentiments of some as a guide to the constitutional rights of others" in the course of declining to make use of religious texts as background to constitutional interpretation (Constitutional Court of South Africa 2005, para. 92). There is a delicate balance between an ability to live out a religious way of life and the ability of others to live out their ways of life as well.

So as not to unduly constrain what is protected by freedom of religion, the Supreme Court of Canada had indicated that its scope extends to a practice based on a "sincere belief" that has a "nexus with religion" (Supreme Court of Canada 2004, para. 46). Lower courts applying the legal test have sometimes been ready to limit particular claims based on non-sincerity in instances where individuals have developed previously unknown religions that seem to offer them only benefits and no burdens (Newman 2016a). But the religious freedom test protects a broad scope of conduct that manifests religious identity, including also collective practices similarly having a nexus with religion (Newman 2016c).

Some – and even some believers from other faith traditions – have mischaracterized the TWU Community Covenant in terms of some type of refusal to study in the same classroom with others. And, indeed, this mischaracterization has unfortunately infiltrated the judicial conceptions of the Community Covenant

(Newman 2016c). However, as a deeper historical and contextual investigation establishes, the TWU Community Covenant has a vastly richer meaning as a community practice of religious belief, both as a way of living out a particular religious way of life and as a way of living out deeply rooted religious traditions that transcend individual believers' lives and embody historically rooted religious identities.

Contemporary examinations by those such as Brad A. Lau and Gerald A. Longjohn, Jr. of why religious educational communities have adopted community covenants have tied them to a variety of specific objectives, including simply the idea that such covenants facilitate the practice of the religion to which community members are committed, that such covenants further the spiritual formation of youth studying within a faith-based educational institution, and that such covenants support an environment facilitating the serious academic mission to which the community is committed (Lau 2005; Longjohn 2013). Those explanations should be sufficient to make community covenants identifiable as expressions of collective religious identity. Such community identity may be countercultural in a broadly individualistic culture; such community identification is a mode of moral life that scholars like Jonathan Haidt have identified as running counterculturally to Western liberalism and thus not always easily recognized by judicial elites, among others, but also as being a mode embraced by many people and no less worthy of recognition (Haidt 2012). However, we can actually go farther than these contemporary explanations of the significance of community covenants within particular faith traditions.

In considering the place of a community covenant within a particular religious community, we can logically also consider how that community covenant is part of the community's identity over time, transcending the generations. Those who join today in that community covenant join a living faith tradition that is rooted deeply in history as well. Scholars like David Novak have traced ways in which the scriptural idea of covenant has had a constitutive political dimension for early Jewish communities on through to more recent Christian communities (Novak 2005). Within the particular Christian traditions at some of the historical roots of the TWU community, the idea of covenant has had particular significance. Early Calvinist communities adopted community covenants as a significant means of aspiring to Christian community (MacCulloch 2003). Community covenants featured prominently among the Puritans in New England and in succeeding political and religious traditions (Elazar 1987). Indeed, the idea of a community covenant has tremendously long historical roots within Reformed Christian traditions, and the modern community covenants in various Protestant educational institutions with some origins in Reformed traditions arguably live out this longer Christian tradition within particular faith traditions. So, if the TWU Community Covenant strikes some outsiders as peculiar or as oriented specifically to some type of isolationism, on the contrary, it actually has religious standing as an embodiment of a living faith tradition. The claim to operate a Christian educational institution with a community covenant is a claim simply to live out the educational dimension of that Christian community's life. The TWU claim is simply one to manifest religious belief, which is well within the core of religious freedom.

That said, as suggested earlier, the claim of LGBT individuals challenging the TWU Community Covenant could also be phrased as one to manifest an identity through practice, in this case a sexual minority identity through sexual practices associated with that identity. The *Whatcott* passage relied upon by some refers to "behaviour that is integral to and inseparable from the identity of the group" in challenging the idea that it is possible in this context to distinguish between status and conduct (Supreme Court of Canada 2013, para. 122). The claim on behalf of LGBT individuals is that something like the Community Covenant, if it is something to which they subject themselves, not only constrains sexual conduct but potentially prevents them from being "who they are."

The discrimination claim arises most obviously in the context of an imaginary member of a legally married same-sex couple who would seek to attend TWU's law school. In this circumstance, the TWU Community Covenant would seem to preclude the individual from sexual intimacy with his or her partner, whereas it would permit sexual intimacy between members of a male-female married couple. However, a charitable reading of the claims of LGBT individuals would also arguably see a broader impact as well. Although there is no reason to argue that unmarried LGBT individuals cannot refrain, in accordance with the Covenant, from sexual intimacy as can unmarried heterosexual individuals, the terms of the Covenant might plausibly be thought to constrain more limited forms of romantic intimacy in same-sex relationships more so than romantic intimacy between those developing in an opposite-sex relationship, insofar as it ultimately specifically precludes any development of that relationship to marriage.

Sexual self-determination is one means by which individuals express and live out a certain model of their lives. Although TWU and those within particular faith traditions have views on the appropriate bounds of this expression, the point here would be that in a pluralistic society and absent harm-based arguments those particular views would not seem easily to provide grounds for legal constraint on this expression by some individuals, particularly when there are no longer (enforced) legal constraints on that expression by others.

The claim to the manifestation of a sexual identity by members of a sexual minority, like the claim to manifestation of a religious identity by members of a religious minority, seeks a right to manifest an identity even in the face of disagreement by others in the society with the manifesting conduct. As with a religious minority, the manifestation represents something that may be an important means of expression but that may be non-mandatory, but members of religious minorities analogously seek the option of engaging in manifestations of religious identity that are not inherently mandatory forms of conduct (Supreme Court of Canada 2004, para. 47). And, as with the religious minority, the manifestation is in the context of a complex identity held by members of a group that may be marginalized by others. As with the religious case, there is also a collective or associative dimension at issue. The *Obergefell* same-sex marriage case from the United States Supreme Court sees Justice Kennedy describing the claim of LGBT individuals seeking to marry as a claim "not to be condemned to live in loneliness" (Supreme Court of the United States 2015, 28). Those seeking a right to sexual expression claim a right to pursue connection (literally) with other human beings as part of a manifestation of their personal identity. At least on a certain surface reading, there are a number of parallels between the two sorts of claims.

4. Distinguishing claims to manifest different identities?

The question that naturally arises is whether there are clear grounds to distinguish between the two claims to manifest identity, the religious and the sexual. In some contexts, the very question would verge on sounding lewd. But the question must be faced in a modern constitutional context, in the particular circumstances of contemporary culture. These circumstances include constitutional interpretations with broad readings adopted of liberty rights and bodily integrity rights. These circumstances also include those of a highly sexualized culture and essentially no legal constraints on consensual heterosexual sexual expression, including widespread practices of cohabitation and no-fault divorce that facilitate widespread serial monogamy. In such circumstances, the denial of equivalent sexual expression to those seeking to engage in LGBT relationships would not have any immediately clear basis explicable in secular terms accepted within pluralistic debate, so it would seem to give rise to discrimination through unequal treatment of a traditionally marginalized group.

The claims to manifest a minority religious identity and to manifest a minority sexual identity might well be criticized by those on each side of the division between them. The TWU law school controversy, as other incidents, shows religious minority communities challenging the claims of sexual minority groups and sexual minority groups challenging the claims of religious minority communities. The decision of whether one has greater standing than the other cannot be made based on the unique premises proffered by each group; rather, it must be made on a more generalizable basis.

The logical candidate for such a basis would be a meaningful distinction between the two types of identity at issue. Religious or spiritual identity might arguably fit better something like Charles Taylor's description of an identity as providing a frame or horizon for one's existence (Taylor 1992, 27; Taylor 2007). Sexual identity might seem more closely related to matters of personal identity and personal authenticity, without necessarily obviously providing the same sort of frame or horizon for existence but fitting within a gradually reconceptualized analysis of the idea of dignity within the law. In this postmodern variant, constitutionally protected liberties "extend to certain personal choices central to individual dignity and autonomy, including intimate choices that define personal identity and beliefs" (Supreme Court of the United States 2015, 20).

One might further distinguish the two as being concerned with the pursuit of some more ultimate truth as opposed to, when concerned with the variety of forms of identity expression at issue, being concerned with forms of personal hedonic pleasure. However, the latter description of sexual identity expression might well be read as understating the significance of individuals expressing "who they are," and the former might be read as implicitly failing to attach sufficient significance to personal authenticity, both of which have become highly popular values. Indeed, the majority in the recent *Obergefell* decision appears to place great weight on individuals defining and expressing themselves; the majority refers to a constitutional right of individuals to "define and express their identity" (Supreme Court of the United States 2015, 2). That this identity is subject to subjective individual definition is consonant, of course, with earlier judicial pronouncements like that of Justice Kennedy, who suggested that "[a]t the heart of liberty is the right to define one's own concept of existence, of meaning, of the universe, and of the mystery of human life" (Supreme Court of the United States 1992, 851). By contrast, my description of the pursuit of religious identity may appear to be based in part on the truth of some claims concerning ultimate reality, which are obviously unlikely to be granted by opponents of religion.

Based on current constitutional approaches, it is arguably not clear that these two forms of expression of identity can be readily distinguished for legal purposes. If that is the case, then religious minority communities seeking legal recognition may put their claim legitimately only if they accept legal respect being accorded to sexual minority communities. Obviously, this is something with which some religious communities have sometimes struggled in the context of historically limited understandings of aspects of the real pain experienced by sexual minorities; that pain has unfortunately sometimes been facilitated by religious groups (Sprinkle 2015). At the same time, though, sexual minority communities seeking legal recognition similarly may put their claims legitimately only if they accept legal respect being accorded to religious minority communities. This, in turn, is something with which sexual minority communities have struggled in what has sometimes become a postmodern moment of triumphalism over religion (Newman 2016c).

This latter triumphalism has, notably, not been uncontested within the LGBT movement. For example, after Mozilla CEO Brendan Eich was forced to resign for having been found to have made a small personal donation against same-sex marriage in a referendum campaign, Andrew Sullivan wrote:

> Will he now be forced to walk through the streets in shame? Why not the stocks? The whole episode disgusts me – as it should disgust anyone interested in a tolerant and diverse society. If this is the gay rights movement today – hounding our opponents with a fanaticism more like the religious right than anyone else – then count me out. If we are about intimidating the free speech of others, we are no better than the anti-gay bullies who came before us.
>
> (Sullivan 2014)

However, Sullivan's view was by no means universally shared. Indeed, the reality is that Brendan Eich was forced to step down from Mozilla.

As I have developed more fully elsewhere, in a number of pertinent senses the legitimacy of the rights claims put by different groups ultimately depends upon their acceptance of rights claims by others that rest upon the same premises

(Newman 2011). If the different claims at issue here rest upon parallel arguments about rights to manifest identity, then there may need to be more respect between groups that have sometimes failed to respect one another.

5. Implications for specific circumstances

The last section ended on a suggestion that groups need to respect one another more fully. Does that imply, for instance, that TWU must change its Community Covenant? On the contrary, I would suggest that the argument at hand supports a claim that TWU should be able to keep its Community Covenant, and that those seeking its change ought to be doing so not through litigation and regulatory efforts to quash TWU's law school, but through mutually respectful engagement with TWU.

This conclusion, I suggest, flows simply from a public-private distinction. Were TWU a publicly established law school, there would be no basis for it to represent a specific religious ethos and there would be compelling bases for it to respect individual expressions of identity through permitting both individual and associative religious belief and expressions of that belief (including in free speech concerning matters of sexual morality, so long as it is not framed in ways that express hatred toward others) and also expression by sexual minority groups, with resulting non-discrimination requirements.

However, TWU is not a publicly established law school, but is the educational activity of a private religious community. If freedom of religion is to be meaningful, those within a private religious community need to be able to manifest their religious beliefs in their ways of living. The deep significance of community covenants within the faith traditions that TWU carries forward highlight that they manifest religious belief in profound senses. Despite the challenging parallelisms of rights claims based on religious identity and sexual identity, there are grounds for TWU to manifest religious belief as a private institution.

At the same time, the types of legal-constitutional parallelisms I have highlighted may also support a call for genuine humility on both sides. If religious believers identify within their own religious traditions bases to distinguish their claims to manifest religious identity from claims by others to manifest minority sexual identity, they may nonetheless wish to recall that, as perceived by outsiders, these claims may rest on similar grounds. They may properly reflect deeply on the fate of the stranger. At the same time, if members of sexual minority groups currently feel that they are triumphing over religious institutions, and feel that this is some sort of historic payback, they may wish to reflect on the deep-seated identity claims of religious believers as well and remember when they were themselves treated as if strangers in a foreign land.

Where rights theory sometimes invites polarization, an engagement with some of the developing sorts of rights conflicts between religious freedom and sexual expression will hopefully invite more mutually respectful engagement and more efforts by all to work toward human flourishing. Saying as much will obviously not resolve in some simple way the range of genuinely difficult conflicts ahead, but there are principled ways of sorting through some of these issues, and some of these principled ways also emphasize the importance of values of humility, respectful engagement, and charity toward one another.

Note

1 I am grateful for comments from and/or discussions with Paul Copan, Joe Gorra, Angus Menuge, Dallas Miller, John Montgomery, Ray Pennings, and others, who participated in the 2015 IVR Special Workshop on Religious Freedom.

Bibliography

Anderson, Ryan T. 2015. *Truth Overruled: The Future of Marriage and Religious Freedom.* Washington, DC: Regnery.

Biddulph, Michelle, and Dwight Newman. 2013. "Eweida v. United Kingdom." *Australian International Law Journal* 20: 183–188.

Burk, Denny. 2015. "The Evangelical Theological Society after Obergefell." Blog post, November 23. Accessed October 21, 2016. http://www.dennyburk.com/the-evangelical-theological-society-after-obergefell.

Civil Marriage Act. 2005. *S.C.* 2005, c. 33 (Canada).

Constitutional Court of South Africa. 2005. *Minister of Home Affairs v. Fourie*, ZACC 19, 2006(3), BCLR 355, 2006(1), SA 524, at paras. 89–90 (CC).

Craig, Elaine. 2013. "The Case for the Federation of Law Societies Rejecting Trinity Western University's Proposed Law Degree Program." *Canadian Journal of Women and the Law* 25(1): 148–170.

Craig, Elaine. 2014. "TWU Law: A Reply to Proponents of Approval," *Dalhousie Law Journal* 37(2): 621–660. https://papers.ssrn.com/sol3/papers.cfm?abstract_id=2446470.

DeFranza, Megan K. 2015. *Sex Difference in Christian Theology: Male, Female, and Intersex.* Grand Rapids: Eerdmans.

Elazar, Daniel J. 1987. *Covenant and Constitutionalism: The Covenant Tradition in Politics*, Vol. 3. New York: Transaction.

Federation of Law Societies of Canada. 2013. "Report on Trinity Western University's Proposed School of Law Program." Canadian Common Law Program Approval Committee. Accessed October 21, 2016. http://docs.flsc.ca/ApprovalCommitteeFINAL.pdf.

Gushee, David. 2015. *Changing Our Mind*, 2nd ed. Canton, MI: Read the Spirit.

Haidt, Jonathan. 2012. *The Righteous Mind: Why Good People Are Divided by Religion and Politics.* New York: Pantheon.

Lau, Brad A. 2005. "Reasons for Student Behavior Codes: A Qualitative Study at Two Christian Liberal Arts Institutions." *NASPA Journal* 42(4): 549–564.

Longjohn, Gerald A.Jr. 2013. *By the Book: Spiritual Formation and Conduct Codes at Selected Christian Universities.* EdD Dissertation, Olivet Nazarene University.

MacCulloch, Diarmid. 2003. *Reformation: Europe's House Divided.* London: Allen Lane.

Marsden, George. 1994. *The Soul of the American University: From Protestant Establishment to Established Nonbelief.* Oxford: Oxford University Press.

Miller, Bradley. 2014. "Proportionality's Blind Spot: 'Neutrality' and Political Philosophy." In *Proportionality and the Rule of Law: Rights, Justification, Reasoning*, ed. Grant Huscroft, Bradley W. Miller and Grégoire Webber. Cambridge: Cambridge University Press, 370–396.

Newman, Dwight. 2011. *Community and Collective Rights: A Theoretical Framework for Rights Held by Groups*. Oxford: Hart.
Newman, Dwight. 2013. "On the Trinity Western University Controversy: An Argument for a Christian Law School in Canada." *Constitutional Forum* 22(3): 1–14.
Newman, Dwight. 2014. "The Desperate Campaign to Thwart a Christian Law School." *National Post*, January 24. Accessed October 21, 2016. http://news.nationalpost.com/full-comment/dwight-newman-the-desperate-campaign-to-thwart-a-christian-law-school.
Newman, Dwight. 2016a. "Implications of the Ktunaxa Nation / Jumbo Valley Case for Religious Freedom Jurisprudence." In *Religious Freedom and Communities*, ed. Dwight Newman. Toronto: LexisNexis, 309–320.
Newman, Dwight. 2016b. "Canadian Proportionality Analysis: 5½ Myths." *Supreme Court Law Review* 73: 93–108.
Newman, Dwight. 2016c. "Ties That Bind: Collective Aspects of Religious Freedom." In *Religious Freedom and Communities*, ed. Dwight Newman. Toronto: LexisNexis, 3–20.
Novak, David. 2005. *The Jewish Social Contract: An Essay in Political Theology*. Princeton: Princeton University Press.
Régimbald, Guy, and Dwight Newman. 2013. *The Law of the Canadian Constitution*. Toronto: LexisNexis.
Saskatchewan Court of Appeal. 2011. *Reference re Marriage Commissioners*, SKCA 3.
Sprinkle, Preston. 2015. *People To Be Loved: Why Homosexuality Is Not Just an Issue*. Grand Rapids: Zondervan.
Sullivan, Andrew. 2014. "The Hounding of a Heretic." *Blog post*, April 3. Accessed October 21, 2016. http://dish.andrewsullivan.com/2014/04/03/the-hounding-of-brendan-eich/.
Supreme Court of Canada. 2001. *Trinity Western University v. British Columbia College of Teachers*, 1 S.C.R. 772, 2001 SCC 31.
Supreme Court of Canada. 2004. *Syndicat Northcrest v. Amselem*, 2 S.C.R. 551, SCC 47.
Supreme Court of Canada. 2013. *Whatcott v. Saskatchewan Human Rights Commission*, SCC 11, 1 S.C.R. 467.
Supreme Court of the United States. 1990. *Employment Division, Department of Human Resources of Oregon v. Smith*, 494 U.S. 872.
Supreme Court of the United States. 1992. *Planned Parenthood of Southeastern Pennsylvania v. Casey*, 505 U.S. 833.
Supreme Court of theUnited States. 2015. *Obergefell v. Hodges*, 135 S. Ct. 1732, 576 U.S. (slip op.).
Taylor, Charles. 1992. *Sources of the Self: The Making of the Modern Identity*. Cambridge: Harvard University Press.
Taylor, Charles. 2007. *A Secular Age*. Cambridge: Belknap.
Webber, Grégoire. 2012. *The Negotiable Constitution: On the Limitation of Rights*. Cambridge: Cambridge University Press.

8 Religious rights of parents and students in US K-12 public education

John Calvert

Introduction

This essay analyzes the religious rights of parents to direct the religious education of their children in a US K-12 public school and the corollary rights of students to not be indoctrinated by the school to accept a particular religious belief under the First and 14th Amendments of the US Constitution. It extends the ideas and conclusions expressed in two of my previous articles, which were published in 2009 and 2013, respectively: "Kitzmiller's Error: Using an Exclusive rather than Inclusive Definition of Religion" (Calvert 2009) and "Human Rights in a Secular State Will Depend on its Legal Definition of Religion" (Calvert 2013). I am a lawyer who has been specializing since 1999 in US constitutional law as it relates to public education regarding religious issues.

Religious rights of parents and students in US K-12 public education

The basis and necessity of human rights in a secular state

"Human Rights in a Secular State" discusses very generally three types of states. A theocracy is a state which endorses and promotes a particular theistic religion. A prime example of one is Iran, where the state actually is an instrument of the religion of Islam. An atheocracy is a state that endorses a non-theistic religion. Examples of this kind of state are Marxist Russia and North Korea. Theocracies often suppress competing theistic sects, while atheocracies suppress theistic religions and beliefs.

A third kind of state is the "secular state." Secular, in this sense, means "not religious." Thus, a secular state purports to be neutral as to religion, not endorsing or favoring any religion or religious belief when a government activity "touches the religious sphere" (*Gillette v. U.S.* 1971, S. Ct., at 450). It is often the preferred idea in a country populated by a plurality of religious beliefs.

The government activity most sensitive to the "religious sphere" is K-12 public education. In the US, parents have the duty to educate their children, but may do so free of charge if they use a public school. The alternatives are limited, consisting of costly home or private schooling. Private schools cost an average of $8,549 per child per year, or $17,090 for a family with two children (The Center for Education Reform 2014). Due to these prohibitive costs, public schooling is effectively compulsory for most parents.

The question then becomes: can a state be truly secular if the public school curriculum promotes or endorses a particular religion or religious belief? It seems not. By teaching a particular religious viewpoint to all children, the state would be indoctrinating the children and interfering with the natural rights of parents to direct the religious education of their children.

This right is incorporated in the European Convention on Human Rights (ECHR), as it provides that "[i]n the exercise of any functions which it assumes in relation to education and to teaching, the State shall respect the right of parents to ensure such education and teaching in conformity with their own religious and philosophical convictions" (Protocol to the Convention for the Protection of Human Rights and Fundamental Freedoms 1952).

The religious rights of parents and students in the US arise primarily under the 1st and 14th Amendments of the US Constitution.[1] The 1st Amendment states that "*Congress* shall make no law respecting an establishment of religion, or prohibiting the free exercise thereof, or abridging the freedom of speech" (emphasis added). After the Civil War, the 14th Amendment was adopted. It prohibits a state from depriving "any person of life, liberty, or property, without due process of law; nor deny to any person within its jurisdiction the equal protection of the laws." In 1940, the Supreme Court held that the 14th Amendment caused the 1st Amendment to be applicable not just to the federal "Congress," but also to any state or local governmental agency, including schools (*Cantwell v. Connecticut* 1940, S. Ct. at 303).

Thus, after the 14th Amendment the Supreme Court construed the two to mean together: "*No governmental agency, whether federal, state or local,* shall make *any* law *or policy* respecting an establishment of religion, or prohibiting the free exercise thereof, or abridging the freedom of speech." This effectively requires all public K-12 schools to be secular and neutral.

The US Supreme Court case that establishes the religious rights of parents and students in public education is the 1987 case of *Edwards v. Aguillard* (1987, S. Ct. at 583–584). *Edwards* involved a challenge to a Louisiana law that required the teaching of a biblical account of origins called "creation science." Creation science had to be taught whenever the curriculum included an objective discussion of biological evolution. The Court found that the law breached a trust owed by the state to the parents and children:

> The Court has been particularly vigilant in monitoring compliance with the Establishment Clause in elementary and secondary schools. Families *entrust* public schools with the education of their children, *but condition their trust on the understanding that the classroom will not purposely be used to advance religious views that may conflict with the private beliefs of the student and his or her family.* Students in such institutions are impressionable and their attendance is involuntary.
>
> (*Edwards*, S. Ct. at 583–584, emphasis added)

The idea of public education initially was that it would teach only secular subjects and therefore not interfere with the religious rights of parents and students. This was explained by Justice Jackson in 1947 in *Everson v. Board of Education*:

> Our public school…is organized on the premise that secular education can be isolated from all religious teaching so that the school can inculcate all needed temporal knowledge *and also maintain a strict and lofty neutrality as to religion.* The assumption is that *after the individual has been instructed in worldly wisdom he will be better fitted to choose his religion.*
>
> (*Everson*, S. Ct. at 23–24, emphasis added)

This is possible when the "temporal knowledge" is confined to subjects like reading, writing and arithmetic, which do not address ultimate religious questions. Thus, by limiting the subject matter of the curriculum, the public school can assure that it will stay in the secular sphere and not touch on the religious sphere.

The idea of restricting subject matter to achieve secularity was addressed in the famous 1971 case of *Lemon v. Kurtzman* (S. Ct. at 610). In *Lemon*, the Court considered a state statute that would reimburse parochial schools for a variety of wholly secular expenses, including the purchase of textbooks deemed to be entirely secular and not religious. In this respect, the statute classified the following subjects as "secular" and not religious: "mathematics, modern foreign languages, physical science, and physical education." In addition, the statute prohibited reimbursement for "any course that contains 'any subject matter expressing religious teaching, or the morals or forms of worship of any sect.'" (S. Ct. at 610). The Supreme Court concluded that "in the abstract" this demarcation was secular and neutral (S. Ct. at 613). However, it concluded that the entire program of providing state aid to religious schools produced an "excessive entanglement" with religion that violated the Establishment Clause.

This case is relevant to the present analysis, as it recognizes a distinction between secular and religious issues or subjects. The list that was deemed secular and neutral did not include curricula relating to historical origins science or classes in behavioral, health and social sciences that deal with issues regarding human sexuality, the sanctity of life, family, morality and ethics.

Subject matter dealing with religious issues must be excluded or taught objectively

But what if the curriculum is expanded to include subjects that address religious issues like the origin of life and what if it is structured so that only a theistic view is presented? This was the issue in the 1968 case of *Epperson v. Arkansas* (S. Ct. at 109), where Arkansas enacted a law that banned the teaching of a materialistic theory of human origins – biological evolution. The court held that the law violated the Establishment Clause because it excluded only one of multiple views of origins, thereby not being neutral. If the law had been fully exclusionary by banning all teaching of origins and not just the materialistic view, the law would have been constitutional (S. Ct. at 109). The court also noted that religious materials, including the Bible, can be taught if they are taught objectively so that the effect is neutral. *Epperson* shows that, if the state wishes to expand the curriculum to teach religious issues, it must teach them objectively so that the effect is religiously neutral.

Religious rights require use of a comprehensive definition of religion that includes theistic and non-theistic beliefs

Religion includes both theistic and non-theistic belief systems. Clear definitions of key words are essential to the protection of religious rights. The words, whose popular definitions produce the most confusion are "religion," "secular" and "science." The popular definition of "religion" is the worship of God. However, billions of those who reject or do not worship a creator god are also "religious." This includes Buddhists, Confucians, members of various Hindu sects, Jainists, Religious ("Secular") Humanists, Freethinkers, Scientologists, Wiccans and Atheists.

The word "secular" means "not religious." However, when used in the context of a theistic definition of religion, then Buddhists and Religious ("Secular") Humanists are not religious. Given this vulgar or popular definition of religion, a so-called "secular" state may be entirely atheistic, as was Marxist Russia and as is North Korea.

The definition of "science" is also important to the definition of religion. If a belief is classified as "scientific," then most assume it to be not religious. The problem is that the word "science" defies definition and has been extended to include opinions and questionable assumptions about religious issues. The Oxford Dictionary of Science (2003) does not include a definition of the words "science" or "scientific." The definitions of religion and science are extensively analyzed in "Kitzmiller's Error" and "Human Rights in a Secular State" (Calvert 2009, 2013). The modern, accurate and constitutionally required definition of religion has moved during the last 100 years from a popular theistic definition to a comprehensive definition that includes both theistic and non-theistic religions.

The popular definition of religion results from the fact that the US was nearly uniformly theistic until the mid-20th century. However, in 1933 Charles Potter, John Dewey and others published the Humanist Manifesto (American Humanist Association 1933), which set forth the tenets of non-theistic "Religious Humanism," a modern version of Epicureanism. The religion was to be advanced by inserting it into public schools.[2] Its tenets include a denial of the supernatural and the idea that life should be led using human reason and materialistic science, not the wisdom of God.

In 1957, the California Court of Appeal held in *Fellowship of Humanity v. County of Alameda* that 14 Religious ("Secular") Humanist churches in Alameda County were religious even though they were atheistic. The Court recognized that religion includes many non-theistic belief systems including Taoism, classic Buddhism, and Confucianism. For Judge Peters, a religion "includes: (1) a belief *about* (rather than 'in') the supernatural, (2) a system of moral practices resulting from the belief and (3) an organization that advocates and observes the tenets of the belief (*Fellowship of Humanity* 1957, Cal. App. at 406).

Since *Fellowship of Humanity*, a number of courts have found Religious ("Secular") Humanism to be a religion, and the Supreme Court has recognized it as one.[3] Similarly, the courts routinely recognize atheism as a religion or religious belief.[4] In many cases, religious advocates have attempted to insert a non-theistic religious belief into public schools under the guise of "science." The first case was *Malnak v. Yogi* in 1979, where a course in transcendental meditation was called the "Science of Transcendental Meditation." The court disregarded the "science" label and found it to be religious (*Malnak* 1979, 592 F.2d. 197 at 211–212). Similarly, in another case, after Humanist Manifesto I (American Humanist Association 1933) proclaimed "Religious Humanism," the authors of Humanist Manifesto II (American Humanist Association 1973) dropped the "Religious" modifier.[5] When cross-examined about what it was if it was not religion, they called the belief system "science," a classification rejected by the court (*Smith* 1987, at 982).

The issue is important, as many opinion-based social subjects have sought and been granted a scientific status even though they are not guided by a scientific method that limits explanations to those which have been empirically derived. Thus, "science" now includes anthropology, archaeology, criminology, economics, education, government, linguistics, political science, psychology, sociology and, in some contexts, geography, history and law.

The inclusive nature of religion is explained by the Supreme Court in the 1992 case of *Lee v. Weisman*. In *Lee*, a school sought to characterize a prayer to an "unnamed God" as "non-sectarian," "non-preferential" and therefore neutral. The Court held it was preferential, as it favored believers over unbelievers – theists over atheists:

> Many Americans who consider themselves religious are not theistic; some, like several of the Framers, are deists.…Thus, a nonpreferentialist who would condemn subjecting public school graduates to, say, the Anglican liturgy would still need to explain why the government's preference for theistic over *nontheistic religion* is constitutional.
>
> (*Lee* 1992, at 617)

According to Justices Souter, Stevens, and O'Connor in their concurring opinion, the "settled law" is that the "clause applies 'to each of us, be he Jew or Agnostic, Christian or Atheist, Buddhist or Freethinker'" (*Lee* 1992, at 611). Similarly, in 2005 the Seventh Circuit held that atheism is a religion (*Kaufman* 2005, at 682–684).

A "religious issue" is one that addresses ultimate questions. Analysis of the scope of the religious sphere leads to the question: what is a religious issue? What is the dividing line between religious issues on the one hand and non-religious, secular issues on the other?

As explained in "Human Rights in a Secular State," the demarcation between the religious and the secular turns on whether the issue relates to an "ultimate question" (Calvert 2013). Two cases decided by Judge Adams of the Third Circuit Court of Appeals explain the demarcation: *Malnak v. Yogi* (1979) and *Africa v. Pennsylvania* (1981). In *Malnak,* Judge Adams found that a public school course in the "*science* of creative intelligence and transcendental meditation" (SCI/TM), developed in India by Maharishi Mahesh Yogi, addressed a religious issue because it "concerns itself with the same search for ultimate truth as other religions and seeks to offer a comprehensive and critically important answer to the questions and doubts that haunt modern man" (*Malnak,* 1979, at 214). However, two years later in *Africa* he found that a prisoner's ad hoc belief system that required a special diet was not religious, as it did not address ultimate questions. In *Africa*, Adams then developed a set of criteria one could use to determine whether a belief system was religious:

> *First*, a religion addresses *fundamental and ultimate questions* having to do with deep and imponderable matters. *Second*, a religion is comprehensive in nature; it consists of a belief-system as opposed to an isolated teaching. *Third*, a religion often can be recognized by the presence of certain formal and external signs.
>
> (*Africa* 1981, at 1032, emphasis added)

The Court further explained that "fundamental and ultimate questions" are those that deal with "certain 'underlying theories of man's nature or his place in the Universe'" and those "having to do with, among other things, life and death, right and wrong, and good and evil" (*Africa* 1981, at 1032–1033, emphasis added). This idea that religions address ultimate questions was succinctly captured by Justice Frankfurter in *McGowan v. Maryland*:

> By its nature, religion – in the comprehensive sense in which the Constitution uses that word – is an aspect of human thought and action which profoundly relates the life of man to the world in which he lives.
>
> (*McGowan* 1961, S. Ct. at 461)

The Adams criteria are similar to those discussed by Judge Peters in *Fellowship of Humanity*: an organized belief *about* (but not necessarily in) the supernatural and "a system of moral practice directly resulting from an adherence to the belief" (*Fellowship of Humanity* 1957, at 406).

If all religions address "ultimate questions," then what are they? Roy Clouser, Professor of Philosophy and Religion, identifies and orders ultimate questions in a natural hierarchy. The ultimate of all ultimate questions is the nature of the ultimate reality that is "unconditional" and "nondependent." He refers to this reality as the "Divine." All else is conditioned and dependent on the Divine (Clouser 2005, 106–111; Calvert 2013). For the theist, the Divine is a creator god who has made the universe and life for a purpose. For the non-theist, the Divine – the ultimate reality – is self-existing matter, energy and the four forces of the universe (i.e., nuclear weak, nuclear strong, gravity, and electromagnetism). Theists are teleologists, while non-theists are materialists. Teleology is the study of design in nature. Materialism, mechanism, or naturalism is "the doctrine that cause-and-effect laws (as of physics and chemistry) are adequate to account for all phenomena and that teleological conceptions of nature are invalid" (Grove 2003).

The ultimate reality, or Divine, is the answer to the popular statement of the ultimate of ultimate questions: where do we come from, what is the cause of the universe and life?

The second question in the hierarchy of ultimate questions is "what is the nature of life?" This question cannot be answered until the first is answered. For a theist, life is a creation made for a purpose – it has an inherent purpose as it has been "made" or created. All creations have a purpose, end or "*telos.*" For the materialist, life is not created, as it just *occurs* without purpose due to the interactions of matter, energy and the four physical forces mentioned above.[6]

Another key aspect of the second question – what is the nature of life? – is what happens when life ends. For the materialist, the answer is simple: the laws of entropy guarantee that it disintegrates into a state of disorder. However, many theists believe that life has both a spiritual and physical nature. The spiritual aspect is referred to as the soul, which continues after physical death. Since it continues after death, one's behavior during physical life will affect one's spiritual life or soul after death. Thus, many theists believe one needs to live one's physical life in a certain way to ensure a good life after death. However, the materialist need not be concerned with how the living of life before death will affect an afterlife, as there is none.

The third ultimate question is "how should life be led, particularly from an ethical and moral standpoint?" Again, the answer to this question depends on how one has answered the first two questions. The theist relies on reason and the wisdom of God reflected in holy scriptures to guide the living of life. For the Christian, one "must first deny himself, pick up his cross daily, and follow" Jesus, based on Scripture and personal experience with Him (Matthew 16:24–25, NIV). For the non-theist, there is no god to follow or believe in. Hence, one should live life to achieve happiness per the use of human reason and materialistic science.

All religions provide answers or solutions to a number of key moral and ethical questions relating to marriage, family, human sexuality and the sanctity of life. The manner in which these issues are resolved depends on one's answers to the prior questions in the hierarchy.

The inclusive definition of religion is necessary for the goal of neutrality to be achieved. A variety of attempts have been made in different contexts to broaden or narrow the definition of religion to achieve a particular goal. They have resulted in a comprehensive, functional and inclusive definition for two reasons. First, as discussed below, it is a fact that many recognized religions are not theistic. Second, a narrow theistic definition of religion is itself not neutral, and the entire goal of the Establishment Clause is to require government to be religiously neutral.

If the definition of religion is gerrymandered to exclude non-theistic beliefs, then those non-theistic beliefs may be systematically endorsed or abridged by the state. The effect is not neutral. Thus, a provision designed to secure neutrality and religious freedom actually becomes a tool to deny it. Accordingly, an inclusive definition is necessary.

Evolution of K-12 public education in the US

Initially, the "wall" that separated religion from government did not apply to the states or schools

The early settlers of North America often immigrated there in order to flee governmental establishment of religions that discriminated against their religious beliefs. They then established "colonies" that embraced their religious beliefs, but subsequently discriminated against later arriving immigrants holding to different religious beliefs. By the time of the Revolutionary War, all 13 colonies, except for Pennsylvania, had established a state religion which preferred one sect over others.

After the Revolutionary War, the need arose to form a national government. A key issue was which religious sect the national government would support. Also, would the national government be permitted to interfere with the various state religions that the colonies had already established? Unwilling to give up their state religions, the colonies adopted a constitution that forbad the "Congress" of the national government to pass any law "respecting an establishment of religion or prohibiting the free exercise thereof." Thus, the 1st Amendment was designed to keep the federal government out of religion so that the states could freely pursue their own. This then enabled the continuance of state religions that limited religious liberty.

The issue regarding federal but not state separation from religion was reflected in a famous 1802 exchange of letters between Thomas Jefferson and the Danbury Baptist Association in Connecticut. The Danbury Baptists complained to Jefferson about a Connecticut Constitution that permitted the state to prefer the Congregational Church over other sects, including the Danbury Baptists. Jefferson replied that although the 1st Amendment erected a "wall of separation between Church and state" [the "state" then being the federal government]," this "wall" of secularity was applicable only to federal, not state governments.[7] However, Jefferson expressed his hope that the state of Connecticut would someday voluntarily erect a wall that would separate that state from religion.

As explained above, the key event which actually imposed the "wall" of secularity on all governments, both state and local, was the 1940 Supreme Court ruling in *Cantwell v. Connecticut* (1940, at 303), which held that the 14th Amendment adopted in 1868 implicitly imposed the 1st Amendment on all state and local governments as well, thereby requiring them to all be secular and neutral.

Since 1940, public education has systematically walled out theistic religious views while walling in non-theistic religious views

The exclusion of theistic religious views. Prior to the separation, public schools were governed by local independent school boards elected by parents that typically promoted Christian views. However, since the separation in 1940, a series of Establishment Clause complaints have effectively eliminated theistic views from all public schools. Generally, the courts have held that any school activity that supports theistic religion may be viewed by an objective observer as state endorsement of "religion."

Thus, to avoid an endorsement schools and other public facilities have systematically excluded theistic activities previously permitted, including: (a) voluntary Bible studies that occur on school premises before the start of school; (b) a teacher's silent reading of the Bible in the view of his English class; (c) teachers providing for a minute of "voluntary prayer or meditation"; (d) mention by a student valedictorian of her theistic religious beliefs during her speech; (e) a kindergartner's reading to his class from his "favorite book" if it is a Bible; (f) a football coach's "bending a knee" with his team during its voluntary collective prayer before or during the game; (g) an invocation to an unnamed god at a high school graduation ceremony; (h) a nativity scene or (i) a copy of the 10 Commandments to be displayed in a court house; (j) a cross to become a part of a city logo; or (k) a cross-shaped memorial to a deceased highway patrolman privately erected in a state highway right-of-way.[8]

Religious issues have been added to the curriculum, but they are taught only from a non-theistic perspective. As discussed above, the Supreme Court in *Everson* viewed the public education system as one in which only secular subjects would be taught, such as "mathematics, modern foreign languages, physical science, and physical education" (*Lemon* 1971, at 610). Since *Everson* (1947) and *Lemon* (1972), the issues addressed by the public school curriculum have been expanded beyond purely secular subjects. They now include subjects that address religious questions, such as origins science and behavioral, health and social sciences that deal with issues regarding human sexuality, the sanctity of life, family, morality and ethics.

Modern curricula lead children to ask and answer "compelling questions" that address religious issues (National Council for the Social Studies 2013, 17). For example, kindergarteners in Connecticut schools are asked this "compelling question:" "How are *we* connected to the past?" A theist would say that we are connected through a god that created each of his children for a purpose. Atheists would claim that we are just connected by a materialistic evolution of random interactions of matter, energy and the four physical forces.

The question then becomes whether these curricula "objectively" provide children with all of the information necessary to make an informed decision about the matter so that the effect of the teaching is religiously neutral. Also, are the "compelling questions" presented when student minds are (a) cognitively mature; and (b) knowledgeable, so that they may make an informed decision? The need for a cognitively mature mind that is knowledgeable is essential for informed decision-making about abstract, highly complex and controversial issues. Origins science, as well as human sexuality, family, and moral and ethical behavior – how a "good citizen" should act – fall into this category.

Another significant change in the public school curriculum is that previously religious issues might arise in isolated instances for brief periods during the

13-year course of public education. Formerly, teaching about origins science might be confined to a week or two in a 10th-grade biology class after the student had (a) formed his religious worldview at home; (b) had mentally matured; and (c) had acquired the background knowledge sufficient to make his own decision about the matter. Today, this isolated, occasional intrusion into the religious sphere is being comprehensively expanded through the implementation of an aligned set of National Education Standards designed to be taught incrementally, progressively and non-objectively to every student in the country. It begins in kindergarten and continues for the entire 13-year education of the child, with the goal of establishing in the child a "worldview" that embraces the core ideas that are taught (National Research Council 2012; Citizens for Objective Public Education Inc. 2012–2013).

Although this formula may make good sense pedagogically with certain subjects like mathematics and English grammar, when applied to matters of opinion, and particularly religious matters, it becomes an instrument for systematic indoctrination in a worldview. This is inconsistent with the right of the parent to direct the religious education of the child and the right of the child to not be indoctrinated by the state to accept a given religious viewpoint. A program of nationalization also moves the educational decisions from the parents and thousands of competing independent school boards to an undefined relatively small group of educators that likely embrace a common set of non-theistic religious beliefs.

The inherent religious problem with the national standards is that they implicitly define religion as just theistic. They then employ a strategy of Establishment-Clause-compliance that excludes "religion" by excluding only the theistic viewpoints. The non-theistic views are taught exclusively as "secular," when they actually promote non-theistic religion.

The Common Core State Standards for English and math (CCSS) were released for adoption by states on June 2, 2010 (National Governors Association 2010): "By November 2013 a total of 45 states and the District of Columbia had adopted the CCSS in both subjects" (Achieve 2013), the states and the district being induced in part by US Department of Education monetary grants and waivers of non-compliance with the requirements of No Child Left Behind (Emma 2014). Although the standards in Math and English do not explicitly address religious issues, they provide the foundation for national standards for all students in all other subjects.

Thus, the 2012 Framework for K-12 Science Education was designed to take advantage of the success of the CCSS and to align science standards with the standards for English and math. As of May 2016, 20 states had explicitly adopted the science framework and standards.

Similarly, in 2012 the National Sexuality Education Standards designed "to promote the institutionalization of comprehensive sexuality education in public schools" were "informed by...the Common Core State Standards for English Language Arts and Mathematics" (Future of Sex Education Initiative 2012, 2). National Social Studies State Standards, released in 2013, were also designed to be aligned with the Common Core Standards, and their acceptance by the states is yet to be determined (National Council for the Social Studies 2013, 7).

A metaphor one might use for this project is a double bacon burger to be fed daily to every child in the US beginning at age 5. The top and bottom buns are the math and English standards. They hold the meal together, but do not provide it with the flavor. In between, one will find a half-pound of meat consisting of the science standards which promote a materialistic/atheistic worldview. Non-theistic Sexuality Education and Social Studies Standards provide the bacon, pickles, lettuce and mustard (or ketchup and mayo if one prefers) that promote non-theistic values regarding human sexuality, family, sanctity of life, social justice, and environmentalism.

The following table reflects the religious issues addressed by National Education Standards, the curricula that deal with the subject, the excluded theistic views, and the included competing non-theistic views, which match the tenets of Religious ("Secular") Humanism.

The following section discusses the issues presented in the table in more detail.

National Education Standards address religious issues without objectivity

National standards for teaching materialistic origins science interfere with the religious rights of parents and students

Origins science, unlike math, physics and chemistry, address the ultimate questions central to all religions. Where do we come from? Do we come from a creator god or simply self-existing matter, energy and the four physical forces? This question is addressed in cosmological, chemical and biological evolution. Along the way, the second question is asked and answered – what is the nature of life? Is it a creation made for a purpose that continues spiritually after physical death, or is it a mere purposeless occurrence that ends on death without an afterlife?

Answers to these questions provide the foundation for the third key question – how should we live life and what should be the basis for making this decision? Should we rely on science, reason and the natural and scriptural revelations of religions that have been tested by thousands of years of human experience, or should we rely only on "reason" and materialistic science?

Modern origins science is historical, materialistic, functionally atheistic and not objective. If origins science was itself an objective non-controversial empirical science that depended only on observations and experimentation for its explanations, then it could be taught by a neutral state even though its explanations were inconsistent with a particular religious viewpoint. This is because its explanations would be inherently objective. That objectivity would render the state's teaching neutral as to religion, as the facts would establish the absence of religious bias.

However, explanations provided by most institutions of science about the origin and nature of life and the universe are inherently non-objective for two reasons. The explanations are necessarily materialistic and functionally atheistic because they are based on a seldom mentioned doctrine called Methodological Naturalism (MN). MN is also called "Scientific Materialism" or "Mechanism." MN requires

Table 8.1 National standards that address religious issues using an exclusive theistic definition of religion

Religious issue addressed	Curricula	Included non-theistic / atheistic views	Excluded theistic views
1. Where do we come from?	origins science	Matter – unguided evolutionary process	Creator god who made the universe and life for a purpose
2. What is the nature of life?	origins science	It is a physical occurrence that ends on death.	It is a creation made for a purpose that includes a soul that continues after death.
3. How should one decide to live life?	sexuality education, psychology, anthropology, social studies	Use reason and science – make evidence-based decisions. "Good and evil" are relative concepts that change with history and culture.	Use God's wisdom derived from Scripture and personal experience along with reason and science. Do good and avoid evil, as reflected in "natural law" and the wisdom of God.
4. Goal of life	sexuality education, psychology, anthropology, social studies	"To live life well and fully." "Working to benefit society maximizes individual happiness."	Various. Christians set goals via a selfless personal relationship with Christ: To have "life," one must "deny himself and take up his cross daily and follow me" (Matthew 16:24–25).
5. Human sexuality	sexuality education	Children should make "safe," reasoned decisions about sex.	Obey religious tenets and laws about sexual activity to optimize the mental and physical health of the individual, the family, and culture.
6. Family – marriage, divorce, duties of mother, father, children and extended family	sexuality education, psychology, anthropology social studies	The family is a very broad concept and includes many different relationships. One should be "tolerant" of another's choice of sexual relationships.	God has defined family relationships through natural and scriptural revelation. Thousands of years of human experience show that God's plan optimizes the mental and physical health of the individual, the family, and culture.
7. Sanctity of life	sexuality education, psychology, anthropology, social studies	Use science and reason to make decisions. Abortion is a woman's choice.	Abortion: Depends on one's interpretation of Scripture. Many believe life begins at conception in the womb and may not be taken by the mother.

one to assume that the apparent design of many natural objects and systems is just an illusion, and that all natural phenomena are due solely to the interactions of matter, energy and the four physical forces.

MN was explained in 1997 by Richard Lewontin, a prominent geneticist and evolutionary biologist, as "a *prior commitment, a commitment to materialism*":

> It is not that the methods and institutions of science somehow compel us to accept a material explanation of the phenomenal world, but, on the contrary, that *we are forced by our* a priori *adherence to material causes* to create an apparatus of investigation and a set of concepts that produce material explanations, no matter how counter-intuitive, no matter how mystifying to the uninitiated. *Moreover, that materialism is absolute, for we cannot allow a Divine Foot in the door.*
>
> (Lewontin 1997, 31)

The second reason origins science is controversial is that it is a subjective historical, rather than empirical, science. MN essentially requires an atheistic historical narrative or "just so" story with respect to deeply religious issues. Its tunnel vision requires that history be written such that events are not due to an intervening mind or intelligence.

As explained by evolutionary biologist Ernst Mayr in 2000,

> evolutionary biology, in contrast with physics and chemistry, is a *historical* science – the evolutionist attempts to explain events and processes that have already taken place. *Laws and experiments are inappropriate techniques for the explication of such events and processes. Instead one constructs a historical narrative*, consisting of a tentative reconstruction of the particular scenario that led to the events one is trying to explain.
>
> (Mayr 2000, 80, emphasis added)

Historical sciences depend on abductive reasoning to determine the best of competing explanations for the cause of unobserved and unobservable past events. Accordingly, historical narratives reduce to opinions not to facts. The opinions are expressed in probabilistic terms – event A was "most likely," or "beyond a reasonable doubt" caused by X. A third possibility is "we don't know" – we lack the evidence necessary to reasonably determine a "best explanation" for the cause of event A.

Origins science is like forensic science, which seeks to determine the cause of a death. Was the death more likely due to an accidental, natural or intelligent cause (suicide or homicide), or do we lack the evidence sufficient to close the case in favor of one of those explanations? However, in origins science we seek to explain the cause of life rather than the cause of a death.

The origin of the universe, of life and much of the diversity of life is mysterious because the universe and life appear to have been designed. The mystery in origins science is that both the universe and life give the appearance of having been brilliantly designed for a purpose. The evidence shows that the universe is not infinite, but rather started with a beginning, or a "big bang," 13.5 billion years ago. Out of the "bang" emerged matter, energy and forces having very precise characteristics. These elements give the appearance of having been fine-tuned for life. Alter any of the forces or the characteristics of matter or energy by a smidgen, and life would not exist. Probabilistic calculations reveal that chance is an implausible explanation. The laws of physics and chemistry also fail to explain the event, as it established those very laws. This suggests that the universe may be due to an intelligent cause, an inference recognized by Francis Collins, Martin Rees and Paul Davies.[9]

Similarly, the origin of life reflects a biological big bang out of which information processors of unimaginable sophistication and complexity arose. E-coli, the simplest form of bacteria, uses an operating system more robust in its "architecture" than the Linux Operating System (Zimmer 2010), and the genetic code has been found to exhibit "eerie perfection," the best of millions of possibilities.[10] Richard Dawkins explains that "biology is the study of complicated things that give the appearance of having been designed for a purpose" and that the design is "brilliant" (Dawkins 1996, 1, 6, 21).[11]

This then raises the core question of origins science. Is the apparently "brilliant design" of the universe and life real or an illusion? Is it an illusion like the illusion of a rising sun which has been disproved by observation? The current state of our actual scientific knowledge is that we simply do not know the answer to the question – origins science is a case not closed. We do not know whether these origins events are due to accidental, natural or intelligent causes.[12]

As a consequence of both the nature of origins science as a historical science and use of the tunnel vision of MN in writing the history of life, the opinions regarding origins provided by modern institutions of science are not objective. Rather, MN causes the two ultimate questions to be answered with only materialistic/atheistic explanations.

New National Science Standards seek to establish a materialistic/atheistic religious "worldview"

In the past, origins science might have been taught for a couple of weeks in a 10th-grade biology class in isolation from other subjects. Thus, by the time the student had learned about a materialistic "core idea" of origins he had already formed his worldview (Barna Group 2009). However, a new Framework for K-12 Science Education (National Research Council 2012) and related Next Generation Science Standards (NGSS Lead States 2013, "Framework & Standards," henceforth "F&S") are designed to establish in the child a materialist / functionally atheistic worldview by teaching the materialistic "core idea" of cosmological, chemical and biological evolution incrementally, progressively, comprehensively and deceptively throughout the student's entire K-12 educational experience, beginning in kindergarten along with other aligned subjects.

The inheritance of traits is to be introduced in kindergarten. Each year, another concept is added. The F&S are based on psychological studies that recognize that children intuitively develop a "misconception" that life is designed by a creator. Inexplicably, the curricula standards are structured to change the misconception by the end of middle school, when the child is 13 or 14 years old. The psychological studies that form a part of the basis for the F&S recognize that it is not an easy task, as materialistic evolution is counterintuitive. However, educational psychologists find that impressionable children tend to naturally accept what authority figures tell them is true. Eventually, like their teachers, they will embrace materialistic explanations of the key questions of life: where do we come from, and what is the nature of life?[13]

The F&S explicitly seek to establish in all students in the US a "scientific worldview" (National Research Council 2012, 41–42, 48; NGSS Lead States 2013, App. G, 1, 4). However, because it employs MN it is one that is actually materialistic and functionally atheistic. This worldview is then designed to cohere with and be aligned with all other aspects of the curriculum. Since many of the subjects involved in the curriculum are themselves classified as science – social science, health science, behavioral science, anthropology – the rest of the curriculum becomes a vehicle to promote the scientific worldview that is materialistic.

Although the F&S include policies designed to promote equity and non-discrimination with respect to students on the basis of sex, race, ethnicity, socio-economic status, language and disability, they make no provision for prohibiting discrimination based on religion, thereby allowing the F&S to promote exclusively a non-theistic religious worldview (NGSS Lead States 2013, App. D, 2).

The F&S make no provisions for causing students to adequately understand and appreciate that MN is used. Nor does the program seek to explain the effect of the use of MN on the explanations students are led to accept about where they come from and the nature of life. Indeed, MN cannot be meaningfully disclosed until the mind of the child is both mature and filled with the necessary background knowledge, a time after middle school when the children have already unwittingly formed their materialistic worldview.

To adequately disclose MN, the curriculum must disclose the banned teleological alternative and the evidence which supports it. In a stock offering, an investor must be shown the other side of the story, or "historical narrative," essential to an informed investment decision. However, the F&S are designed to lead children to believe that there is no other "reliable" side to tell, when in fact the teleological argument is based on functional patterns in nature that appear brilliantly designed for a purpose, that are not attributable to physics and chemistry, and that have not been shown to be due to chance using statistical analysis and probability theory.

State adoption of such an extensive, sophisticated and comprehensive policy of religious indoctrination of students in the garb of science education would seem contrary to the religious rights of students and their theistic parents.

Non-theistic sexuality education interferes with the religious rights of parents and students

Sexuality education addresses ultimate religious questions about how life should be lived. Sexuality education is another subject not included in the list of "secular" subjects mentioned in the *Lemon* case. It is typically taught in health science classes. However, it is now being expanded by National Sexuality Education Standards to be taught progressively throughout the child's 13-year educational experience (Future of Sex Education Initiative 2012).

Based on our answers to questions about the cause and nature of life, religions then explain how we should live our lives, ethically and morally. The most profound of these ethical issues deals with human sexuality, namely, when, how and with whom one may engage in a variety of sexual activities. Next are decisions about family and the duties of members of a family, and finally decisions about the sanctity of life, including abortion.

All major religions of the world address issues relating to when, where and with whom one may engage in sexual activity. The Abrahamic religions (Judaism, Islam and Christianity) generally prohibit sex out of marriage including adultery (Deuteronomy 22:13–22, NIV), incest, sex with animals, and homosexuality (Leviticus 18:6–22, NIV). Buddhists follow a set of five precepts, including one that requires abstention from sexual misconduct. Since the Buddhist precepts do not derive from God, they derive from the logical necessity of seeking a "pure life" – one that will avoid suffering and enhance society, as adherence to moral precepts optimizes the mental and physical health of the individual, the family, and culture (Dahlke et al. 2008).

An article in *Psychology Today* shows that Religious Humanists have a significantly different view of sex – one typically advanced by comprehensive sexuality education:

> As opposed to conservative Christian beliefs about pre-marital sex, the secular humanist view – *which is atheistic or, better, non-theistic* – doesn't start with "pre-ordained" assumptions about right and wrong but attempts to understand this basic libidinal drive holistically. By seeing sexuality not from the perspective of *established religious dogma*, but from a bio-socio-cultural vantage point, humanists *endeavor to help young people better* grasp the complex nature of sexual intimacy. To prompt them to consider the various ramifications – ethical and otherwise – of unrestrainedly letting loose their libido. And to have them question whether giving *unmitigated expression* to their erotic impulses is finally in their best interests.
>
> (Seltzer and Niose 2010, emphasis added)

Sexuality education address all of these religious issues, which include the following questions: *what is a family, and does family include unmarried couples whether or not they are heterosexual? Is having sex a decision a child may make? When is it appropriate for a child to decide to have sex, if at all? With whom is it appropriate for a child to have sex, if at all? What sexual acts are okay? When one has sex, how should it be done "safely"? What does "safe sex" mean?*

Since religions take a position on all of these issues, then how can a school address these issues and still preserve the religious rights of parents to direct the religious education of the child and the right of the child to not be indoctrinated by the state? How should sexuality education be taught, if at all? Can these subjects be taught objectively and neutrally to a 5-year-old or a 10-year-old, or to a 13-year-old? Is it even possible to teach all the various religious views objectively when the curriculum strays into issues relating to when, with whom and how one may have sex and whether abortion is a permissible solution to an unwanted pregnancy?

Most sexuality education incorrectly assumes the subject is not religious, as it is classified as "science." In fact, the issue of human sexuality goes to the very heart of religion, as it addresses fundamental questions about morality, marriage, family, parenting and the sanctity of life.

A number of problems arise from a "scientific" classification of sexuality education. First, modern science, as discussed previously, uses a materialistic assumption that permits only materialistic/atheistic explanations. When sex is treated as science, it will be treated within a functionally atheistic frame of reference. God did not create human sexuality in a particular way for a purpose, it just occurred via unguided evolutionary processes.

Second, since all "science" is incorrectly thought to be empirical, students will be misled into believing that the non-theistic "scientific" explanations are valid, while the theistic religious views may be disregarded as simply faith-based dogmas, not empirically derived and evidence-based, and therefore not reliable.

Third, the scientific and "not-religious" classification permits the total exclusion of theistic views as "religion." The standard curriculum is then implicitly grounded in the argument that one should act based on "reasoned" and "evidence-based" scientific conclusions, not unreliable "faith-based" adherence to religious dogmas. This is the core tenet of Religious ("Secular") Humanism – life should be led based on science and reason. However, the inherent problem with reason is that its output is only as good as its input. If the so-called "evidence-based" subjective opinion input is faulty, so too will be the output – garbage in, garbage out.

So-called "evidence-based" input regarding human sexuality can easily be garbage, as the input also depends on emotions, fallible human speculations, assumptions, biases and opinions, and often on a dearth of human experience. On the other hand, the rejected so-called "faith-based" conclusions are ones that have actually been tested by thousands of years of human experience, have been embraced by eastern religions, and have been shown by human experience to actually optimize the mental and physical health of the individual, the family, and culture.

The following very briefly discusses comprehensive sex education as incorporated in the National Sexuality Education Standards. These are designed to be taught uniformly by all schools to every child in the US (Future of Sex Education Initiative 2012, 12–13).

Comprehensive sex education is comprehensive, as it addresses practically every issue regarding human sexuality one might imagine. This includes how, when, where and with whom one may engage in sexual activity. The sanctity of life enters the discussion, as abortion is discussed as a "family" planning option.

Although the issues are comprehensive, the discussion is not, as it omits traditional theistic views. The modern curriculum reflected in National Sexuality

Education Standards begins the education of children in kindergarten. At age 5, children are taught that they have the right to not be touched by others "when they do not want to be touched" (Future of Sex Education Initiative 2012, 6). However, many religions (and criminal law) simply do not permit any sexual touching, regardless of whether the child "want[s] to be touched." Furthermore, the age of the "toucher" is not limited to adults, but includes other children. Thus, the child does not have the right to touch his or her friend in particular ways and places even if the friend wants to be touched.

Psychology Today explains that theistic and non-theistic religions have different views about touching: "Andersen notes that Atheists and agnostics touch more than religious types, probably because religions often teach that some kinds of touch are inappropriate or sinful" (Chillot 2013).

A regional state conference on comprehensive sex education in 2004 addressed a critical issue: what should children be taught about *when* it is permissible for them to have sex, when does the light turn green for them? The discussion was fascinating, as the question addressed the more fundamental question of what "love" is. There appeared to be a consensus among the educators that love should precede sex. Hence, sex is apparently okay if it is not promiscuous. But what is "love?" The instructor suggested that true love certainly does not occur on the first day of school, but might occur by spring break. Also, one should not engage in it with a "shark," but rather find a personality like that of a "dolphin" (Calvert 2004). The discussion did not mention laws that make it criminal for anyone, including other children, to have sex with a child below a specified age, which in some cases is the age of 18.

The following are summaries of some of the concepts that National Sexuality Education Standards expect children to learn during the ages of 5 to 7 and in middle school. By age 7, students should know

> "[h]uman sexual anatomy"; "*different kinds of family structures*"; "ways to show respect for different types of families"; "healthy ways for friends to express feelings to each other"; "why bullying and teasing [about homosexuality is] wrong"; that you "have the right to tell others not to touch [you] *when [you] do not want to be touched*"; "how boys and girls may be expected to act"; and "how friends, family, media, society and culture [but not religion] influence ways in which boys and girls think they should act."
>
> (Future of Sex Education Initiative 2012, 12–13, emphasis added)

Between 11 and 14, students who will not be legally able to consent to engage in any sexual activity until the age of 16, 17 or 18 should know

> how to make good decisions about engaging in sexual activity, the differences "between gender identity, gender expression and sexual orientation" and "the range of gender roles" and how to "promote dignity and respect for all people in the school community"; that "sexual intercourse" includes anal and oral sex, the physical health benefits, risks and effectiveness of "various methods of

> contraception," and "pregnancy prevention," "negotiation skills about the use of contraception," "emergency contraception" (the morning after pill), "the use of effective communication skills to reduce or eliminate risk for STDs, including HIV." [sic] "the characteristics of healthy and unhealthy relationships," the "differences between friendships and romantic relationships," "communication skills that foster healthy relationships," how "to communicate personal boundaries," "behaviors that constitute bullying, sexual harassment, sexual abuse, sexual assault, incest, rape and dating violence," who are "trusted adults" that one may communicate with "about bullying, harassment, abuse or assault," and that you have the right to not be touched if you "do not want to be touched."
>
> (Future of Sex Education Initiative 2012, 16–19)

The high school standards (Future of Sex Education Initiative 2012, 20–23) include a discussion of abortion, which is defined in the glossary as nothing more than "a medical intervention that ends a pregnancy" (Future of Sex Education Initiative 2012, 39). Many religions consider an abortion to be the taking of the life of another, as life is believed to begin at conception. Students in high school are to "compare and contrast the laws relating to pregnancy, adoption, abortion and parenting," thus educating themselves on how to have one if they decide to do it. Notice that only the "laws" are to be analyzed, not the various religious views about the matter. Nor do the Standards suggest a discussion of the impact of an abortion on the long-term mental health of the mother, which includes the symptoms of post-traumatic stress disorder (PTSD).[14]

The comprehensive sexuality education model implicitly assumes that decisions about sex are not to be guided by "parochial" scriptures, but rather by reason and logic. The goal is to focus on the teaching of "*functional knowledge* and essential *personal and social skills* that contribute directly to *healthy sexuality*" (Future of Sex Education Initiative 2012, 8, emphasis added).

The program is problematic because it ignores the fact that the issue is religious and not entirely secular. Therefore, the state should not take a position (other than one required by law) on how, when and with whom a child may have sex and what "healthy sexuality" is. Otherwise, it interferes with the religious rights of the parent and the student. Second, it assumes that children have the capacity to make good decisions, when in fact their decision-making capacity does not fully mature until the mid-20s, when the frontal cortex finally completes its development. Finally, the law simply does not permit a child to decide to have sex until the age of consent, which is 16 to 18. Thus, to imply that it is permissible for a child to decide to have sex at an earlier age amounts to a tacit granting of permission to break the law.

Non-objective social studies interferes with the religious rights of parents and students

Social studies includes a number of subjects that address religious issues. These include (a) the morals and ethics deemed necessary to be a "good citizen," such as issues regarding human sexuality, discrimination, family, care for the environment, and "social justice"; and (b) the impact of various religions on civilization and how globalization is affecting religious views and values.

As with those of other "sciences," social studies curricula often treat the subject as a non-religious or secular "science" that promotes only non-theistic solutions to the problems of humanity. As explained under origins science, modern institutions of science use Methodological Naturalism (MN), a doctrine that assumes that ultimate reality is self-existing matter, not a universe brought into being by a creator god. Given the absence of a creator god, one should use reason and materialistic science to solve the problems of life – not "parochial opinions" (National Council for the Social Studies 2013, 5).

This idea, which reflects the core tenet of Religious ("Secular") Humanism, appears to be the basis of the College, Career, and Civic Life (C3) Framework for National Social Studies Standards (henceforth, the "C3 Framework"), which was developed by the National Council for the Social Studies (2013). According to the C3 Framework, "students need the intellectual power to recognize societal problems; ask good questions and develop robust investigations into them; consider possible solutions and consequences; separate evidence-based claims from *parochial opinions*; and communicate and act upon what they learn."

The C3 Framework is general and ambiguous by design; that is, it has no real content (specific learning objectives). It simply suggests ways in which social studies should be taught, emphasizing such concepts as critical thinking, collaboration and inquiry. All of the actual learning objectives must be supplied by the states that develop their standards. Thus, the C3 Framework doesn't provide specific guidance on religious issues. States could choose to stress theistic religious concepts or ignore them entirely. But overall, the C3 Framework tends to emphasize reasoning skills that do not mention traditional theistic ideas.

The National Council for the Social Studies (2010, 5) has also published National Curriculum Standards for Social Studies (NCSSS). NCSSS are a "framework for professional deliberation and planning." NCSSS do have some content (learning objectives), but these tend to be broad and not very specific. Nevertheless, one can gain a better understanding of the philosophy of social studies from NCSSS as compared to the C3 Framework.

NCSSS divide social studies content into 10 themes. Learning objectives from some of these themes, as described below, often show a lack of regard for traditional theistic principles:

Culture. NCSSS state: "By recognizing various cultural perspectives, learners become capable of understanding diverse perspectives." Multiculturalism starts with the premise that all cultures are equally valid. However, cultural equivalence is a myth; the fact is that some cultures have moral and ethical values that many find abhorrent.

Time, Continuity and Change comprise the history theme. History is a narrative of the past that may be written or constructed through omission and misrepresentation to support a particular belief or view. Given the non-theistic bias, many theists complain about history curricula that emphasize exploitation of indigenous peoples, colonial expansionism, victimization (of minorities, the working class and women), the lives of "ordinary" people, and social justice rather than the impact of Christianity, which has shaped Western civilization.

Individual Development and Identity is a theme that explores human behavior and development. Students learn that "individual choices are influenced by personal and social factors." They are not led to acquire their basic value system at home (from parents) and in their religious community. When discussing human development, particularly values and ethics, only non-theistic views are suggested for consideration.

Individuals, Groups and Institutions is a theme that explores interactions between individuals and groups or organizations. Students look at conflict and how to deal with it, but no specific approaches or methods are recommended. As in the previous theme, there is no consideration of theistic principles of ethics and morality.

Power, Authority and Governance is a theme that focuses on the workings of government. Students study the "fundamental values of constitutional democracy (e.g., the common good, liberty, justice, equality, and individual dignity)." However, it lacks any mention of traditional theistic values, despite the fact that the American system was based on Christian principles.

Global Connections. Globalization is a ubiquitous theme, along with the subtheme of universal human rights. However, there is no mention of the view that fundamental rights come from God rather than from governments.

Civic Ideals and Practices. This is the civics theme. Rights and responsibilities of citizenship are listed as follows: "respecting the rule of law and due process, voting, serving on a jury, researching issues, making informed judgments, expressing views on issues, and collaborating with others to take civic action." This is a good list for participation as a citizen in the workings of government, but it says nothing about the personal characteristics of a citizen. Many believe that, for a democracy to succeed, its citizens need to assume personal responsibility for themselves and their family. This includes a strong work ethic and a caring attitude. Instead, the standards emphasize social justice and wealth redistribution.

The difficulty with NCSSS is that they assume a completely non-theistic context while essentially endorsing all of the tenets of Religious ("Secular") Humanism. To protect the religious rights of theistic parents and children, at a minimum, the theistic context needs to be objectively included, so that the overall effect (of children's education) is religiously neutral.

Suggestions for the protection of the religious rights of parents and students

Since the state enters the religious sphere when it teaches origins science, sexuality education and social studies, the curriculum needs to be designed to teach the subjects objectively in order to protect religious rights. The following are general suggestions for such a difficult task:

1 *The audience should be mature and knowledgeable.* A curriculum dealing with religious issues such as origins science, sexuality education and controversial areas of the social sciences should be delayed until the child has (a) formed a basic religious worldview per the direction of parents, typically by age 13; and (b) developed the basic background knowledge necessary to understand and make an informed decision about the matter.
2 *The audience should know a religious issue is involved.* Students should be adequately informed that the curriculum they are about to be taught addresses opinions regarding religious issues. They should also know that the issues have not been decided by the state or by science, that explanations about origins, sexuality education and what it means to be a "good citizen" often reduce to controversial opinions rather than established facts, that there are many competing and conflicting views about the issues, and that they should keep an open mind with respect to the issue and seek parental guidance about it.
3 *The audience should know that the school must be neutral.* Students should be informed that teachers may not present one of competing explanations about a religious issue as valid or as the best explanation, and that their job is to objectively explain the actual state of our scientific or other knowledge about the competing sides of the issue.
4 *The audience should be adequately informed about MN and other assumptions.* Any "scientific" explanation that deals with a religious issue that is based in part on Methodological Naturalism, must be accompanied by an extensive discussion of that doctrine, the extent of its use or influence on the development of the explanation, the competing explanations excluded due to the use of the doctrine, and the evidence that supports the excluded views.
5 *The audience should know that the goal is to objectively inform them about the actual state of our scientific and other knowledge.* If students know this goal, then they and others may assess the extent to which it has been achieved and whether the effect of the presentation is religiously neutral. Students should be told what we don't know as well as what we do know.
6 *Parents and the public should be informed of the content of curricula that address religious issues.* Public school websites should describe the content of religiously sensitive curricula so that parents may make informed decisions about how they should respond to the content. Without adequate information, parents will not be able to effectively exercise their religious rights or those of their children.

The effect of public education on the rights of other citizens

Public education that favors a particular religion interferes not only with the rights of parents and students, it also interferes with the rights of the citizens who live, vote and pay taxes in the state to fund the discriminatory public education. It stigmatizes them as outsiders in the community, deprives them of the equal protection of the law, and interferes with their right to seek to influence members of the community to embrace their particular religious beliefs. An educational system that effectively produces voters that favor a particular religious view will eventually disenfranchise the citizen who holds a different religious view. This is exceedingly important, as much legislation addresses religious issues, particularly in the areas of health care, abortion, euthanasia, marriage and adoption.

As a consequence, a religiously biased public education system affects practically all aspects of the state. If the education system is not substantively neutral, then the state will become religious and thereby restrict the religious freedom of non-adherents.

Conclusion

To adequately protect the religious rights of parents, students and citizens of a pluralistic state that is required to be secular, public education needs to be designed so that it either avoids entirely the religious issue or treats it with scrupulous objectivity.

As explained above, scrupulous objectivity is probably not possible with respect to the discussion of extremely complex or subjective and abstract concepts with immature children and those who lack the necessary background information. However, even where the children are knowledgeable and mature, the burden of providing all sides of many religious issues objectively in a manner that produces a religiously neutral effect will likely take more time and resources than are available during the public school day.

The state could also achieve neutrality by providing parents with education vouchers which they could then endorse to the public or private school of their choice. This would enable a Muslim parent to educate their children in schools that endorse the Koran, or a Christian parent to educate their children in a Catholic or Protestant school. The competition might actually be quite healthy for the educational progress of the country as a whole, as schools would be competing for the educational dollars controlled by the parents.

Notes

1 "That Amendment requires the state to be neutral in its relations with groups of religious believers and non-believers; it does not require the state to be their adversary. State power is no more to be used so as to handicap religions, than it is to favor them" (*Everson* 1947, 18).

2 "Education is thus a most powerful ally of humanism and every American public school is a school of humanism. What can the theistic Sunday schools meeting for an hour once a week and teaching only a fraction of the children do to stem the tide of a five-day program of humanistic teaching?" (Potter, 1930, 128).

3 *Washington Ethical Society* 1957; *Smith* 1987; *Strayhorn* 2003; *Torcaso* 1961.

4 *Torcaso* 1961, S. Ct., holding that the free exercise rights of an atheist were abridged by requiring him to take an oath to God; *Lee* 1992, S. Ct., holding under the Establishment Clause that a so-called "non-preferential" or "non-sectarian" prayer to an unnamed god was in fact preferential and sectarian, as it preferred "theistic over *non-theistic religion*"; and *Kaufman* 2005, 7th Cir., holding that prison regulations denying religious status to atheists violated the Establishment Clause.

5 That is, Paul Kurtz and Edwin H. Wilson.

6 "ABILITIES TO DISTINGUISH BETWEEN NATURAL OBJECTS AND OBJECTS MADE BY HUMANS: Some objects *occur* in nature; others have been *designed and made by people to solve human problems* and enhance the quality of life.... Objects can be categorized into two groups *natural and designed*" (National Research Council 1996, 138, emphasis added). This standard teaches 4th graders that natural objects are not designed.
7 The letter used the word "state," but the 1st Amendment then was only applicable to the "Congress" of the federal government. The letter from the Danbury Baptists and Jefferson's reply are posted at http://www.wallbuilders.com/libissuesarticles.asp?id=65. Jefferson's 1802 letter is published by the Library of Congress at http://www.loc.gov/loc/lcib/9806/danpre.html.
8 (a) *Bell* 1985, 10th Cir; (b) *Roberts* 1990, 10th Cir at 1057; (c) *Wallace* 1986, S. Ct. at 70; (d) Boroff (2013); (e) *Busch* 2009, 3rd Cir.; (f) *Borden* 2008, 3rd Cir.; (g) *Lee* 1992, S. Ct.; (h) *County of Allegheny* 1989, S. Ct.; (i) *McCreary County* 2005, S. Ct.; (j) *Robinson* 1995, 10th Cir.; (k) *American Atheists* 2010, 10th Cir.
9 Many scientists, including Francis Collins, the head of the Human Genome Project, find that the data imply that the universe is "fine-tuned" for life and therefore is a design; see Collins (2006, 75) and Gonzalez and Richards (2004, 195–218). Martin Rees recognizes the inference, but does not prefer it; see Rees (2001, 146–148). For Paul Davies, "[t]he seemingly miraculous concurrence of numerical values that nature has *assigned to her* fundamental constants must remain the most compelling evidence for an element of cosmic design" (Davies 1983, 189).
10 In *Life's Solution: Inevitable Humans in a Lonely Universe*, paleontologist Simon Conway Morris devotes a sub-chapter to the extraordinary efficiency of the genetic code, which he describes as "eerie perfection" (Morris 2003, 13). *See also* Freeland and Hurst (1998, 238–248).
11 Dawkins explains to Susan Mazur: "I see value in looking to physical principles to explain the form of organisms; however, it absolutely neglects the question where does the illusion of design come from? Where do animals and plants get this powerful impression that they have been *brilliantly designed for a purpose?* Where does that come from? That does not come from the laws of physics on their own. That cannot come from anything that has so far been suggested by anybody [who is a materialist] other than natural selection" (Mazur 2010, 99).
12 According to Suzan Mazur in *The Origin of Life Circus: A How to Make Life Extravaganza*, "Freeman Dyson's statement that 'We are all equally ignorant' when it comes to origin of life still holds." "Three of the great remaining mysteries are: (1) origin of the universe, which we may never solve; (2) origin of life, which is a huge problem in my opinion; and (3) how the brain works" [quoting origin of life expert Harry Lonsdale (Mazur 2014, 3, 20)].
13 Harris and Koenig (2006); National Research Council (2012, 249); National Research Council (2009, 113); and Evans (2001).
14 "Events that typically trigger PTSD include: war, rape, witnessing a murder, being a victim of a violent crime, or surviving the devastations of an earthquake or hurricane. For the woman, or man, who has had an abortion, it is the loss of their unborn child" (Abortion Recovery International 2016).

Bibliography

Abortion Recovery International. 2016. "The Impact of Abortion on Women." Accessed August 29, 2016. http://www.abortionrecovery.org/abortionaffects/womenmothers/tabid/230/default.aspx.

Achieve, Inc. 2013. *Closing the Expectations Gap, 2013 annual Report on the Alignment of State K–12 Policies and Practice with the Demands of College and Careers.* Accessed

August 29, 2016. http://www.achieve.org/files/2013ClosingtheExpectationsGapReport.pdf.

American Humanist Association. 1933. *Humanist Manifesto I.* Accessed August 29, 2016. https://americanhumanist.org/what-is-humanism/manifesto1/.

American Humanist Association. 1973. *Humanist Manifesto II.* Accessed August 29, 2016. https://americanhumanist.org/what-is-humanism/manifesto2/.

American Humanist Association. 2003. *Humanism and Its Aspirations: Humanist Manifesto III, a Successor to the Humanist Manifesto of 1933.* Accessed August 29, 2016. https://americanhumanist.org/what-is-humanism/manifesto3/.

Barna Group. 2009. "Barna Survey Examines Changes in Worldview among Christians over the Past 13 Years." Accessed August 29, 2016. https://www.barna.com/research/barna-survey-examines-changes-in-worldview-among-christians-over-the-past-13-years/#.V8RC3jWb2-A.

Boroff, David. 2013. "Texas High School Valedictorian Cut Off after Mentioning 'God' in Graduation Speech." *New York Daily News*, June 11. Accessed August 29, 2016. http://www.nydailynews.com/news/national/valedictorian-cut-mentioning-god-graduation-speech-article-1.1369065.

Calvert, John. 2004. "Touring a Quagmire: Public Sex Education." *Family Concerns: Bridging the Information Gap*, June 17 and 24. Concerned Women of America of Kansas. Accessed August 29, 2016. http://www.intelligentdesignnetwork.org/Touring_a_quagmire_Public_sex_education.pdf.

Calvert, John. 2009. "Kitzmiller's Error: Using an Exclusive rather than Inclusive Definition of Religion." *Liberty University Law Review* 3(2): 213–328. Accessed August 26, 2016. http://www.intelligentdesignnetwork.org/Kitzmiller%27s_Error.pdf.

Calvert, John. 2013. "Human Rights in a Secular State Will Depend on its Legal Definition of Religion." In *Legitimizing Human Rights: Secular and Religious Perspectives*, ed. Angus J. L. Menuge. Farnham, UK: Ashgate, 105–125.

Chillot, Rick. 2013. "The Power of Touch." *Psychology Today*, March 11. Accessed August 29, 2016. https://www.psychologytoday.com/articles/201302/the-power-touch.

Citizens for Objective Public Education, Inc. 2012 and 2013. "*Analyses of the Framework and Standards.*" Accessed August 29, 2016. http://copeinc.org/docs/COPE-Letter-Achieve-Inc-June-1-2012.pdf and http://copeinc.org/docs/NGSSJan2013F.pdf.

Clouser, Roy. 2005. *The Myth of Religious Neutrality: An Essay on the Hidden Role of Religious Belief in Theories.* Notre Dame: University of Notre Dame Press.

Collins, Francis. 2006. *The Language of Life: A Scientist Presents Evidence for Belief.* New York: Free Press.

Dahlke, Paul, Bhikku Silacrara, L. R. Oates andG. Constant Lounsbery. 2008. *The Five Precepts: Collected Essays.* Buddhist Publication Society. Accessed October 31, 2016. http://www.bps.lk/olib/wh/wh055.pdf.

Davies, Paul. 1983. *God and the New Physics.* New York: Touchstone.

Dawkins, Richard. 1996. *The Blind Watchmaker: Why the Evidence of Evolution Reveals a Universe without Design.* New York: Norton.

Emma, Caitlin. 2014. "Common Core Repeal Costs Oklahoma its NCLB Waiver." *Politico*, August 29. Accessed October 21, 2016. http://www.politico.com/story/2014/08/oklahoma-common-core-no-child-left-behind-waiver-110421.

Evans, E. Margaret. 2001. "Cognitive and Contextual Factors in the Emergence of Diverse Belief Systems: Creation versus Evolution." *Cognitive Psychology* 42(3): 217–266.

Freeland, Stephen J., and Laurence Hurst. 1998. "The Genetic Code is One in a Million." *Journal of Molecular Evolution* 47(3): 238–248.

Future of Sex Education Initiative. 2012. *National Sexuality Education Standards: Core Content and Skills, K-12*." (A special publication of the *Journal of School Health*). Accessed August 29, 2016. http://www.futureofsexed.org/documents/josh-fose-standards-web.pdf.

Gonzalez, Guillermo, and Jay Richards. 2004. *The Privileged Planet: How our Place in the Cosmos is Designed for Discovery*. Washington, DC: Regnery.

Grove, Philip Babcock (ed.). 2003. *Webster's Third New International Dictionary of the English Language*. Springfield, MA: Merriam-Webster.

Harris, Paul, and Melissa Koenig. 2006. "Trust in Testimony: How Children Learn about Science and Religion." *Child Development* 77(3): 505–524.

Lewontin, Richard C. 1997. "Billions and Billions of Demons." *New York Review of Books*, January 9. Accessed October 21, 2016. http://www.drjbloom.com/Public%20files/Lewontin_Review.htm.

Mayr, Ernst. 2000. "Darwin's Influence on Modern Thought." *Scientific American*, July: 79–83.

Mazur, Suzan. 2010. *The Altenberg 16: An Exposé of the Evolution Industry*. Berkeley: North Atlantic.

Mazur, Suzan. 2014. *The Origin of Life Circus: A How to Make Life Extravaganza*. New York: Caswell.

Morris, Simon Conway. 2003. *Life's Solution: Inevitable Humans in a Lonely Universe*. Cambridge: Cambridge University Press.

NGSS Lead States. 2013. *Next Generation Science Standards: For States, by States*. Washington, DC: National Academies Press.

National Council for the Social Studies. 2010. *National Curriculum Standards for Social Studies: A Framework for Teaching, Learning and Assessment*. Accessed August 29, 2016. http://www.socialstudies.org/standards.

National Council for the Social Studies. 2013. *The College, Career, and Civic Life (C3) Framework for Social Studies State Standards: Guidance for Enhancing the Rigor of K-12 Civics, Economics, Geography, and History*. Silver Spring, MD.

National Governors Association. 2010. "*National Governors Association and State Education Chiefs Launch Common State Academic Standards*." Accessed August 29, 2016. http://www.ccsso.org/News_and_Events/Press_Releases/NATIONAL_GOVERNORS_ASSOCIATION_AND_STATE_EDUCATION_CHIEFS_LAUNCH_COMMON_STATE_ACADEMIC_STANDARDS_.html.

National Research Council. 1996. *National Science Education Standards*. Washington, DC: National Academies Press.

National Research Council. 2009. *Learning Science in Informal Environments: People, Places and Pursuits*. Washington, DC: National Academies Press.

National Research Council. 2012. *Framework for K-12 Science Education: Practices, Crosscutting Concepts and Core Ideas*. Accessed August 29, 2016. http://www.nap.edu/catalog/13165/a-framework-for-k-12-science-education-practices-crosscutting-concepts.

Oxford Dictionary of Science. 2003. New York: Oxford University Press.

Potter, Charles. 1930. *Humanism: A New Religion*. New York: Simon and Schuster.

Protocol to the Convention for the Protection of Human Rights and Fundamental Freedoms. 1952. Paris: 20.III.

Rees, Martin. 2001. *Just Six Numbers: The Deep Forces that Shape the Universe*. London: Weidenfeld and Nicolson.

Seltzer, Leon, and David Niose. 2010. "Teen Sex: The Holy vs. Humanistic Approach: How Do Secular Humanists Look at Teenage Sexuality?" *Psychology Today*. Blog post,

August 5. Accessed August 29, 2016. https://www.psychologytoday.com/blog/evolution-the-self/201008/teen-sex-the-holy-vshumanistic-approach.

The Center for Education Reform. 2014. "K-12 Facts as of September 2014." Accessed August 26, 2016. https://www.edreform.com/2012/04/k-12-facts/.

Zimmer, Carl. 2010. "Linux v. E-Coli." *Discover*. Blog post, May 3. Accessed August 29, 2016. http://blogs.discovermagazine.com/loom/2010/05/03/linux-versus-e-coli/#.UOxfRXexXQg.

Legal decisions cited

Africa v. Pennsylvania [1981] 662 F.2d 1025, 3rd Cir.

American Atheists, Inc. v. Davenport [2010] 637 F.3d 1095, 10th Cir.

Bell v. Little Axe ISD [1985] 766 F.2d 1391, 10th Cir.

Borden v. School Dist of East Brunswick [2008] 523 F.3d 153, 3rd Cir.

Busch v. Marple Newton School District [2009] 567 F.3d 89, 3rd Cir.

Cantwell v. Connecticut [1940] 310 U.S. 296.

County of Allegheny v. American Civil Liberties Union [1989] 492 U.S. 573.

Edwards v. Aguillard [1987] 482 U.S. 578.

Epperson v. Arkansas [1968] 393 U.S. 97.

Everson v. Board of Education [1947] 330 U.S. 1.

Fellowship of Humanity v. County of Alameda [1957] 315 P.2d 394.

Gillette v. U.S. [1971] 401 U.S. 437.

Kaufman v. McCaughtry [2005] 419 F.3d 678, 7th Cir.

Lee v. Weisman [1992] 505 U.S. 577

Lemon v. Kurtzman [1971] 430 U.S. 602.

Malnak v. Yogi [1979] 592 F.2d 197, 3rd Cir.

McCreary County v. ACLU of Kentucky [2005] 545 U.S. 844.

McGowan v. Maryland [1961] 366 U.S. 420.

Roberts v. Madigan [1990] 921 F.2d 1047, 10th Cir.

Robinson v. City of Edmond [1995] 68 F.3d 1226, 10th Cir.

Smith v. Board of School Commissioners of Mobile County [1987] 655 F. Supp. 939, S.D. Ala., *rev'd on other grounds* [1987] 827 F.2d 684, 11th Cir.

Strayhorn v. Ethical Society of Austin [2003] 110 S.W. 3d 458, Tex. App.

Torcaso v. Watkins [1961] 367 U.S. 488.

Wallace v. Jaffree [1986] 472 U.S. 38.

Washington Ethical Society v. District. of Columbia [1957] 249 F.2d 127, D.C. Cir.

9 Over the secular ridge of human wants

The constitutional legitimacy of secular-state funding of chaplaincy programs in Australia

Vito Breda

Williams n.2: A case of illiberal utilitarianism?

In common law systems, judicial institutions are normally vested with the task of finding solutions to legal dilemmas under the epistemic guidance of rules and precedents. Democratically elected institutions are instead vested with the task of fostering the common good, which, in most liberal societies, is associated with the reasoned implementation of utilitarian policies and the redistribution of resources to those in need. Hegel's philosophy of rights delivers one of the most succinct analyses of the issue: "The essence of the modern state binds together the universal and the full freedom of the particular, including the welfare of the individuals" (Hegel 2008, 138). The balance between the two activities (that is, the promotion of free enterprise and the protection of the weak) varies. So, for instance, the allocation of redistributive policies that support families in Sweden is different from said allocation in Australia. The Swedish Parliament might, for instance, provide up to 65 weeks of parental leave (at 80% of pay) shared between the two parents. It is logical to assume that, first, the Swedish Parliament considers such a policy an appropriate response to the desire of parents to care for their children and, second, that the majority of the Swedish population perceives the policy as beneficial for the whole community (Addati, Cassirer and Gilchrist 2014, 137). The Commonwealth of Australia, instead, entitles newborn primary carers to up to a maximum of 18 weeks at the minimum wage and their partner to 2 weeks at minimum wage (Fair Work Ombudsman 2015).

There is, in this example, a great disparity in how the Australian and Swedish deliberative institutions decided to balance the requirement of the economic efficiency of their respective workforces with the legitimacy of redistributive policies aimed at engaging an individual aspiration. This aspiration includes a desire that carers might have for spending time with their children. In both instances, parliaments select whom the beneficiary of the policy might be (e.g., the mother, the father, the adopted mother, the adopted father and the carer in a same-sex couple) and how he or she might receive such a benefit. It is important to note that the carers *might need* such support; however, both parliaments decided that they could access these benefits. A court intervention in the evaluation process carried out by parliament might be limited to deciding whether the deliberative institution has the power to make such a decision or, for instance, whether such a policy hinders the rights of other groups. It would be improper, for instance, for the High Court of Australia (hereafter, the HCA) to suggest that a policy that provides paid maternity leave for Australian parents is, by way of comparison to the one granted in Sweden, inadequate. The suggestion would be unacceptable in court, even if a hypothetical plaintiff were to present objective evidence of the inadequacy of the federal policy. This is the case because the accommodation of the parents' desiderata with the policy aim of fostering the common wealth of a country is a political task (Tully 2002), and constitutional law should be "conceived as a structure of rules and principles which provides the foundation of the political order" (Loughlin 2003, 193).

Constitutional law deals with how law shapes and limits the conduct of politics. In *Williams v. The Commonwealth* ([2012] HCA 23) – hereafter, Williams n.1 – the federal government tried to allocate resources to a series of schemes aimed at providing pastoral care for students in state schools. The Commonwealth relied exclusively on its executive power to do so, and the HCA considered the policy, quite rightly, as unconstitutional. Williams n.1 might have been perceived as the comeuppance of a final appellate jurisdiction, yet in Williams n.2 the chaplaincy scheme was supported by a series of statutory measures which were, according to the intention of Parliament, directly linked to a federal head of power set out in Section 51 (xxiiiA) of the Constitution. Again, the HCA, in *Williams v. The Commonwealth of Australia & Ors* ([2014] HCA 23) (hereafter, Williams n.2), considered the statutory measure as unconstitutional.

I will return to the technical aspect of the decision in the last section of this paper, but it is important to note that the HCA questioned the legitimacy of a series of federal statutes. These were the Financial Framework Legislation Amendment Act (No. 3) 2012, the Financial Management and Accountability Act 1997, and the Financial Management and Accountability Regulations 1997. In particular, the HCA considered the National School Chaplaincy and Student Welfare Program (hereafter, the NSCSWP), which derived its legitimacy from the above statutes, incompatible with Section 51 (xxiiiA) of the Constitution. The aims of the NSCSWP's policy were, as drafted by the Commonwealth, "[t]o assist school communities to support the wellbeing of their students, including by strengthening values, providing pastoral care and enhancing engagement with the broader community" (Financial Framework Legislation Amendment Act (No. 3) 2012 (Cth)). The NSCSWP's policy authorized the agreement between the Commonwealth and the Scripture Union Queensland (hereafter the SUQ), which provided pastoral care in the school in which Mr. Williams sent his children. Before engaging with the jurisprudential shortcoming of the HCA's decision, I will explain why the HCA should not have tried to define a human want.

The Commonwealth argued that Section 51 (xxiiiA) includes a federal competence to draft legislation that is directed at providing a benefit to students. The HCA argued, instead, that a benefit could only be considered as "material aid given pursuant to a scheme to provide for human wants." A policy that provides a service within a state school could not be considered part of federal distributive policies because that type of support does not meet a human want. The narrative appears to have been thrown pell-mell into the decision.

The issue in Williams n.2 was whether the "benefits to students" could support the legislation that allowed for non-denominational pastoral care in state schools. At first sight, the answer ought to be in the affirmative. Historically, the HCA's jurisprudence has been at odds with other final appellate jurisprudence in common law courts (Aroney and Allan 2008). Aroney and Allan suggest that the HCA has a tendency to construct narrow literal interpretations of constitutional norms that, in turn, deliver decisions in direct contrast with the constitutional text from which they originated. For instance, the HCA has, over the years, endorsed a series of narratives that might appear articulated and plausible, but that support flawed or paradoxical decisions. They deliver such a conclusion in a pungent narrative:

> The ironic result – to adopt Herbert's terminology – has been a most uncommon body of constitutional law, generated by a most uncommon court, using what appear to be the most orthodox techniques of common law reasoning, applied to the text of the Constitution.
>
> (Aroney and Allan 2008, 245)

In Williams n.2, the HCA does it again, so to speak, and, in this case, the penchant for strict textualism has the effect of transferring a prerogative to the court that no common law court has claimed, as far as I know: the prerogative to set out what a human want ought to be in a liberal democracy.

This is not to say that Australian Justices are the votaries of the paradoxical or that they disport themselves in producing mildly elaborate casuistries. Aroney and Allan's (2008) narrative shows instead the epistemic limitations of textualism, and the Williams n.2 case confirms the claim. In particular, the HCA argued that a human want in areas of benefits to students is a monetary benefit given to a specified group of individuals: "And in the case of benefits to students, the relief would be material aid provided against the human wants which the student has by reason of being a student" (Williams n.2, 46). Even within the restricted realm of public-sponsored education, the possibility that a court would be able to qualify the basis of utilitarianism appears difficult to accept. For instance, if we were to return to the example of differences between parental leave policies in Sweden and Australia, and we assumed that parliaments in both countries had the prerogative to set up legislative policies that have the effect of helping new parents, it would be reasonable to assume that jurisdictional institutions are not entitled to decide on what new parents want. However, in Williams n.2, the HCA accepted Mr. Williams' claim and affirmed a lack of legislative competence in respect of the Commonwealth for policies that do not provide a pecuniary benefit to students.

This conclusion is not underpinned by a sound understanding of utilitarianism. For instance, it would be equivalent to the court saying that Parliament could not pass legislation that would give unpaid parental leave to parents if their child were in the hospital. Indeed, the hospital staff would provide for the care of the child, and perhaps the parents' desire to stay with their children might not be materially or psychologically beneficial to the child. It might also be the case that giving the parents the opportunity to spend time with their child in the hospital would directly hinder the interests of the community. One or both parents might already be providing critical services within the community; they might be, for instance, police officers or firefighters. However, it is a prerogative of the political arena to evaluate those human desires and to set up policies that might accommodate those desires.

Similarly, setting up policies that accommodate the demand for religious support for children in public education is a manifestation of power allocated to a parliament. More precisely, it is a manifestation of the prerogative to balance economic efficiency with the promotion of a common good by caring for a chosen group of individuals (e.g., parents and carers). This evaluative process cannot simply be derived from the selective reading of jurisprudence, the method apparently adopted by the HCA, without undermining the proper role of democratic institutions.

Before I support my narrative, I would like to briefly discuss a series of important issues. First, in Williams n.2 the issue is not whether the wording "benefits to students" in Section 51 (xxiiiA) could be interpreted so broadly that it has the effect of giving the Commonwealth full power over primary and secondary education. We might call this narrative the "Australian endangered federalism thesis." There are two reasons for rejecting the Australian endangered federalism thesis. One reason is that it is relatively clear that the Commonwealth does not have a head of power over education. It is a state responsibility. Section 51 (xxiiiA) was inserted as part of a constitutional amendment that allowed the Commonwealth Parliament to promote distributive policies (*Constitution Alteration (Social Services) 1946 – SECT 2*). Following the reform, the new Section 51 allocated the power to legislate in several new areas, which included benefits to students: "The Parliament shall, subject to this Constitution, have power to make laws [...] with respect of: [...] (xxiiiA) the provision of [...] benefits to students and family allowances."

The HCA has a tendency to interpret the Australian Constitution literally, and that has the effect of unbalancing federalism in a way that favors the Commonwealth over the states (Aroney and Allan 2008). Constitutional courts in federal systems have a tendency to fill the constitutional text with significances. Yet the HCA has, over the years, embraced literal textual interpretations which are seldom adopted by other final appellate constitutional jurisdictions in federal systems such as those of Canada, Germany or the US (Aroney and Allan 2008, 247). However, the acceptance of a legislative unbalance between states and the Commonwealth might not provide a plausible justification for Williams n.2. To start with, it would be a self-defeating argument to suggest that the HCA in Williams n.2 manifested an intention to swing the balance of Australian federalism in favor of the states. That is per se a political endeavor that would cast a serious doubt over the present and past legitimacy of the HCA's jurisprudence. In addition, the NSCSWP's program cannot be considered an educational program that overlaps with a state's competence.

The other reason why the Australian endangered federalism thesis can be rejected is that the specific aim of the NSCSWP was to help students who, for whatever reason, elected to make use of such a service. The objective of the policy is clearly stated: "Objective: To assist school communities to support the wellbeing of their students" (Financial Framework Legislation Amendment Act (No. 3) 2012 (Cth)). In other words, the Parliament's NSCSWP scheme did not set up an education policy which altered state schools' pedagogical curricula. It also did not foster a change in state policies by stealth, so to speak, by promoting a change in school policies in exchange for a financial incentive. The financial beneficiaries of the NSCSWP's scheme were the third parties that provided the pastoral care (not the schools). In short, the Australian endangered federalism thesis cannot provide an explanation for Williams n.2.

Second, the Australian Constitution does not include a section that has an equivalent effect on public education as the so-called "Establishment Clause" (U.S. Const. amend. I) in the US Constitution. At first sight, the wording of Section 116 of the Australian Constitution appears to be similar to the one in the Establishment Clause: "The Commonwealth shall not make any law for establishing any religion, or for imposing any religious observance, or for prohibiting the free exercise of any religion, and no religious test shall be required as a qualification for any office or public trust under the Commonwealth." The relationship to the Establishment Clause is obvious: "Congress shall make no law respecting an establishment of religion, or prohibiting the free exercise thereof" (U.S. Const. amend. I). However, in Australia, public education is a state legislative competence, and states are not bound by Section 116, which applies only to the Commonwealth.

The narrow interpretation of the term "religion" might appear controversial. Section 116 is inspired by the Establishment Clause, yet there are strong indications that the historical conditions that justified the 1789 Establishment Clause in the US, as well as Bentham's critique of the Anglican Church in 1768, lapsed before the approval of the Australian Constitution. In particular, during the 19th century the coupling of sectarianism and elitism mentioned in Bentham was radically reduced by the UK Parliament. The Universities Test Act 1871, for instance, removed the religious requirements for students and staff at the universities of Oxford, Cambridge and Durham: "No person shall be required [...] to conform to any religious observance" (Section 3). The Universities Test Act was preceded by the Northcote-Trevelyan Report, which prepared conditions for the development of an independent civil service (Northcote and Trevelyan 1854) and a series of commissions that substituted the English patronage system with exams and meritocracy (Fukuyama 2012, 110). Furthermore, Australian immigration policies historically favored British immigration in a way that fostered the expansion of a large community of Anglicans and Catholics. These communities maintained a strong connection with the political sphere, and that connection had the effect of reducing the state and federal commitment to maintaining the separation between public institutions and religion (Chavura 2013). In short, Section 116 of the Australian Constitution might mimic the wording of the Establishment Clause, but it does not carry a similar effect in the Australian constitutional system.

Third, the Commonwealth Parliament, by using Section 96, might allocate financial resources to state governments in areas that would otherwise be outside of federal legislative competences. In the aftermath of Williams n.2, the Commonwealth went back and used Section 96 to give money to the states on the condition that it would be used for pastoral care programs. In short, the Commonwealth is still able to fund chaplains in schools, but has to channel the monies through state governments. At the time of the writing of this essay, the new procedure has not been challenged in court.

The constitutional boundaries of utilitarianism

In Williams n.2, the HCA's narrative could not be redeemed by considering the decision an attempt to rebalance Australian federalism. However, instead, there might be an attempt to impose a political evaluation on a deliberative arena. In this section, I will explain the current understanding of the relationship between the utilitarian renderings of human wants.

In describing Jeremy Bentham's "unfavorable affection" for the Church of England, Philip Schofield draws the reader's attention to two episodes. The first episode is most likely to have happened in 1768. Bentham witnessed the expulsion of six fellow students from Oxford University (Schofield 2009, 171). The students, all Methodists, were accused of heresy. They were meeting in private houses, where they prayed and sang hymns. Bentham, at the time at Queen's College, tried to plea against expelling the six Methodists but was reminded by one of the college fellows of the insignificance of his individual opinions: "His answer was cold: and the substance of it was – that is was not for the uninformed youth such as we, to presume to set up our private judgements against a public one, formed by some of the holiest, as well as best and wisest men that ever lived" (Bentham 1818, xx). The second episode mentioned by Schofield is the undersigning of the Thirty-Nine Articles of the Anglican Church. Bentham was, as were all the Oxford graduates, required to sign them, but this last episode left him with the perception of having compromised his intellectual integrity (Schofield 2009, 173; Bentham 1818, xxiii).

Both anecdotes give us a strong indication of the possible motivation for Bentham's unfavorable affection for the Church of England, but they might also shine a beam of light on the role of the freedom of expression of religious beliefs in legal systems that endorse utilitarianism (Schofield 2009, 173; Bentham 1988). It is worth remembering that in 1789 Bentham's *Introduction to Principles of Morals and Legislation* prepared the theoretical framework which inspired, among others, H. L. A. Hart's (1961) legal positivism (Schofield 2010), Rawls' studies in political philosophy (Rawls 1993; Rawls 1972) and Dworkin's theory of adjudication (Dworkin 1978; Dworkin 1998). However, utilitarianism and its well-reproduced separation thesis, that is, between law and morals, and not between law and religion, should not be understood as arguing for an incompatibility between individual religious aspirations and human wants (Chavura 2013).

Bentham, for instance, was quite explicit in advocating a separation between the state and religious indoctrination, his model of indoctrination being that which he had received at Oxford University (Bentham 1818, 231). The separation, for

Bentham, included a prohibition to allocate fiscal resources, which were, he explained, from unwilling contributors, for the benefit of religious institutions such as the Church of England. Yet, on the same page, Bentham explained that such a limitation would not apply to "the administering of instruction of the sort in question [that is, religious education]" (Bentham 1818, 232). For Bentham, there is, in other words, an intrinsic benefit in having the state support religious education. The logical assumptions from this narrative are, first, that non-denominational religious education could be part of, at least for Bentham, a utilitarian society and, second, that religious aspirations are legitimate human wants. This last logical deduction is particularly relevant to a debate over the legitimacy of the Commonwealth policy that seeks to provide for students' desire to have access to non-denominational pastoral care in school.

Since 1768, the debate over types of state-sponsored education has been rehearsed in several spaces (Dewey 2012; Weber 2008; Fukuyama 2014; Rawls 1993, 196). Rawls, for instance, advocates the connection, albeit minimal, between education and the necessity of knowing the basic rights protected by the US Constitution (Rawls 1993, 199). The example chosen to explain the importance of education directly engages with the necessity of knowing about religious claims. Rawls proposes that "children's education include such things as knowledge of their constitutional and civic rights so that, for example, they know that liberty of conscience exists in their society and that apostasy is not a legal crime" (Rawls 1993, 199). There is, from the quote, grounds for speculating that Rawls envisages a type of childhood education that explicitly engages with and recognizes the role of religion in society. It is, therefore, reasonable to assume that Rawls does not advocate the benefit of endorsing religion as a comprehensive justification for a political system. Rather, Rawls argues that children should be made aware of the existence of religious communities and of the claims these religious communities might make in the political arena and of the fact that some of these claims might not be legitimate.

Even thinkers such as Stephen Macedo, who seeks in his work to reduce the role of religion in public education to a bare minimum, do not plead for excluding the knowledge of religion therefrom. Macedo's narrative is, instead, that political liberalism should have a logical priority in the school curriculum (Macedo 1995, 487; Calvert 2013, 120). In short, there is little, even in the current conception of utilitarianism, suggesting an incompatibility between spiritual needs and a utilitarian rendering of the concept of human wants.

This point is delicate, so I must be precise. My contention is not that religion is a constitutive part of a liberal society, or that we should assume that students' wants in relation to private religious aspirations must be considered. The issue in Williams n.2 is rather this: in the debate over the interpretation of Section 51 (xxiiiA), is a student's desire to have pastoral care from a non-denominational organization an expression of a human want that is incompatible with the utilitarian underpinning of the Australian Constitution? The short answer should be "no" for two reasons.

First, there is no explicit prescription within the text of the Australian Constitution which prevents the Parliament from legislating in this area. Quite the opposite, Section 51 (xxiiiA) explicitly gives the prerogative to legislate in this area. This point was conceived, albeit indirectly, in Williams n.1. Second, once it was ascertained that NSCSWP was not an education policy that was reserved for the states, the decision on how to provide for student wants, and that included those desiderata that are a manifestation of religious belief, should have been (within the limit of reasonableness) allocated to Parliament.

However, the HCA appears to narrow Macedo's stance even further by requiring that services provided to students by a non-denominational organization, such as the service provided by the NSCSWP, be measurable in pecuniary terms and directed to individuals. There is, however, little in the Australian Constitution and in the HCA's jurisprudence that would require a connection between such a farrago of assumptions and the evolution of a human want. If we were to return to the example of the newborn child in hospital, a parallel narrative would suggest that the parents' desire to take parental leave could not be measured in pecuniary terms, and so the federal policy that provides for parental leave would not be one directed toward an expression of a human want.

Williams n.2: Cognitive dissonance or jurisprudential orthopraxy?

In the previous sections, I explained that utilitarianism might not support the use of fiscal revenues to promote proselytism in an educational establishment, but that is not to say that a pastoral service provided by a company that has a religious affiliation is incompatible with a modern liberal and capitalist society. In this section, I will review the line of authority that underpins Williams n.2 and show that the decision is affected by a manifest error. It will be argued that, if the criteria extracted from the previous qualifications of Section 51 (xxiiiA) were correctly applied to Williams n.2, the decision should not have favored Mr. Williams.

The Williams n.2 case is indeed multifarious, yet the decision to reject the Commonwealth argument was linked, the HCA argued, to two intrinsic limitations to the Commonwealth legislative competences set out in Section 51 (xxiiiA). First, legislation that provides for a benefit has to be for a monetary benefit (or a benefit evaluated in monetary terms). Second, a benefit should be direct in order to engage a student demand:

> The meaning of the word "benefits" accepted by the majority in *British Medical Association v. The Commonwealth* was that expressed by McTiernan J: "material aid given pursuant to a scheme to provide for human wants…under legislation designed to promote social welfare or security." And that material aid may be provided in various ways. McTiernan J referred to the provision of benefits in the form of "a pecuniary aid, service, attendance or commodity."
>
> (Williams n.2)

These two criteria (aid that is pecuniary and that corresponds directly to a human want) are not stated in the aforementioned Australian Constitution. It might be worth reminding the reader of the text of Section 51 (xxiiiA):

> [T]he provision of maternity allowances, widows' pensions, child endowment, unemployment, pharmaceutical, sickness and hospital benefits, medical and dental services (but not so as to authorize any form of civil conscription), benefits to students and family allowances.
>
> (Commonwealth of Australia Constitution Act 1900 c. 12 (UK))

The two requirements are instead drawn from two precedents. The first one is *British Medical Association v. Commonwealth* [1949] HCA 44 (hereafter, BMA). In BMA, the HCA explained that handing out free medicines could not be considered as a form of civil conscription. The reasons for inserting the criteria in Williams n.2 as a requirement of a legitimate human want is a matter of speculation, yet it is possible to suggest that in Williams n.2 the HCA misread the BMA case.

The second case considered in Williams n.2 was *Alexandra Private Geriatric Hospital Pty Ltd v. Commonwealth* [1987] HCA 6 (hereafter, Alexandra Private Geriatric Hospital). The case discussed whether the statutory measure that allowed the government to enter into a contractual relation with a third party, that is, the hospital which provided a service, was considered as legitimate by making reference to Section 51 (xxiiiA). In the Alexandra Private Geriatric Hospital case, the court confirmed the decision based on the BMA case. It was a case of confirming rather than qualifying it. In BMA, the issue of the inclusion of the possibility of paying for a third-party service to the beneficiary, who is the patient, was already engaged. In BMA, the HCA explained that the process of providing a pharmaceutical good required the payment to two third parties: the doctor who filled in the prescription using the approved government form, and who thus provided a service, and the pharmacy that handed out the prescribed remedy. In Alexandra Private Geriatric Hospital, the HCA included private hospitals on the potential list of service providers that might receive money for medical care. Again, given that Section 51 (xxiiiA) explicitly allocates a competence to provide for sick benefits and hospital benefits, the decision that a federal government could pay for a third party to deliver its policy was, as the HCA noted, relatively uncontroversial.

In Williams n.2, the HCA was asked eight questions, but only question four and question six are relevant to the issue discussed in this essay. In question four, the HCA restated the *dictum* in Williams n.1. In particular, the court stated that the Commonwealth had no executive power (without legislative support) to provide money for a chaplaincy scheme. In the case of Williams n.2, the SUQ had a funding agreement with the Commonwealth and provided pastoral care at the school to which Mr. Williams sent his children: "Question 4. Was the Commonwealth's entry into, and expenditure of monies under, the SUQ Funding Agreement, as varied by the First to Fourteenth Variation Deeds, supported by the executive power of the Commonwealth? Answer. No" (Williams n.2, 3).

In answering question six, the HCA stated that payments made to the SUQ were illegitimate because the power used by the government exceeded the legislative competence of Section 51 (xxiiiA):

> Question 6. Was the making of the January 2013 Payment and the February 2014 Payment and, to the extent that the answer to question 5 is "Yes," the January 2012 Payment and the June 2012 Payment, unlawful because it was not authorised by statute and was beyond the executive power of the Commonwealth? Answer. Yes.
>
> (Williams n.2, 3)

In the aftermath of Williams n.1, the Parliament approved a series of statutory measures that had as one of their aims the provision of legislative backing to government chaplaincy schemes such as the one that supported the SUQ. The approved statutes were set out in the Financial Framework Legislation Amendment Act (No. 3) 2012 (Cth) (hereafter, the FFLA Act). The FFLA Act incorporated aspects of the Financial Management and Accountability Act 1997 (Cth) (hereafter, the FMA Act) and the Financial Management and Accountability Regulations 1997 (Cth) (hereafter, the FMA Regulations). Schedule 1AA of the FMA Regulations asserts that (in item 407.013 in Pt. 4) one of the FMA's objectives is to assist "school communities to support the wellbeing of their students." This objective was, as intended by the Parliament, sufficient for providing a legislative umbrella for the chaplaincy program and, in particular, for legitimizing the agreement between the Commonwealth and the SUQ.

In Williams n.2, the HCA decided that such an aim could not be considered as included in the legislative power of Section 51 (xxiiiA). In particular, the SUQ activity within the school could not be financially supported by making reference to benefits to students in Section 51 (xxiiiA) (Williams n.2, 38–48). The HCA argued that the word "benefit" in Section 51 (xxiiiA) has a distinctive lexical significance. That is, a pecuniary aid, service, attendance or commodity. This rendering of the word "benefit" was, as intended by the HCA, established by Justice McTiernan in the BMA case.

However, there are strong indications that McTiernan intended to qualify what should not be considered to be civil conscription, rather than explaining what a pharmaceutical benefit ought to be. There are two reasons supporting this analysis. First, in the BMA case a group of pharmacists, who represented the British Medical Association, argued that the list of subsidized prescriptions constituted a manifestation of a civil conscription:

> Latham C.J. It will be necessary to consider the effect of s. 7A with particular reference to the provision contained in s. 51 (xxiiiA.) of the Constitution with respect to civil conscription. It is contended for the plaintiffs that s. 7A compels doctors to practise their profession in a particular way, and therefore amounts to a form of civil conscription.
>
> (BMA, 27)

Civil conscription is the only explicit limiting criterion on the head of power set out in Section 51 (xxiiiA): "[T]he provision of [...] pharmaceutical, sickness and hospital benefits, medical and dental services (***but not so as to authorize any form of*** *civil conscription*), benefits to students and family allowances" [my emphasis]. In particular, the BMA contested the constitutional legitimacy of the Pharmaceutical Benefits Act 1947–1949 and the related Pharmaceutical Benefits Regulations (S.R. 1948 No. 56–1949 No. 44). The statute required medical doctors (who wanted to prescribe a treatment from the list of subsidized medicines) and the pharmacists to use a government-approved form (ex. in Section 7 (1) Pharmaceutical Benefits Act 1947–1949). The issue is repeated several times in the decision: "Rich J. I have confined my judgement to what I conceive to be the crucial question in this matter, namely, whether the provisions of s. 7A of the Act can be regarded as a form of civil conscription" (BMA, 1). The obligatory use of the form should be considered, according to the BMA, as a manifestation of a civil conscription which would make the Act exceed the legislative power of the Commonwealth. The majority of the HCA rejected the claim by explaining that "a pecuniary aid, service, attendance or commodity" cannot be considered a form of civil conscription on the agencies which were asked to deliver a welfare policy. The full quote might give a clearer understanding of McTiernan's trope:

> The material aid given pursuant to a scheme to provide for human wants is commonly described by the word "benefit." When this word is applied to that subject matter it signifies a pecuniary aid, service, attendance or commodity made available for human beings under legislation designed to promote social welfare or security: the word is also applied to such aids made available through a benefit society to members or their dependants. The word "benefits" in par. (xxiiiA.) has a corresponding or *similar meaning*.
>
> (BMA, 1, my emphasis)

The definition allowed for the use of similar significance and thus did not intend to be literally prescriptive.

So, the doctors and the pharmacists represented by the BMA, the HCA explained, are not precluded from using other forms, or indeed from using any pharmaceutical treatment, but the Commonwealth will only pay for the ones that are listed and that have been ordered via the form. Similar reasoning might apply to the beneficiaries. Those individuals who are considered unwell by a doctor would be able to obtain a similar service from a pharmacist if they would be willing to pay for it. The point is made in a clear narrative by Chief Justice Latham: "The dilemma which the legislative choice of the first of these alternatives presented to chemists of either coming in or staying out of the scheme does not seem to me to be civil conscription or to place the measure outside the power to provide pharmaceutical benefits" (BMA, 26).

In short, McTiernan's words, which misled the HCA in Williams n.2, were not reported in the BMA case to explain that Section 51 (xxiiiA) does allow Parliament to allocate only money and government-sponsored services to achieve a social aim. Rather, the definition says that Section 51 (xxiiiA) cannot underpin legislation that obliges agencies or beneficiaries to take advantage of such a policy. It is reasonable to suggest that, if the criteria set out in the BMA case by McTiernan were considered coherently in Williams n.2, they would have supported the legitimacy of the FFLA Act, the FMA and, finally, the SUQ Funding Agreement, which provided pastoral care in Mr. Williams' son's school. In Williams n.2, the government policy's aims, as described in the NSCSWP, were "[t]o assist school communities to support the wellbeing of their students, and they should have been compatible, within the margin of appreciation that is normally allocated to a Parliament, with the wording of Section 51 (xxiiiA)." Furthermore, like the Pharmaceutical Benefits Act 1947–1949, the method that the government chose to deliver the NSCSWP's aims included, as McTiernan stated in the BMA case, a pecuniary aid, service, attendance or commodity that both the agencies (the public schools and the entities that offer the pastoral care) and the beneficiaries might never use. Lastly, like the doctors in the BMA case, in Williams n.2 it was a third-party institution (the state's education policies) that defined who should be considered a beneficiary.

There is indeed a correlation between McTiernan's test and the concept of a benefit in Section 51 (xxiiiA); yet, McTiernan's trope cannot be used to define what a benefit *must be*. The conclusion appears to have been reached without adequate critical engagement. McTiernan simply stated that the correlation between the Australian open market for medical and pharmaceutical services (and goods) and a pecuniary aid, service, attendance or commodity cannot be constructed as a civil conscription. Again, Chief Justice Latham comes to reinforce this narrative: "If persons or institutions choose to remain outside the benefits of the scheme there is not in my opinion anything in the Act to compel them to accept those benefits [...] It only offers to them an opportunity of coming into the Commonwealth scheme if they think fit" (BMA, 62). A similar narrative should be applied to Williams n.2.

The second reason supporting my analysis is that one cannot argue that a benefit to students should be tested in practice. In the BMA case, the HCA does engage the issue directly. It was not possible, the British Medical Association argued, to make a direct correlation between the Pharmaceutical Benefits Act 1947–1949 and an effective patient benefit. Given that a benefit to patients was a legitimacy requirement of the Pharmaceutical Benefits Act 1947–1949 and that it could not be ascertained in all instances, the British Medical Association argued that the Act should be considered unconstitutional. However, the majority of the HCA rejected the reasoning and explained that an allocation of services or goods which provides for unforced demands should be considered, in principle, as beneficial. So, a statutory measure that is intended for the benefit of patients does not need to be beneficial in practice for all the recipients of the policy. It is also plausible to assume that, at a general level, policies which provide gratuitous allocations of resources (money and services) to a constitutionally recognized policy end will produce a beneficial effect. If all the narratives taken from the BMA criteria were applied correctly in Williams n.2, it would be very difficult to dismiss, as the HCA did, the Commonwealth's argument that considers its statutory measure as legitimate. The Commonwealth policy provided financial support for a service that a school might elect to provide and that might benefit some students.

In the BMA case, there is little help from Justice Dixon's definition of the word "benefit." His rendering of the word was not accepted by the majority of the HCA:

> The general sense of the word "benefit" covers anything tending to the profit, advantage, gain or good of a man and is very indefinite. But it is used in a rather more specialized application in reference to what are now called social services; it is used as a word covering provisions made to meet needs arising from special conditions with a recognized incidence in communities or from particular situations or pursuits such as that of a student, whether the provision takes the form of money payments or the supply of things or services.
>
> (BMA, 9)

The definition is lexically well formulated, but it was rejected by the majority because the reasoning that followed was perceived as unconvincing. In particular, none of the Justices considered Section 7A (2) of the Pharmaceutical Benefits Act 1947–1949 as incompatible, as Justice Dixon did, with the Constitution.

However, in Williams n.2, Dixon's minority opinion is referenced in tandem with McTiernan's qualification, as they were part of an uninterrupted line of reasoning (Williams n.2, 30–40). A closer reading of the case would note that McTiernan's qualification restricted the concept of civil conscription, whereas Dixon's narrative attempted but quite importantly failed to convince the rest of the judges that Section 51 (xxiiiA) did not include a civil conscription limitation for pharmaceutical policies. In Dixon's opinion, the civil conscription restriction would apply only to medical and dental services: "The purpose no doubt was to prevent laws made with respect to medical or dental services imposing duties which would amount to a form of civil conscription" (BMA, 11). So, the pairing of Dixon's trope with McTiernan's test should be considered to be a manifest casuistry. Dixon's narrative denied the relevance of civil conscription that McTiernan sought to qualify.

It is reasonable to suggest that the HCA misread the case. McTiernan's test of civil conscription and Dixon's minority opinion are drawn from different assumptions and produce different conclusions in the BMA case. It is the case even without considering that Dixon's minority opinion should not have been considered binding in Williams n.2. The HCA surmised, for an unexplained reason, that both Justices' opinions were equivalent, but failed to apply them to the object they were originally designed to engage.

Conclusion

In Williams n.2, the HCA confirmed its reputation for being an uncommon court in a common law system. It has done so in a way that is, perhaps, unique for a final appellate jurisdiction in a modern democratic society. It misinterpreted the correlation between the constitutional allocation of legislative competences in a federal system and the parliamentary prerogative to draft legislation which engages a human want. I have argued here that constitutional law in a liberal and utilitarian society should be considered as a set of prescriptions and innumerate principles that provides the limits of the political sphere. Those limits need, for very good reasons, to be protected, yet the debate within the walls of Parliament cannot be policed. A comparative analysis shows, for instance, that legislation might have similar intentions in areas such as paid parental leave, but the way in which such legislation engages parents' desires changes drastically. These variations might be difficult to justify rationally. They might produce a negative financial impact on the community and a large relocation of resources from other essential public services, yet it is an exclusive parliamentary prerogative to set up the best policy, within the limit of reasonableness, to engage political desires.

However, in Williams n.2 the HCA concluded that a policy supporting non-denominational pastoral care for students was not an appropriate legislative response to a human want. In this essay, I explained that Williams n.2 is a precarious decision in terms of two sets of self-standing explanations. First, a desire to have religious-based pastoral care in a public school cannot be considered antithetical to the liberal underpinning of a modern society. Given that the Australian Constitution does not impose a separation between religion and public institutions, the unforced desire to access religious-based pastoral care in public schools should be considered as a manifestation of a human want. In the literature on utilitarianism, there is little to suggest that the manifestation of a desire to obtain a benefit from a religious organization should be perceived as incompatible with the principles endorsed by a utilitarian society. Even the most robust argument for the separation between state and church accepts, for instance, that education policies might accommodate the desire to know about religion and that public money might be used to support such a policy. In Williams n.2, the debate is, by way of a comparison of educational policies that in Australia are the states' competence, subdued. In Williams n.2, students are not forced to learn about religion and institutions are not compelled to teach it. The pastoral care scheme allowed students attending schools (that requested access to a government scheme) to use a service. This political desire should be considered as a manifestation of a "human want" that a parliament might decide to engage.

The second argument for considering Williams n.2 as unsupported is internal. There are strong indications, from the reading of the decision, that the HCA misread its own line of authority. In Williams n.2, the court asserted that the Parliament has the prerogative to legislate on policies that provide benefits only in the form of "a pecuniary aid, service, attendance or commodity." The services have to be used to meet a human want, as defined by Dixon. Both restrictions are not mirrored in the Constitution.

The limits on the Parliament's discretion are instead taken from a line of authority which commenced in 1949 with a position put forward by the British Medical Association. However, in the BMA case the majority opinion repeatedly and consistently considered the Parliament's competence to set policies in areas covered by Section 51 (xxiiiA) as only being limited by the prohibition of civil conscription. Given that the policy engaged in the BMA case, which allowed for the free distribution of pharmaceutical goods, was, in McTiernan's words, "a pecuniary aid, service, attendance or commodity," it could not be considered as a form of civil conscription. The policy did not prevent doctors and chemists from prescribing and selling medicines which were not subsidized. Thus, the requirement of "a pecuniary aid, service, attendance or commodity" was not a requirement of the benefits, but a test for assessing whether the agencies that deliver such a policy and the beneficiaries have been forced to accept it. If McTiernan's test had been applied correctly in Williams n.2, it would have denied Mr. Williams' claim. The schools were not forced to adopt the government policy, and the students were not obliged to take advantage of it. A further indication of the HCA mishandling its own line of authority is the reference to Dixon's minority opinion in the BMA case. In Williams n.2, Dixon's narrative is coupled with one of McTiernan's, but the two decisions are cognitively dissonant. Dixon's reasoning is rejected by the majority, and its qualification does not engage the same object as the one in McTiernan's test. The coupling of the two qualifications shows either a lack of cognitive awareness of the Justices or a misunderstanding of the role of final appellate jurisdictions in modern liberal democracies.

Bibliography

Addati, Laura, Naomi Cassirer and Katherine Gilchrist. 2014. *Maternity and Paternity at Work: Law and Practice across the World.* Geneva: International Labour Office.

Aroney, Nicholas, and James Allan. 2008. "An Uncommon Court: How the High Court of Australia Has Undermined Australian Federalism." *Sydney Law Review* 30: 245–294.

Bentham, Jeremy. 1818. *Church-of-Englandism and its Catechism Examined.* London: E. Wilson.

Bentham, Jeremy. 1988. *The Principles of Morals and Legislation.* Buffalo: Prometheus.

Calvert, John H. 2013. "Human Rights in a Secular State Will Depend on Its Legal Definition of Religion." In *Legitimizing Human Rights: Secular and Religious Perspectives*, ed. Angus J. L. Menuge. Farnham, UK: Ashgate, 105–125.

Chavura, Stephen. 2013. "The Secularization Thesis and the Secular State: Reflections with Special Attention to Debates in Australia." In *Religion and the State: A Comparative Sociology*, ed. Adam Possamai, Bryan S. Turner and Jack Barbalet. New York: Anthem, 65–92.

Dewey, John. 2012. *Democracy and Education.* LaVergne, TN: Simon and Brown.

Dworkin, Ronald. 1978. *Taking Rights Seriously.* Cambridge: Harvard University Press.

Dworkin, Ronald. 1998. *Law's Empire.* Oxford: Hart.

Fair Work Ombudsman. 2015. "Paid Parental Leave." Government of Australia. Accessed June 10, 2016. http://www.fairwork.gov.au/leave/maternity-and-parental-leave/paid-parental-leave.

Fukuyama, Francis. 2012. *The Origins of Political Order: From Prehuman Times to the French Revolution.* London: Profile.

Fukuyama, Francis. 2014. *Political Order and Political Decay: From the Industrial Revolution to the Globalisation of Democracy.* London: Profile.

Hart, H. L. A. 1961. *The Concept of Law.* Oxford: Clarendon.

Hegel, Georg W. F. 2008. *Philosophy of Right*, trans. S. W. Dyde. New York: Cosimo.

Loughlin, Martin. 2003. *The Idea of Public Law.* Oxford: Oxford University Press.

Macedo, Stephen. 1995. "Liberal Civic Education and Religious Fundamentalism: The Case of God v. John Rawls?" *Ethics* 105(3): 468–496.

Northcote, Stafford, and Charles E. Trevelyan. 1854. *The Northcote-Trevelyan Report.* London: Eyre and Spottiswoode.

Rawls, John. 1972. *A Theory of Justice.* Oxford: Oxford University Press.

Rawls, John. 1993. *Political Liberalism.* New York: Columbia University Press.

Schofield, Philip. 2009. *Utility and Democracy: The Political Thought of Jeremy Bentham.* New York: Oxford University Press.

Schofield, Philip. 2010. "Jeremy Bentham and HLA Hart's 'Utilitarian Tradition in Jurisprudence'." *Jurisprudence* 1(2): 147–167.

Tully, James. 2002. "The Unfreedom of the Moderns in Comparison to their Ideals of Constitutional Democracy." *Modern Law Review* 65(2): 204–228.

Weber, Eric Thomas. 2008. "Dewey and Rawls on Education." *Human Studies* 31(4): 361–382.

Case law

Alexandra Private Geriatric Hospital Pty Ltd. v. Commonwealth [1987].
HCA British Medical Association v. Commonwealth [1949] HCA.
Williams v. The Commonwealth [2012] HCA 23 (Williams n.1).
Williams v. The Commonwealth of Australia & Ors [2014] HCA 23 (Williams n.2).

Statutes

Commonwealth of Australia Constitution Act 1900 c. 12 (UK).
Constitution Alteration (Social Services) 1946 – SECT 2 (Cth).
Financial Framework Legislation Amendment Act (No. 3) 2012 (Cth).
Financial Management and Accountability Act 1997 (Cth).
Financial Management and Accountability Regulations 1997 (Cth).
Pharmaceutical Benefits Act 1947–1949 (Cth).
Pharmaceutical Benefits Regulations (S.R. 1948 No. 56–1949 No. 44).
The Universities Test Act 1871 (UK).
U.S. Const. amend. I.

10 Modern hostage-taking: A serious problem for religious liberty today

Paul Cliteur

Article 18 of the Universal Declaration of Human Rights (UDHR) of 1948 states:

> Everyone has the right to freedom of thought, conscience and religion; this right includes *freedom to change his religion or belief*, and freedom, either alone or in community with others and in public or private, to manifest his religion or belief in teaching, practice, worship and observance.[1]

The freedom to change your religion or belief is also to be found in other human rights declarations. For example, Article 9 ("Freedom of Thought, Conscience and Religion") of the European Convention on Human Rights (ECHR) is almost identical to Article 18 of the UDHR and includes the exact same clause that I have emphasized.

But this freedom to *change* your religion for another religion, and the freedom to change your religion for no religion at all (so basically to become an *apostate* or an *atheist*) is in jeopardy nowadays. The reason is that what, in human rights language, is called the freedom "to change your religion" is "apostasy," "atheism," and "heresy" to religious terrorists. And these are to be punished by no less than capital punishment. If the state fails to apply this sentence, the religiously motivated individual has to step in, and that is precisely what happens nowadays.

Modern religious terrorism (or "theoterrorism"), more in particular the Islamist kind, makes it difficult, if not impossible, to criticize (radical) Islam (see Cliteur 2013, 15–41; 2012, 127–152). This is one of the most serious factors limiting religious liberty in our time. The effective limits of religious liberty are now drawn not by nation states, not by ordinary judicial tribunals, but by informal theoterrorist vigilante groups applying *their* interpretation of religious law in the modern world. In this essay, I try to develop this issue by explaining how what I call "modern hostage-taking" has developed. This process started with the death verdict on Salman Rushdie in 1989 and came to a peak (for the time being) with the murder of the cartoonists of *Charlie Hebdo* on January 7, 2015. This new situation takes us all hostage, as I hope to explain more fully in the paragraphs that follow.

The first "modern hostage" is the author Salman Rushdie, whose book *The Satanic Verses* caused the Islamist religious dictator Ayatollah Khomeini to put a price on his head. Since 1989, many new cases have arisen where religious criticism, religious satire, apostasy, heresy or simply "change of religion" have been hit by this new terrorist technique.

Let me try to explain what I mean by this.

Hostage-taking in general

A "hostage" is a person seized and brought under the power of another person or organization, usually in order to compel another person or organization (including the state) to do something that would not have been done without this compulsion. There is a long history of political or military use of hostage-taking in which sometimes one organization, or one state, *willingly* brings certain hostages into the power of another organization, or state, as a guarantee of good faith, or in the observance of obligations. This element is clearly included in the definition of "hostage" that we find in *The Oxford Companion to the Law*:

> A person, usually of importance, taken from, or surrendered by agreement by one belligerent to another, to be held as security.
>
> (Walker 1980, 582)

The Oxford Companion continues by saying that the practice was formerly common as a means of securing legitimate warfare. But this is no longer the case. Nowadays, seizing people and holding them as hostages is a tactic resorted to by hijackers of aircraft and trains, usually to force governments to give in to the their demands (Walker 1980, 582).

Jean-Paul Laurens' (1838–1921) painting *Les Otages* (1896) shows us two young boys, ostensibly one of about 10 years old, the other a little older, who, as we gather from their sophisticated clothing, must be of noble birth (Figure 10.1).

In combination with the title of the painting, *Hostages,* we may conjecture that this refers to a situation that was more common in former times than it is nowadays. The Romans sometimes took sons of tributary princes and educated them in Rome. There they were held as a security for the continued loyalty of a conquered people. This also served the purpose of educating possible future leaders in the ways and dealings of Roman civilization (Allen 2006).

Hostage-taking was also a very common practice in 14th-century France and England. In September 1339, Edward III attacked France. He had a force of around 15,000 men under his command (Clarke 2010, 87). In the protracted war that followed, there were also sea battles, one of which took place in 1340. During that confrontation, the English took the rich Frenchmen prisoner and threw the rest overboard, where – in the lively depiction of that practice by Stephen Clarke – the armor of the Frenchmen "did not help them swim to safety" (Clarke 2010, 91). The French leaders Quiéret and Béhuchet tried to save their skin by surrendering, hoping they would be held for ransom. This was not accepted by the English, unfortunately, and both were killed.

During the war on the French mainland, the nobles who were taken prisoner were sometimes luckier; they were sent to England, where heavy prices were

Figure 10.1 Les Otages (1896)

demanded to get them back (Clarke 2010, 93). Anyone not rich enough to hold for ransom was killed. Later, Edward also started something of a market for hostages, as Clarke writes, and anyone returning from France with a valuable prisoner stood a good chance of selling him or her to the King. Edward would then contact the relatives of the rich captive and extort the full price (Clarke 2010, 110, 121).

One may also compare the ancient hostages with prisoners of war. The practice of taking hostages as security for adherence to treaties has now become obsolete in international law.[2]

Hostage-taking and terrorism

Taking hostages is nowadays considered an act of *terrorism*. But in the modern experience, the identification of taking hostages with acts of terrorism is relatively new. It dates from the 1970s, when armed terrorists kidnapped civilians of their own nation state or another nation state to force their will upon the state or society at large.

In 1979, the United Nations General Assembly adopted the International Convention against the Taking of Hostages. The United States also made hostage-taking a federal criminal offense pursuant to 18 U.S.C. § 1203 (1984), with the relevant clause being "whoever, whether inside or outside the United States, seizes or detains and threatens to kill, to injure, or to continue to detain another person in order to compel a third person or a governmental organization to do or abstain from doing any act as an explicit or implicit condition for the release of the person detained, or attempts or conspires to do so, shall be punished by imprisonment for any term of years for life and, if the death of any person results, shall be punished by death or life imprisonment." Famous hostages throughout history include such people as Julius Caesar; Richard I of England, returning from a crusade; Emperor Theodoric the Great; and Terry Waite.

The most famous hostage situation in the recent history of the United States is undoubtedly the Iran Hostage Crisis (1979–1981). Iran seized 66 American citizens at the US embassy in Tehran, holding 52 of them for more than a year. The crisis, which took place during the chaotic aftermath of the Islamic Revolution (1978–1979) and its overthrow of the Pahlavi monarchy, had a dramatic effect on the domestic politics of the United States. It poisoned US-Iranian relations for decades, and it proved a deadly blow to the popularity of the Carter administration.

In the recent past, kidnapping Europeans for ransom has become a global business for Al Qaeda and other terrorist organizations. One of the reasons for this is that it is extremely profitable because, although they deny doing this, European governments in particular appear willing to pay ransoms to free their citizens. An investigation by *The New York Times* found that Al Qaeda and its affiliates have taken in at least $125,000,000 dollars from kidnappings since 2008. Approximately half of that amount was paid in 2013, which makes clear that the business is booming. As reporter Rukmini Callimachi writes, "put bluntly, Europe has become an inadvertent underwriter of Al Qaeda" (Callimachi 2014). Kidnapping for ransom has become today's most significant source of terrorist financing, and each transaction encourages another transaction.

Taking hostages has also become a specialty for particular organizations. Terrorists do not do the work themselves: they outsource it to criminal groups that work on commission. Only the United States and Great Britain resist paying ransoms.

Knowledge on how to successfully kidnap victims is also shared by terrorist organizations. In 2004, Abdelaziz al-Muqrin, an Al Qaeda operative, published a guide on how to conduct a successful kidnapping operation (Callimachi 2014).

Quite successful in the "kidnapping business" (this phrase could be mistaken for cynical commentary, were it not that what is described is so real), is the Islamic State (ISIS or ISIL). As Islam scholar Robert Spencer writes in *The Complete Infidel's Guide to ISIS*, the Islamic State demanded $100,000,000 for the release of journalist James Foley (Spencer 2015, 111). No ransom was payed, and Foley was beheaded. The Islamic State also demanded $200,000,000 for the life of Japanese hostage Haruna Yakawa. When no payment was provided by the Japanese government, Yakawa was beheaded. The Treasury Department estimates that in 2014 alone, the Islamic State took in $20,000,000 in ransom payments (Spencer 2015, 112).

This proves that in many instances the Islamic State is successful in having a ransom paid. The *Daily Mail* tells the story of a hostage of the Islamic State who was forced to call his family during a torture session, so that his screams would bring the family to a point where they would pay the $80,000. When the money was paid, the victim was released (Spencer 2015, 113).

Modern hostage-taking

Let me now address what I want to call *modern* hostage-taking. This is *not* the "modern" hostage-taking that arose in the 1970s that was referred to above: the situation in which armed terrorists kidnapped civilians to enforce their will upon the state or society at large. I am also not referring to the hostage-taking by terrorists for mainly financial reasons, as described in the previous paragraph. Modern hostage-taking, in the sense I want to use that concept here, arose with the Rushdie Affair and is driven by an "idealist" motive: to spread fear among the citizens and governments of the nations targeted.

This modern hostage-taking, in the sense in which I describe this phenomenon, did not start, perhaps, with a master plan. Initially, people did not even understand what was happening. It started in 1989, with the inconvenience for a writer (Rushdie) – that, supposedly, he would be "hidden from the public" for a few days. It turned out differently, as we can say in hindsight.

The British intellectual historian Peter Watson (b. 1943) starts his *The Age of Nothing* with a most hilarious anecdote. And it is one of the most bitter ones I have read as well, although it is highly relevant for the matter I want to discuss in this essay. It is about Salman Rushdie, who in 1990 had been living in hiding for more than a year. In July of that year, the police, Watson tells us, had "a further refinement for his safety – a wig" (Watson 2014, 1). The idea was that if Rushdie were to wear a wig he would be able to walk down the street without attracting attention.

Rushdie decided to go along with the wig experiment. When he had put it on, and the police said that it "looked great," the author of the controversial novel decided to "take it for a walk" (Watson 2014, 1). Once he was on the street, Rushdie noted that several people broke into wide grins or even laughter. He heard one man say: "There's that bastard Rushdie in a wig" (Watson 2014, 2).

The anecdote, which is told by Rushdie (2012) himself in his autobiography *Joseph Anton*, and commented upon by Watson (2014), is interesting for several reasons. First, it confronts us with the question: are we less naïve now than in 1990, or is the level of awareness of the theoterrorist threat still the same? Second, it forces us to ask another one: what about the attitude of the general public? The man who recognized Rushdie on the street spoke of "that bastard Rushdie." Apparently, the man on the street had no idea that the situation had something to do with himself. That it was also *his* freedom that was at stake, not only Rushdie's.

He had no idea, so to speak, that it was not the individual British author Salman Rushdie who was wearing the wig, but the whole of British society, the British government, the British state. The wig is a kind of symbol for the predicament of Great Britain at that moment in time.

It was also Margaret Thatcher (1925–2013) wearing the wig. Or Geoffrey Howe (1926–2015). But it was also the man who made the remark about the wig. *He* was the "bastard" that he was talking about. It was, after all, *he* who had voted for the laws governing Great Britain. These laws and individual human rights were not the brainchild of a silly Indian writer, but they were the laws of

England: *his* England. The British, by upholding the Magna Carta or the Universal Declaration of Human Rights, have chosen those values (see Vallance 2009). And now, one of those citizens, Rushdie, was a hostage in his own country, because for him some of these values seem abrogated.

But before I elucidate what I mean by the notion of "modern hostage-taking," let me first emphasize that the way I will portray the situation is undoubtedly very different from the way that the principal agents frame it. And with "principal agents," I mean the Iranian regime, Western governments (those of the United States and Great Britain, among others), Salman Rushdie himself, and also the fellow novelists who supported him (see MacDonogh 1993; Chervel 1992; Abdallah et al. 1993). Needless to say, the way I see the whole affair is through *my* angle of looking at things. But I think it makes sense to consider the affair under the angle chosen here, and it seems important (at least, that is what I hope to show in what follows) that governments learn to look at it in this way as well. It could, I hope, make the nature of the terrorist threat, as it manifests itself in the contemporary world, clearer. It would make clear that modern religious liberty (including the controversial liberty to change your religion or abandon your religion) is far from realized. It seems an ideal which is further away than it was in the 19th century. *Pace* the formal human rights declarations which make the freedom to apostatize a basic human right, theoterrorist organizations are so effective in stifling this right that we are in a serious condition nowadays with regard to religious liberty.

Traditional hostage-taking, that is, the way Terry Waite (b. 1939) and other hostages were taken, often means that someone who is physically present on the territory of another state is taken into captivity to exert pressure on a foreign regime. *Modern* hostage-taking is different. Here, someone (Rushdie, the Danish cartoonist Kurt Westergaard, the Swedish artist Lars Vilks, the American anti-Islam activist Pamela Geller, the Dutch politician Geert Wilders, and others in the same predicament) is not physically taken captive, but the targets are seriously threatened *in the state or the country where they live* by foreign powers (either state powers, as is the case with Iran, or religious or criminal organizations such as Al Qaeda and the Islamic State) who, by operating in the way indicated, terrorize the individual targeted and also the state where that person lives (or, in the case of great international solidarity, the international community).[3]

This threat is so severe, and the countries in which people are threatened are so much in confusion about what has happened to them, that this kind of terrorist tactic is very effective. Basically, it leaves the country hit by the new strategy in great turmoil and embroiled in perplexing and protracted discussions about decency, national guilt, the freedom to offend, and the limitations of free speech (see Hume 2015; Cohen 2012). Modern hostage-taking, as it manifested itself in the Rushdie Affair (and to a lesser extent in the Carrell Affair), has caused governments and important politicians to start doubting their most sacred principles. Now this is a great success for terrorism indeed. Modern hostage-taking is therefore much more effective, in fact, than the old physical hostage-taking. It is *so effective* even, that the expectation seems justified that it will continue, and even augment, in the future.

Why modern hostage-taking is so effective

From a certain perspective, making this claim can be deemed to be "alarmist." The one who engages in this type of analysis is often accused of being panicky or in the grip of fear (see Bourke 2006). But from another perspective, it might also be deemed realistic. And that modern hostage-taking will increase also seems realistic. There are five reasons why this relatively new technique is so effective.

First, it does not require complicated actions to get the person targeted in your power. If you take someone hostage in the traditional way, then you have to capture the person first and subsequently keep him or her alive in some hidden place. In other words, you have to spend money and resources on this. This is all fairly complicated. One of the complications is also that the people perpetrating the hostage-taking are working under stressful conditions. Usually, they start quarreling with their fellow criminals about what has to happen, about the ransom to be paid, and other matters. The Dutch movie *De Heineken Ontvoering* (Treurniet 2011), about the kidnapping of beer mogul Freddy Heineken, gives a lively picture of these quarrels.[4] These quarrels make the kidnappers weaker.

A *fatwa* of the type that Ayatollah Khomeini issued in 1989 (our main case of "modern hostage-taking") does not have this inconvenience for the "kidnappers." The only thing you have to do is, from another part of the world, make the statement that will cause all the havoc. Afterwards, you can continue with your own business. This shows, according to Daniel Pipes (b. 1949), one of the first writers to produce a monograph on the Rushdie Affair, how easily such a "kidnapping" can be organized (see Pipes 2010, 30–35). Khomeini proceeded to summon a secretary and then took the single most important step in the entire incident. On February 14, 1989, he dictated the following legal judgment (*fatwa*) against Rushdie and his publishers:

> I inform all zealous Muslims of the world that the author of the book entitled *The Satanic Verses* – which has been compiled, printed, and published in opposition to Islam, the Prophet, and the Koran – and all those involved in the publication who were aware of its contents, are sentenced to death.
>
> I call upon all zealous Muslims to execute them quickly, wherever they may be found, so that no one else will dare to insult the Muslim sanctities. God willing, whoever is killed on this path is a martyr.
>
> In addition, anyone who has access to the author of this book but does not possess the power to execute him should report him to the people so that he may be punished for his actions.
>
> (Quoted in Pipes 2010, 30–35; Pipes 2003, 27)[5]

So you do not have to organize a spectacular seizure of the victim in a faraway country, as the Israelis had to do with Adolf Eichmann (1906–1962) (Mulisch 2005). You do not have to ponder over the matter of where to hide the victim after he or she has been brought under your control. You do not have to bother about internal discussions about the legitimacy of continuing with an act once perpetrated. You only have to call your secretary and formulate the death sentence, and subsequently the person or organization intimidated (in this case, Rushdie and the government of the United Kingdom) is brought into a most precarious (if not hopeless) position.[6] It is up to him or her, the victim, to convince his or her fellow countrymen that *they*, those fellow countrymen, have lost their freedom as well, and that *they*, those fellow countrymen, would do well to bear the colossal costs of the protection. But before that message gets across, years will have passed – if he or she succeeds at all.

The second reason why modern hostage-taking is so effective is that it has a greater terrorizing effect on the people targeted than traditional hostage-taking, because you send a much more frightening message to the people living in a foreign country than you do with traditional terrorist techniques. An example from the United Kingdom may make this clear. Mohammad Sidique Khan (1974–2005), one of the four suicide terrorists responsible for the London underground bombings on July 7, 2005, said: "Until we feel security you will be our targets and until you stop the bombing, gassing, imprisonment and torture of my people we will not stop this fight. We are at war and I am a soldier. Now you too will taste the reality of this situation" (BBC News 2005; also quoted in Desai 2007, 6).

This is an important passage because it teaches us something about the *motives* of theoterrorists. The aim is, apparently, to make people feel uncomfortable in their daily lives. The idea is to get the message across that, although people may feel safe on the territory of their own state, in fact they are not. This is very effective. The reason why this is the case is this: many people have the idea that if Terry Waite, for example, goes to Lebanon to try to secure the release of four hostages and is subsequently seized and held captive himself (as happened between 1987 and 1991), they will feel great unease. But this particular feeling of unease is nothing compared to the feeling people experience when, *on the territory of their own state*, they appear not to be immune from terrorist attacks and other types of aggression. It in fact brings modern societies back to earlier stages of development, when physical security was less well-developed than it is today.[7]

It is for that very reason that Rushdie is called "that bastard Rushdie" (and not Khomeini "that bastard Khomeini") by the man who recognized him despite the wig. From the point of view of the man in the street, it is Rushdie (not Khomeini) who is the primary cause of that loss of security in England. The essential reasoning is this: no book, no fatwa, no problem.

It is a misguided conception of causality, of course, because this would mean that the cause of the death of the victim is *not* the villain's knife stab, but the vulnerability of the human body (for which the person himself or herself is to blame, not his or her attacker). And yet, this mistaken conception of causality is, in the controversy I am discussing in this essay, hugely popular – not only with the man on the Clapham omnibus, but with Members of Parliament, influential philosophers and intellectuals (Taylor 1989, 118–122), and professors of logic and metaphysics (see Dummett 1990 for a glorious manifestation).

Third, the modern tactic of hostage-taking is so popular with the aggressors because it is extremely humiliating *for the country* (and especially the government of the country) where it occurs. Usually, people concentrate on the immediate victim, be it Rushdie, Westergaard or Carrell (Cliteur 2013, 15–41). But we should not forget (and this is one of the reasons why this has a very nice cherry on top from the perspective of the terrorist) that also "the British" and "the Danish," as peoples, are involved – as are their respective governments.

When, in 1979, the American embassy in Tehran was occupied and 66 Americans were seized, the United States felt a great deal of humiliation (see Carter 1982, 431ff). When, in April 1980, a rescue operation was organized and ultimately failed, the sense of humiliation only became greater. And when Terry Waite was captured in Lebanon, this was, of course, a difficult situation for the Government of Great Britain. But no one – and here comes the point that I want to make – will think that the United States is weak because it could not forestall the taking of hostages abroad during the aforementioned crisis. And nobody will reproach the British government for not being able to maintain the civil order in Lebanon. But when a government cannot fulfill its primary function, that is, to protect its citizens *on its own territory*, it becomes a matter of grave concern. It is, in fact, an utter humiliation and – consequently – a great boon for the terrorizing agency.

This boon for the terrorist agency is so great (and the corresponding humiliation of the state whose nationals are taken captive on the territory of the state), that this partly explains, I think, Margaret Thatcher's negative feelings toward Rushdie. In his conversation with Rushdie, the French philosopher Bernard-Henri Lévy (b. 1948) indicated that he had heard Margaret Thatcher saying that Rushdie deserved this, and also that Prince Charles was chuckling in Paris about the Rushdie Affair, saying that Rushdie was quite expensive for the British crown (Lévy 1999, 78, 96).

It is no secret that Thatcher had very negative feelings about Rushdie. A common explanation for this is that Rushdie wrote unfavorably about the British prime minister (Weatherby 1990). I do not think this is the most likely reason for her aversion to Britain's most controversial author. A much more likely reason is that the Rushdie Affair made Thatcher seem weak. His case, the *fatwa*, made the Iron Lady look silly and vulnerable, and, in other words, not very "iron-like."

There is a famous anecdote about Thatcher and President H. W. Bush that is relevant here. When Bush was hesitant about how to react to the seizure of Kuwait by Saddam Hussein in 1990, Thatcher helped the American president to overcome his hesitations with the words: "This is no time to go wobbly, George" (Coughlin 2013). In the Rushdie Affair, which was in a certain sense much more delicate, Thatcher and the British government were (as all Western governments) "wobbly" the whole time.

I think this is the most important reason why we do not find any mention of Salman Rushdie anywhere in Margaret Thatcher's autobiography (Thatcher 1995). He made the British government feel embarrassed – not because of what he wrote, but because it found it difficult to fulfill its most important duty: safeguarding the territory of the state against physical threats by other actors. Although the British government has been able to keep Rushdie alive (which is to their credit), it is still a humiliating situation for a country that it has to *hide* one of its citizens and deprive him of his elementary right to move about freely on its territory in order to keep him alive.

In Rushdie's autobiography, there is an interesting quote from his bodyguards that is relevant to this discussion. Regarding the matter at hand, Benny and Stan were reassuringly saying: "It can't be allowed. [...] Threatening a British citizen. It's not on. It'll get sorted. You just need to lie low for a couple of days and let the politicians sort it out" (Rushdie 2012, 146). This is a great passage because it so wonderfully reflects what people who are not familiar with all the higher politics might think. "It'll get sorted." Unfortunately not. And it will least of all get sorted out *by the politicians.* They have been struggling with the matter for years and years, and slowly it has begun to dawn on us (and on them, one may hope) how little the matter has improved. Is it over the top to say that, with regard to Rushdie, Westergaard, and some other people, the Westphalian state can hardly fulfill its primary obligations regarding their physical safety and freedom to move about at the same time? Are we back in a pre-1648 geopolitical situation?

This brings me to the fourth reason why modern hostage-taking is so effective. The tactic of modern hostage-taking is also superior to the older tactics because it proves to be much easier to stimulate a confusing debate about the moral foundations of Western countries. I will try to elaborate this point a little further in the following paragraph.

Let us try to imagine what the discussion on *The Satanic Verses* would have been had there *not* been terrorist intimidation toward the author. Would Jimmy Carter (Carter 1989), the Vatican, John Le Carré, and all the other detractors of Rushdie have taken a stance against the book had Khomeini *not* taken offense? This cannot be proven with absolute certainty, of course, but it does not seem very bizarre to speculate that they probably would not have done so. Now, the consequences of this state of affairs are far-reaching. It means that the indignation of Western intellectuals and Western politicians regarding Rushdie's stances on the Prophet Mohammed and other topics that are deemed sacred by religious believers are heavily dependent on the ideas of Khomeini. Simply by threatening violence (or even the expectation that he may threaten violence), Khomeini was able to elicit a reaction from Jimmy Carter, who declared that "Rushdie's book is an insult" on March 5, 1989 (Carter 1989; Appignanesi and Maitland 1990, 236–237). If Khomeini had not indicated that the book was an insult three weeks earlier, on February 14, 1989, Carter would not even have thought of reacting to the contents of a novel. In other words, Carter felt insulted *because* Khomeini felt insulted. Or perhaps Carter felt insulted because Khomeini *claimed* to have felt insulted.[8]

One may object that this is all too obvious. Of course, one might say, Carter would not have taken offense had Khomeini not taken offense. The British author Margaret Atwood (b. 1939) opined that, when she read *The Satanic Verses,* she could not understand that some Muslims would be concerned about what was written there. The most controversial passage was, after all, what appeared in a dream to one of the characters in a novel (Atwood 1992, 62–65). Suppose Jimmy Carter did not read Rushdie's novel (assuming that he did in fact read the novel) at the height of the protests against and the death threats made to the author, but as a book he had taken on holiday to read on a beach somewhere far removed from all the sound and fury that is the modern media – would he have been just as enraged by the contents of the book? The answer is: probably not. And that brings us to an important consequence for the subject of theoterrorism: indignation is contagious. And simply *affecting* indignation can have a tremendous effect on others. It seems to me not unduly speculative to presume that some Islamist leaders purposefully used this indignation to rally confused Western intellectuals to their cause (see Landes 2013, 621–634). And this makes it very rewarding for potential terrorists, and those sympathizing with their ideology, to walk around with an air of being "insulted" all the time. Insulted about pornography on the Internet, insulted by satire of the Prophet, even insulted about the way women dress on the streets in Europe and the United States.[9]

The curious situation arises that in the past decades we have come to live in a world where a pretense of "feeling insulted" is an important precondition for implementing the terrorist agenda – and for realizing it in a *very* effective way. Khomeini's *fatwa* has effectively undermined Western society's confidence in its own values of free speech, freedom of conscience and freedom of religion to such an extent that you can now find the Secretary-General of the United Nations denouncing the Universal Declaration of Human Rights (UDHR), the Chairman of the European Parliament denouncing the European Convention on Human Rights (ECHR), and the President of the United States distancing himself from an American citizen who defends the First Amendment (Herrenberg 2015; Cliteur and Herrenberg 2016).

And this brings me to a fifth and final reason why modern theoterrorists are so effective at intimidating Western politicians: the victims can never know *when the situation has been terminated*. In fact, there *is* no termination, no end. There was no end when Khomeini died. There was no end with new declarations of the Iranian government. In fact, there never is an end. The only end is the natural death of Salman Rushdie, as some wistful early commentaries pointed out.[10]

Suppose Khomeini had cancelled the *fatwa*. There would still be the chance that some fanatic who is "more popish than the Pope" could come along.[11] And suppose the Iranian government issues a declaration that, from now on, they will concentrate on another target (e.g., not a novelist, but a politician). Would this save Salman Rushdie? Not completely: there can always be a zealous terrorist who aspires to outdo the official leaders of the Iranian regime (which has now begun to grow decadent, less committed to the cause, has it not?). And this never-ending existence of the threat is precisely what is so characteristic of contemporary theoterrorism.

The most recent assault on religious liberty

Directly after the shooting in the editorial offices of *Charlie Hebdo* on January 7, 2015, Cherif Kouachi, one of the two Kouachi brothers who conducted the attack, commented on what had happened. A French television network managed to get Kouachi on the phone while the brothers were holed up inside a printing factory outside Paris. A journalist for France's BFMTV, Igor Sahiri, asked Cherif what the motives for the attack were (Saliba 2015):

> Kouachi: We're telling you that we are the prophet's defenders, peace and blessings be upon him, and that I, Cherif Kouachi, was sent by Yemen's Al-Qaeda.

The journalist asked Kouachi whether it was his plan to kill more people. The theoterrorist answered with a semantic commentary on the concept "killer." Here was his response:

> Kouachi: We are not killers. We are defenders of the prophet, we don't kill women. We kill no one. We defend the prophet. If someone offends the prophet then there is no problem, we can kill him. We don't kill women. We are not like you. You are the one killing women and children in Syria, Iraq and Afghanistan. This isn't us. We have an honor code in Islam.

What follows is an interesting commentary on the notion and significance of the concept of "revenge":

> Interviewer: But you just sought revenge here, you killed 12 people.
> Kouachi: Yes, because we sought revenge. You just said it well. You said it yourself, we sought revenge.

Authors like Noam Chomsky and John Esposito will focus on the part of Kouachi's comments where he says: "You are the one killing women and children in Syria, Iraq and Afghanistan." Is his killing not revenge for interventions by Western powers in the Middle East? Interpreted in this way, the religious or theological dimension vanishes and the Kouachi brothers are political actors. But there is another dimension, as it appears from this exchange of words between the theoterrorist and the journalist, which is that Cherif Kouachi will kill anyone who, in his view, offends the prophet. And his killing is seen as some sort of "defense." This defense is not something that takes place in Syria, Iraq or Afghanistan alone, but in Paris, Amsterdam, Aarhus and any place in the world as well where this so-called "offense" takes place, irrespective of the national legislation of the countries involved.

If European nation states and the United States are not successful in curbing this danger, their cartoonists, playwrights, novelists and talk-show hosts are a potential target as long as they do not comply with the holy legal order that the theoterrorists aim to protect. It makes them hostages in their own countries because they are basically outlaws struggling to survive while their official leaders do not know how to react to this new phenomenon.

The tactic of modern hostage-taking is so effective because the targets (and the states supposed to protect the targets) have to be active and alert, while the potential perpetrators of an attack can relax and prepare themselves at the pace they deem appropriate. The only possible effective remedy against the attack is perhaps the announcement that possible attackers will be killed themselves, but even then one would have to think about the following: how does one scare off people who do not fear death? So the whole matter becomes a war of attrition (Pantucci 2015).

Whose force and determination will prevail in this conflict is hard to predict at this point in time. Sometimes it seems that the theoterrorists are *so* determined to realize their goals, and the weakness of Western leaders looks *so* embarrassingly manifest, that we must fear the worst. In countries where there have been no recent official executions for blasphemy (like Pakistan), extremists have not infrequently killed the accused before and during the trials, and also when the accused were acquitted (wrongly, as the extremists claim) (see Marshall and Shea 2011, 8).

This revival of the importance of religiously motivated lynch mobs in the contemporary world is the dubious legacy of Khomeini's highly successful *fatwa* on the British author Salman Rushdie.

Notes

1 My emphasis.
2 This was decided in the International Convention against the Taking of Hostages in New York in 1979: http://www.un.org/en/sc/ctc/docs/conventions/Conv5.pdf.
3 What distinguished the Rushdie Affair from the Cartoon Affair, the Jones Affair, and the Trial of Wilders was that Rushdie generated international support from fellow writers (see MacDonogh 1993; Chervel 1992). The Cartoon Affair did not result in such mass-scale support. The Jones Affair did lead to reactions from all over the world, but in the case of Jones it was people rejecting his activities.
4 This film is about the kidnapping of the Dutch businessman Freddy Heineken (1923–2002). Heineken and his driver, Ab Doderer, were kidnapped in 1983 and released on a ransom of EUR16,000,000.
5 In "Religion and Murder in the Middle East," Bernard Lewis writes that Ayatollah Khomeini "knew no English and had apparently never read the novel" (Lewis 2004, 105).
6 As the legal philosopher Jeremy Waldron so well understood (see Waldron 1989, 248, 260; 1993, 134–143). His more recent contributions to this subject are, unfortunately, less convincing (see Waldron 2012).
7 Steven Pinker's (2001) *The Better Angels of our Nature: Why Violence Has Declined* offers a comparison of our own time with previous epochs with regard to physical safety.
8 That Khomeini was a complicated person who was more a man of the world than we think appears clearly from Oriana Fallaci's insightful interview with the Iranian dictator (see Fallaci 2011, 172–262).
9 One of the preoccupations of Sayyid Qutb, a foremost Islamist ideologue (see on him: Berman 2010, 42–41; 50–53; 186–187).
10 Saramago wrote at the end of his open letter to Rushdie that he did not know whether they would meet one day or whether Rushdie would be forever forced to live disconnected from the rest of the world (see Saramago 1992, 38). That same pessimism, or realism, you also find in Jeremy Waldron's essay on the matter (Waldron 1989, 248, 260; Waldron 1993, 134–143).
11 Karima Bennoune describes this mechanism when referring to Anwar al-Awlaki: "Anwar al-Awlaki was indeed killed by the U.S. government about a year later, something I did not celebrate. Unfortunately, he never rescinded his own death list, which remains out there in cyberspace with a long half-life" (Bennoune 2013, 24).

Bibliography

Abdallah, Aouar, et al. 1993. *Pour Rushdie: Cent intellectuels arabes et musulmans pour la liberté d'expression*. Paris: La Decouverte.

Allen, Joel. 2006. *Hostages and hostage-taking in the Roman Empire*. Cambridge: Cambridge University Press.

Appignanesi, Lisa, and Sara Maitland (eds.). 1990. *The Rushdie File*. Syracuse, NY: Syracuse University Press.

Atwood, Margaret. 1992. "Traum im Kopf eines Taugenichts." In *Redefreiheit ist das Leben: Briefe an Salman Rushdie*, ed. Thierry Chervel. Munich and Zurich: Piper, 62–65.

BBC News. 2005. "London Bomber: Text in Full." September 1. http://news.bbc.co.uk/2/hi/uk/4206800.stm.

Bennoune, Karima. 2013. *Your Fatwa Does Not Apply Here: Untold Stories from the Fight against Muslim Fundamentalism*. New York and London: W. W. Norton.

Berman, Paul. 2010. *The Flight of the Intellectuals*. New York: Melville House.

Bourke, Joanna. 2006. *Fear: A Cultural History*. Emeryville, CA: Shoemaker and Hoard.

Callimachi, Rukmini. 2014. "Paying Ransoms, Europe Bankrolls Qaeda Terror." *New York Times*, July 29.

Carter, Jimmy. 1982. *Keeping Faith: Memoirs of a President*. Toronto: Bantam.

Carter, Jimmy. 1989. "Rushdie's Book Is an Insult." *New York Times*, March 5.

Chervel, Thierry (ed.). 1992. *Redefreiheit ist das Leben: Briefe an Salman Rushdie*. Munich and Zurich: Piper.

Clarke, Stephen. 2010. *1000 Years of Annoying the French*. London: Black Swan.

Cliteur, Paul. 2012. "State and Religion against the Backdrop of Religious Radicalism." *International Journal of Constitutional Law* 10(1): 127–152.

Cliteur, Paul. 2013. "The Rudi Carrell Affair and its Significance for the Tension between Theoterrorism and Religious Satire." *Ancilla Iuris* 15: 15–41.

Cliteur, Paul, and Tom Herrenberg (eds). 2016. *The Fall and Rise of Blasphemy Law*. Leiden: Leiden University Press.

Cohen, Nick. 2012. *You Can't Read this Book: Censorship in an Age of Freedom*. London: Fourth Estate.

Coughlin, Con. 2013. "Margaret Thatcher: It Was An Iron Law that there Should Be no Surrender to Terrorism." *The Telegraph*, April 13.

Desai, Meghnad. 2007. *Rethinking Islamism: The Ideology of the New Terror*. London and New York: L.B. Tauris.

Dummett, Michael. 1990. "Open Letter to Rushdie." *The Independent*, February 11.

European Union. 2012. *Charter of Fundamental Rights of the European Union*, 26 October 2012, 2012/C 326/02.

Fallaci, Oriana. 2011. *Interviews with History and Conversations with Power*. New York: Rizzoli.

Herrenberg, Tom. 2015. "Denouncing Divinity: Blasphemy, Human Rights, and the Struggle of Political Leaders to defend Freedom of Speech in the Case of Innocence of Muslims." *Ancilla Iuris* 1: 1–19.

Hostage Taking. 18 U.S.C. § 1203 (1984).

Hume, Mick. 2015. *Trigger Warning: Is the Fear of Being Offensive Killing Free Speech?* London: William Collins.

Landes, Richard. 2013. "From Useful Idiot to Useful Infidel: Meditations on the Folly of the 21st-Century 'Intellectuals'." *Terrorism and Political Violence* 25(1): 621–634.

Laurens, Jean-Paul. 1896. *Les Otages*. Painting. Lyon: Musée des beaux-arts de Lyon.

Lévy, Bernard-Henri. 1999. *Avec Salman Rushdie: Questions de principe six. Le Livre de Poche*. Paris: Librairie Générale Française.

Lewis, Bernard, 2004. "Religion and Murder in the Middle East." In *From Babel to Dragomans: Interpreting the Middle East*. London: Weidenfeld and Nicolson, 100–108.

MacDonogh, Steve (ed.). 1993. *The Rushdie Letters: Freedom to Speak, Freedom to Write*. Kerry, Ireland: Brandon.

Marshall, Paul, and Nina Shea. 2011. *Silenced: How Apostasy and Blasphemy Codes Are Choking Freedom Worldwide*. Oxford: Oxford University Press.

Mulisch, Harry. 2005. *Criminal Case 40/61: The Trial of Adolf Eichmann*. Trans. Robert Naborn. Philadelphia: University of Pennsylvania Press.

Pantucci, Raffaello. 2015. *"We Love Death as You Love Life": Britain's Suburban Terrorists*. London: Hurst.

Pinker, Steven. 2011. *The Better Angels of our Nature: Why Violence Has Declined*. London: Viking.

Pipes, Daniel. 2003. *The Rushdie Affair: The Novel, the Ayatollah, and the West*. 2nd ed. New Brunswick, NJ and London: Transaction.

Pipes, Daniel. 2010. "Two Decades of the Rushdie Rules." *Commentary* (October): 30–35.

Rushdie, Salman. 2012. *Joseph Anton: A Memoir*. London: Jonathan Cape.

Saliba, Emanuelle. 2015. "Paris Killer Cherif Kouachi Gave Interview to TV Channel Before He Died." *NBC News*. Trans. *NBC News*. January 9.

Saramago, José. 1992. "Die Strasse von Santiago." In *Redefreiheit ist das Leben: Briefe an Salman Rushdie*, ed. Thierry Chervel. Munich and Zurich: Piper, 36–39.

Spencer, Robert. 2015. *The Complete Infidel's Guide to ISIS*. Washington, DC: Regnery.

Taylor, Charles. 1989. "The Rushdie Controversy." *Public Culture* 2(1): 118–122.

Thatcher, Margaret. 1995. *The Path to Power*. London: HarperCollins.

Treurniet, Maarten (dir.). 2011. *De Heineken Ontvoering*. The Netherlands: IDTV Film.

Vallance, Edward. 2009. *A Radical History of Britain*. London: Abacus.

Waldron, Jeremy. 1989. "Rushdie and Religion." First published under the title "Too important for Tact" in *The Times Literary Supplement*, March 10, and reprinted in Jeremy Waldron. 1993. *Liberal Rights: Collected Papers 1981–1991*. Cambridge and New York: Cambridge University Press.

Waldron, Jeremy. 2012. *The Harm in Hate Speech*. Cambridge, MA and London: Harvard University Press.

Walker, David M. 1980. *The Oxford Companion to Law*. Oxford: Clarendon Press.

Watson, Peter. 2014. *The Age of Nothing: How We Have Sought to Live since the Death of God*. London: Weidenfeld and Nicolson.

Weatherby, W. J. 1990. *Salman Rushdie: Sentenced to Death*. New York: Carroll and Graf.

11 Religious non-freedom traditions and the lack of universal education in the Indian social system

A WV3 case study of Jotirao Phule

Thom Wolf

Introduction

For a half-century, various global observers, while disagreeing on many issues, have seen the power of allegiances and the impact of ideas on social problems which now face us all in the 21st century. These observers range from France's (former) Minister of Finance and economist Alain Peyrefitte, professor of comparative literature Abdelwahab Meddeb, Switzerland-based philosopher Francis Schaeffer, State University of New York philosopher David Dilworth, Tufts University economist Lawrence Harrison, Harvard/Stanford historian Niall Ferguson and Singapore United Nations representative and public policy academic Kishore Mahbubani, to India's Hyderabad University political scientists Jyotirmaya Sharma and Aparna Devare, activist thinkers Kancha Ilaiah and Vishal Mangalwadi, and Jawaharlal Nehru University social scientists Parimala Rao and Dipankar Gupta, as well as Canadian Islamic scholar and political scientist Mojtaba Mahdavi and African Muslim Marxist Samir Amin (Peyrefitte 1986; Meddeb 2003; Schaeffer 1969; Dilworth 1989; Harrison 1985, 2000, 2013; Ferguson 2012; Mahbubani 2002, 2013; Sharma 2011, 2013; Devare 2011; Ilaiah 2004; Mangalwadi 2013; Rao 2010; Gupta 2004; Mahdavi 2005; Amin 2011). And there are many others (Tarnas 1991; Meddeb 2003; McGrath 2007; Nasr 2007; Berger and Redding 2011; Hannan 2013; Stuenkel 2016; Mitchell 2013; Kahan 2015; Wolf 2007a, 2012a, 2012b).

In South Asia, the power of allegiances and the impact of ideas on social problems can be seen in Nepal as well as in India. Both nations have approximately 80% Hindu populations. With a recent decline of 0.7%, India's Hindu population dipped below 80%. India's population by religion is approximately Hindu (79.8%), Muslim (14.2%), Christian (2.3%), Sikh (2.08%), Buddhist (0.7%), Jain (0.4%), Other (0.6%), and "religion-not-stated" (0.1) (Chowdhury, Ghosh and Tewari 2015; Mampatta 2015).

Similarly, Nepal is slightly over 80% Hindu. Nepal's *National Census of 2011* statistics show that Hindus (81.3%), Buddhists (9%), Hindu-Buddhist-animist Kirant/Yumaists (3%), and Muslims (4.4%) constitute 97.7% of Nepal's population. The remaining 2.3% are Christians (1.4%) and Others (.9%) (National Population and Housing Census 2012; Malla 2012).

Nepal: Addressing social maladies stemming from religious origin

The National Inter-Religious Network – Nepal (NIRN) is an umbrella network of Nepal's faith-based organizations in the world's only officially Hindu nation until 2008. NIRN wants Hindu, Buddhist and Muslim leaders, representing some 98% of the Nepali population, to play a key role in bringing social reform.

The goal is for Nepal to address her "social maladies…stemming from religious origin." Sangeet Sangroula draws attention to efforts of the Government of Nepal and NIRN to diminish "various social evils prevalent in the Nepali society in the name of religious belief, tradition and culture" (Sangroula 2014. See also Thapliyal 2014; Wolf 2011c, 2012a; Roche and Mehta 2014; Gellner 2007; Miklian 2009; Jensen and Mandozai 2014).

Nepal's NIRN initiative and Sangroula's framing offer a most helpful expression for considering society as a culture tree and, specifically, for discussing the intersections and relationships between spirituality and development, and their implications for India's social system. For, as Bishnu Upreti, Director of the South Asia Studies Centre at the University of Rajasthan, reminds us: "Religion is a major binding factor between India and Nepal," and, as a Hindu kingdom, Nepal has been "the farthest place in the north where Hindu culture is dominant. It is on account of reverence towards a Hindu monarch that the king of Nepal had been accorded privileges in India. For instance, in the temple of Puri [Odisha, India], other than priests of the temple, the king of Nepal alone had the exclusive right to enter the innermost sanctuary of Lord Jagannath and offer worship" (Upreti 2014, 8).

In Nepal, according to Narendra Pandey of NIRN, "superstition and harmful social practices in the three religions are widespread. So, the role of the leaders of these religions is really crucial for social transformation" (Sangroula 2014). Identified maladies include child marriage, caste-based discrimination, violence against women, witchcraft, as well as *Chaupadi* (female squat-hut isolation during their menstrual periods) (Gaestel 2013; Das 2014; Kapoor 2014; George 2014) and the traditions of *Ghumto* (face-covering), *Deuki* (girl temple dedication) (Jha 1997) and *Jhuma* (girl monastery dedication) (National Discovery Channel 2013).

The *Deuki* and *Jhuma* traditions involve selling and/or dedicating young girls to Hindu temple deities (*Deuki*) or to Buddhist monasteries (*Jhuma*) as a sacrifice to recover health, bear a son, or see other things accomplished. Parents offering their young daughters understand that the Brahmin Hindu temple priests (*Deuki* dedication) or the Buddhist monastery monks (*Jhuma* dedication) may well have sex with the girls. In *Jhuma,* any infant born from the girl is said to become a Lama in a future reincarnation (Mahto 2012; National Discovery Channel 2013). Such beliefs and behaviors are what the late, distinguished anthropologist Robert Edgerton at University of California, Los Angeles,[1] Darla Martin-Gorski at State University of New York Buffalo, Pace University historian Reza Afshari, University of Adelaide anthropologist Peter Sutton, political scientist Alvin Edgell at Kent State University, Asian Human Rights Commission activist Sujata Paudel, and others call "maladaptive practices" – entrenched practices that harm a society's members (Edgerton 1992, 65–74, 101–104, 144, 202–209; Martin-Gorski 2002;

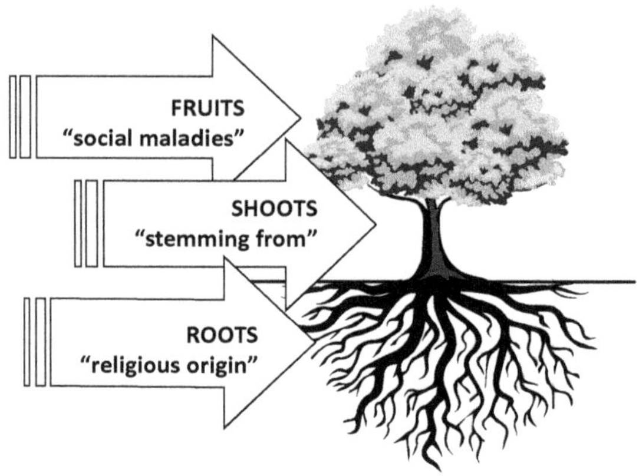

Figure 11.1 Society as a culture tree

Afshari 2001; Sutton 2005, 2011; Edgell 2003; Paudel 2011; Wolf 2007a, 2007b, 2010c).

How can we intellectually frame and practically approach development in a social system in order to mobilize change? My proposal is to compare societies as "cultural trees," so research can be conducted, assessments can be made, prunings can be initiated, and grafts and/or transplants can be proposed by local activists as well as academic scholars. In summary, a culture tree is ***a cultural matrix, a lifezone system of roots (worldvoice), shoots (worldview), and fruits (worldvenue)*** (Wolf 2011b, 9–21; 2012b; Kaplan 2013, 2015; Khanna 2016) (see Figure 11.1). Here, through the vision and vocabulary of Mahatma Jotirao Phule, 19th-century India as a culture tree is explored.

WV3 tree: A culture tree of roots, shoots and fruits

When you see a culture as a tree, it becomes clear that every WV3 tree produces its own lifezone in character with its internally generated roots, shoots and fruits. In other words, each cultural tree produces its own worldvenue fruits, ***its mazeway practices***, and its social behaviors. But those fruits grow from that society's supporting cultural worldview shoots, ***its mindset perspective***. And those systemic beliefs are organically related to the underlying worldvoice roots, ***the model person***, that culture's spiritual benchmark person (Wolf 2012c, 2012d). Each culture tree's particular cultural matrix either releases-and-enables or restricts-and-inhibits its people. The WV3 culture paradigm can be graphed as follows (see Figure 11.2).

Jotirao Phule's enduring and exceptional significance is that he always insisted on addressing the issue of India's cultural motif of religious non-freedom and the lack of universal education within the total cultural system. As Govind Deshpande of the Centre for East Asian Studies, Jawaharlal Nehru University, explains, "Phule's canvas was broad, his sweep majestic. He identified and theorized the most important questions of his time – religion, the varna system, ritualism,

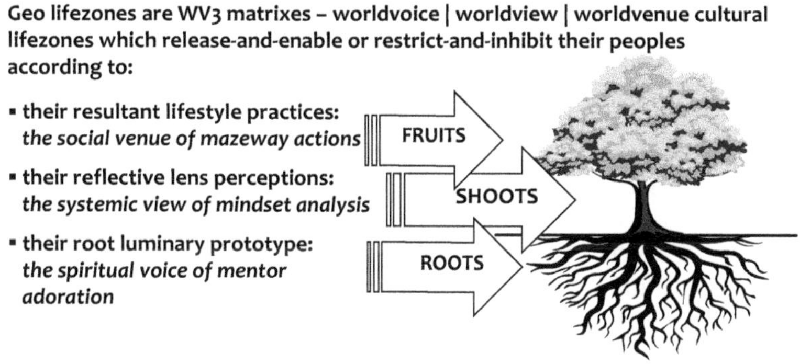

Figure 11.2 WV3 geo lifezones

language, literature, British rule, mythology, the gender question, the conditions of production in agriculture, the lot of the peasantry," and "no other Indian figure of the 19th century comes to mind who displayed this sort of range" (Phule 2002b, 20; Malik-Goure 2013).

But it must be emphasized that Phule was an activist, not an academic. His personal engagement was obvious, his vocabulary was bold, and his comments were blunt, at times belligerent (Wolf 2010d). Even Phule's close associates Lokhande and Bhalerao reacted to *Farmer's Whipcord* as too "*kadak*" (too hard, vitriolic). Lokhande himself said it was "overstated beyond necessity" (*vazvipeksha phajil*) (Phule 2002b, 11).

Perhaps Lokhande and Bhalerao had a point; no better example would be Phule's "*kadak*" (almost ribald) treatment of Brahma's mouth, Brahma's genitals, Brahma's daughter and Brahma's body sets (Phule 2002b, 48–49). But then again, certainly no one ever misunderstood Phule's pathos-filled voice for the poor, oppressed and humiliated; his public opposition to the matrix of misery from the hegemonic culture; or his piercing intellectual analysis of causes and effects.

Nevertheless, what follows are the actual words of Phule. For his original and continuing impact as India's father of social revolution, his statues are erected outside the Parliament House Building and outside the Maharashtra Sadan in New Delhi (Maharashtra Sadan 2016; Dailyhunt 2015).

Phule's own picture of choice for India's traditional social system was that of a "prison," "prisons of the Brahmans," "the age-old prison house," "this slavery system," not that of a culture tree as employed here (Phule 2002b, 21, 44, 98–99). Comparing India to other lands, Phule observed and commented on both pleasant houses and prison houses. With that metaphor, like the Mother Goose nursery rhyme *This Is the House that Jack Built*, each geographical region's life-space house is seen as having constructed its own dynamic yet distinctive house, building on its spiritual meaning foundation, structured according to its systemic mindset scaffolding, and experiencing its social mazeway lifestyle.

As a result, living in the pagoda patterns of Buddha is a distinctly different life experience from the mosque modes of Muhammad (Goucher, LeGuin and

Walton 2004; Berzin 2006, 2016; Wolf 2007b; The Economist 2013; Strathern 2013). Or, the South Asian Indian caste house of Brahma mythology, Vishnu jurisprudence and Shiva Linga spirituality stands a world apart from the Socrates rationality, Caesar jurisprudence and Jesus spirituality of the Western Euro-American church house (Kakar and Kakar 2007; Madan 2010, 64–251; Stevenson, Haberman and Wright 2012; Thakur 1969; Braunthal 1979; Nelson 2010; Shain 1996; Verma 2000).

And of course, there was that 20th-century house-of-horrors that Karl built. That toxic spiritual-intellectual-social matrix cocktail of the Marx master prototype with the communist worldview and its gulag prison house created the same oppressive life-neighborhood everywhere it spread (Courtois et al. 1999).

But everywhere, "This is the house that ____ built" is obvious to ordinary people on the street, and those obvious differences (between the different houses) drive global immigration flows toward cultural pleasant-house nations (Collier 2015; Eisenstadt 1986; Amin 2011; Nolan and Lenski 2010). Here, Phule's prison-house / slavery-system image is integrated with that of the WV3 culture tree. Using the WV3 framework, Mahatma Phule's themes are clear.

Roots: The worldvoice mentor of Phule's India

Taittiriya Brahmana II.8.9.6 (ca. 450 BCE) says: "The Brahman was the wood: Brahman the tree from which they shaped heaven and earth" (Taittiriya Brahmana 2011). That root, that worldvoice luminary of South Asia's WV3 was accurately located by Phule in the "earth-born gods, the Brahmins...certain groups of individuals who are called super-sacred and indeed are worshipped as gods on earth." As the worldvoice mentor, their collective voice has directed the Indian cultural system "for many centuries past" – for "probably more than 3,000 years." And that root-voice Phule describes with precision: "The Brahmin is styled the Lord of the Universe, even equal to the God himself. He is to be worshipped, served and respected by all. A Brahmin can do no wrong" (Phule 1991a, 28, 230, 31, 27, 29; Sood 2005, 3–13).

In Phule's systemic thinking, then, what India is, she owes to the prototype person, the cultural *virtú*, the Brahmin. The Brahmin is the root, the spiritual luminary, of the WV3 Chaturvarna lifezone, which extends geographically across the entirety of South Asia (*chatur* = four, *varna* = caste: the four castes that compose the karma-created and birth-based hierarchy that is irrevocable, unchangeable, unequal, and purity-pollution-graded; the Hindu social system. See Ambedkar 1946; Shah 2007, 162–173). Nineteenth-century Phule advocated that a spiritual revolution is an essential prelude to a social revolution; anything less is a formula for an incomplete revolution.

Indeed, Pratap Mehta of the Centre for Public Research, a New Delhi think tank, suggests that "India was one of the few societies where a political revolution preceded a social one," leaving India's classic "society of inequality" intact. As a result, for Indians, Mehta regretfully records, "in all our social and political relationships, procedures, habits of thought, patterns of conduct...the influence of

inequality is palpable." And this "palpable inequality" of contemporary India illustrates what Mehta calls the four characteristics of "inegalitarian societies": (1) fierce competition for dominance; (2) abject servility; (3) volatile violence (to announce one's power and worth); and (4) routine humiliating discrimination (Mehta 2003, 35–57; Rousseau 1755).

Others have addressed the same issue of India's "palpable" experience as a society of inequality. In 1873, for example (over 125 years before Mehta), Jotirao Phule published his life experience in one word, *Gulamgiri/Slavery*, which was his book dedicated to the people of the United States who had just bled out a civil war to end slavery; and 1873 was also the year in which Phule founded *Satyashodhak Samaj* (The Society of Truth Seekers).

In fact, Phule ended 1873 with his startling December 25 protest ceremony: India's first ever wedding with no Brahmin priest, no priest-donation, no dowry, and no caste restriction: just the equality of a man and a woman, with an elder of honor officiating. Is it, then, a mere insignificant happenstance that 23 years later (1896) Gandhi delivered a condemnation of the harshly inequitable social conditions of South Africa on December 25? Or that 31 years after Ghandi's protest (1927), Dr. Bhimrao Ramji Ambedkar publicly burned a copy on December 25 of the *Manusmriti*, a foundational record of Hindu law, thus rejecting the legal code of India's Hindu civilization (Phule 1991a; Emilsen 2001; Ambedkar 2004)?

Phule made what I call his "cultural superstition/stagnation observation": "To this system of selfish superstition and bigotry, we are to attribute the stagnation and all the evils under which India has been groaning for many centuries past" (Phule 1991a, 31). For along with (but before) the 20th-century Ambedkar (father of the Constitution of India) and Gandhi (father of the nation of India), Phule fully understood the social lesson: that India's future would always include, and even be based on, a spiritual solution, that is, what Boettke, Berger, Harrison, Inglehart, Welzel, scholars at Yale University's "Spiritual Capital Initiative," and others refer to as "cultural capital" or "spiritual capital" (Boettke 2011, 29–30; Berger 2011, 1–14; Harrison 2011, 15–28; 2013; Inglehart and Welzel 2005).

This, then, must be emphasized: For Phule, the cultural base for a transformed India lay neither in Gandhi's Brahmanism nor in Ambedkar's Buddhism (Parekh 2001; Chowdhury 2006). Instead, Phule saw the future of a progress-prone India flourishing only through the cultural mentorship of Baliraja – the *bali* (sacrifice) *raja* (king). In stark contrast to Bal Gangadhar Tilak and Swami Vivekananda, Phule had no vision for constructing Vivekananda's "European society with India's religion" (Sharma 2013, 113–119). Instead, comparing European and North American societies to his India, Phule called for transforming Indian society with Baliraja's religion.

Phule remained in the Hindu community throughout his life. Because of his argumentation, his Brahmin opponents in Pune often accused him of being a Christian (O'Hanlon 2002, 122–135; Devare 2011, 43–50) – small wonder, considering Phule's insistence that progress would come to India not by *adjusting* the old system, but by *adopting* a different system. In his 1873 *Gulamgiri/Slavery*, his best known work, Phule gives a succinct history of the radical worldvoice he advocated for India. Blending world history and indigenous mythology, Phule (2002b) wrote:

> [The] one great champion of the downtrodden, the holiest of the holy, the great sage and lover of Truth, Baliraja, came into this world. He realized that the great Almighty God, our great Father and Creator, had given us the true and holy knowledge and had granted everyone an equal right to it. He fathomed the Divine Will: that this knowledge be shared by all alike.
>
> Therefore he undertook the task of releasing his poor oppressed brethren from the bondage of slavery by the wicked, cunning and treacherous hunters like the Brahmins and to establish the kingdom of God on earth. Thus the prophecy of our ancient women – that one day Bali's kingdom will be established on earth once again, was realized at least to some extent.
>
> Millions became the followers of this Baliraja in Europe where he had brought about tremendous upheaval. All of them began to work ceaselessly for this noble task of establishing God's kingdom on earth (73–74).
>
> Several American and Scottish missionaries, followers of the Baliraja in the West, this Jesus Christ, came to this country, without the least regard for what their governments would say. They preached the true teachings of Jesus among the shudras and freed them from the deceit and slavery of the Brahmins (75).
>
> You know, I had written a play about how the *bhat-joshis* deceive the shudras with the rigmarole of their self-serving religion, and how the Christian missionaries disseminate true knowledge of their impartial religion among them to lead them onto the path of Truth (93).

When asked to explain the teachings of this "Baliraja" – this "Sacrifice King" – Phule, in succinct summary, replied that Baliraja was the one whose "great teaching is: 'You must love your enemy and do him a good turn'" – the "great teaching" paragraph that ends with the rule worth its weight in gold in terms of moral and civilizational transformation: "Do to others as you would have them do to you" (Phule 2002b, 236; Luke 6:27–31).

"'You must love your enemy and do him a good turn…and do to others what you would have them do to you.'" That core teaching of "the Baliraja in the West, that is Jesus Christ," was being received by Shudras and resisted by Brahmins in Phule's generation (Phule 2002b, 75). But that very "great teaching," by Phule's confrontational reasoning, was the exact initiating of a radically egalitarian social ethic that would uproot the caste tree and grow a new kind of society for his India, where "the code of proper conduct" would be to "judge others as you would judge yourself" (Phule 2002b, 236, 232).

Thus Jotirao Phule – who described India from Pune in the middle of the generation of Karl Marx (Blackburn and Dunaevskaya 2011), Abraham Lincoln (McPherson 2009; Wolf 2013, 47–49), Charles Darwin (Baum 1988; Barzun

1981), and Sir Syed Ahmad Khan (Troll 2013; Hasan 2006) – stands as a breathtaking conceptualizer for a new kind of India even today.

Shoots: The worldview mindset of Phule's India

The worldview lens by which those of India "generally view men and things" are "Brahmin spectacles." The character of those "spectacles" Phule delineated in detail. It is not a neutral description, but it is Phule's own voice piled up phrase upon phrase. It is a litany of disdain, a distaste born from what Phule discerned was the intent of that mentored way of seeing things: "Innumerable Bhut [Brahmin; literally, demon or spirit, especially a malevolent spirit] writers, with the selfsame objects as those of Manu and others of his class, added from time to time to the existing mass of legends, the idle phantasies of their own brain, and palmed them off upon the ignorant masses as of Divine inspiration, or as the acts of the Deity himself" (Phule 2002b, 31–32).

The goal of the Brahmin hegemony, Phule wrote, was "domination." "To achieve this devious goal," he argues, "they created the fraudulent rigmarole of the caste system and wrote several books to legitimize the caste system." In fact, to Phule's way of thinking, "their main object in fabricating these falsehoods was to dupe the minds of the ignorant and to rivet firmly on them the chains of perpetual bondage and slavery which their selfishness and cunning had forged" (Phule 2002b, 29, 45, 30). Thus the spectacles' power grew over time, magnifying misery to the Shudra and Atishudra masses. To Phule, it was "a mass of specious fiction," so that the masses themselves "still remain ignorant and captive in the mental slavery which the Brahmans have perpetuated through their books" (Phule 2002b, 30, 45) – ignorant of basic human rights, captive to Brahmanic hierarchical rites.

Finally, Phule often piled up multiple descriptors around the triad of "magic"/ "mantras"/"Manu," with a special place reserved for Manu-related literature. To Phule, the lens of the "earthborn gods" produced a comprehensive view, a systemic mindset perspective. A sampling from *Slavery* reveals that prevailing mindset as one of "magic," "black magic," or "Brahman black magic", which was often described by Phule as "all manner of ghosts and creatures and…mumbo-jumbo and magic." He assigns an entire section of *Slavery* to the exposure of what he calls Vedic magical incantations, the power of magic, being possessed by spirits, and "telling the beads" (recitation of sacred words using rosary beads) (Phule 2002b, 71–73; Wolf 2012e).

All told, Phule considered such a package to be a cohesive unit. Those intellectual shoots, to Phule, conveyed the worldvoice which instructed all the castes and was responsible for what he said were "poisoning their minds against each other," which was compiled from "books such as *smrutis, shastras, puranas, samhitas*" (compare translations of Phule 2002b, 71–73 with Phule 1991a, 32–35).

For Phule, then, those "Brahman spectacles" (the "mass of incredible fiction… found in the books of the Brahmins") were the cultural lens of analysis, the worldview shoots, which grew vigorously from the roots of Manu and

Manusmriti. With very non-neutral terms, Phule described the "fraudulent tales from the Bhagawata and rigmarole of the Vedic incantations," a wide and numerous assembly of "spurious religious books of the bhats," which he summarized as "fraudulent make-believe stories concocted by the Brahmans."

To Phule's thinking, then, those worldview "arguments" formed the shoots of India's WV3: the stories and interlocking-and-reinforcing ways of viewing everything from people to plants to planets, from cosmos to conception to caste to cremation (compare Parry 1994 and Parry 2004, 79–106, with Phule's 1873 "Now I will explain a little..." WV3 examples, Phule 2002b, 30, 123–130) – a thick grove of mantras, magic, myths and manipulations. It was precisely those "arguments" which were firmly "imprinted" and "implanted" in the secluded minds and social mazeways of the illiterate and uneducated Shudra and Atishudra masses (Phule 2002b, 32, 28, 74, 38, 119).

Fruits: The worldvenue mazeway of Phule's India

What were the fruits, the results, and reinforcements of such roots and shoots? "Thraldom" was Phule's one-word definition, a "system of slavery" (Phule 2002b, 31). And Phule allowed no one to mistake his evaluation about that "age-old prison house" social system: "To this system of selfish superstition and bigotry, we are to attribute the stagnation and all the evils under which India has been groaning for many centuries past" (Phule 2002b, 99, 31).

Phule profiled this system at one point by some eight recognizable worldvenue attributes of lifestyle attitudes and/or actions in his blunt, street-level conversation: (1) "they do not know they are human;" (2) they do not know "what their rights are;" (3) "they have worshipped stone and metal idols, cows, and snakes, and plants, and treated them as gods;" (4) "the farmers do not have the power of balanced thought;" (5) they "believe in all manner of ghosts and creatures;" (6) they "practice all manner of mumbo-jumbo and magic;" (7) they "waste their own money;" and (8) "they lose their lives, too, because they do not believe in medicine, but turn to shamans and magicians" (Phule 2002b, 170–171).

The fruits of the system had been cultivated and continued by perpetual isolation and by prohibitive exclusion. "From the prisons of the Brahmins," by Phule's reckoning, the Shudras "were like a prisoner who has been imprisoned for a long time and desperately looks forward to the day when he will be set free...because 1/10 of the total population, the Brahmans, had deprived 9/10 of the people of strength, intelligence, knowledge, skill and courage in matters of religion and state [worldvenue], hiding behind their scheming religion [worldvoice] and on the strength of their pens [worldview]" (Phule 2002b, 44, 151).

Completing the picture of his Maharashtra WV3 culture tree, Phule in *Slavery* concludes: "They strictly prohibited education of the Shudras and made strict rules about their books like the *Manusamhita*." To Phule, this strict prohibition of education had a built-in benefit: "Keeping the Shudras illiterate also enabled them to make whatever changes in their books they wanted to suit their interests" (Phule 2002b, 73).

And Phule made sure every reader felt the sting that all this was not simply by benign neglect. In *Whipcord*, Phule emphasizes that the non-education motif of these cultural non-freedom traditions was not shriveled and incidental fruit, but was full and intentional fruit: "This knowledge and education the ancestors of the Brahmins shut tight by prohibiting it in their selfish books" (Phule 2002b, 175).

For Phule had come to clearly see that, while some societies had been passive toward, and others neglectful of, the universal education of the masses, the Brahmin worldvoice and its caste worldview had a prominent and mandated worldvenue cultural distinctive: "They strictly prohibited education" of the backward and outcastes. "And now, even though they speak sweetly to all the farmers," Phule concluded that still "they avoid educating the farmer," being as they are a tree without shade for the poor (Phule 2002b, 73, 169).

Universal education: Savitribai and Jotirao Phule

But Jotirao and his wife Savitribai provided just such a shade for the children of Pune under the Baliraja tree. For their Baliraja worldvoice transformed their worldview, and they had an enormous worldvenue: education for all (Wolf and Andrade 2008; Brinkmann 2016). When asked to identify this "Baliraja" – this "Sacrifice King" – Phule replied that Baliraja was the one whose "great teaching is, 'Do to others what you would have them do to you'." That root teaching of a radical social ethic, Phule argued, would uproot the caste tree and grow a new kind of society, where "the code of proper conduct" would be to "judge others as you would judge yourself" (Phule 2002b, 236, 232).

As I have mentioned above, for Phule the cultural base for a transformed India lay neither in Gandhi's Brahmanism nor in Ambedkar's Buddhism (Parekh 2001; Chowdhury 2006). Instead, he could only see the flourishing of India in the cultural mentorship of Baliraja – the "Sacrifice King." Phule had no space in his vision, for example, for constructing Vivekananda's "European society with India's religion." Instead, recalling India's long history of non-freedom traditions and comparing European and North American societies to his 19th-century India, Phule was a wilderness voice when he cried out for the transformation of Indian society by Baliraja (Wolf 2010a, 2010b). But Phule saw that as the only way India could flourish. In the words of Govind Deshpande, seasoned by some 40 years of studying the man, Phule often "returned to this [Baliraja-Vamana] myth which, in his view, was central to all subsequent history. If that terminology were available to him, he may almost have said that all recorded history is the history of the Vamana-Baliraja struggle. Indeed he did describe Jesus as Baliraja" (Deshpande 2002b, 32, 48–68, 74–77, 83–84).

In Pune, then, Jotirao and Savitribai founded in 1848 the first ever Indian-originated school to educate Shudras (backward castes) and Atishudra (untouchables, now referenced as scheduled castes and scheduled tribes) children, including the girl child. By operating from a fresh-and-foreign kind of WV3 matrix, Savitribai (now widely acknowledged as India's "Mother of Education") designed an exemplary education program.

Starting from her core understanding that every child is unique and created by the Creator, Savitribai developed a framework of education that sought to revolutionize Brahmin Hindu India. The Savitribai educational framework was marked by four key features: it (1) conceived the scope of education as *universally available*; (2) introduced a teaching style that was *child-sensitive*; (3) insisted on a learning experience that was *intellectually critical*; and (4) concluded with an education system that was *socially reforming* (Wolf 2011a, 78–104; O'Hanlon 2002; Omvedt 2008).

The key social benefit, the experience of learning-for-all, was a concept totally unthinkable and hotly forbidden in the Brahmin system, as vividly preserved in the writings of Pune's other renowned resident, Bal Gangadhar Tilak (Rao 2010; Devare 2011). For as Jawaharlal Nehru University researcher Chinna Rao Yagati summarizes, "the old Indian system of education was non-universalistic, parochial and partisan…the product of an Indian outlook on knowledge and a corresponding scheme of life and values" (Yagati 2002, 84; O'Hanlon 2002; Devare 2011; Gupta 2002).

But Savitribai and Jotirao Phule's Baliraja radically reached out to teach and share all learning with all persons: a universal education for the backward castes, those without caste (the "outcastes" or those "without caste," and thus without humanity – Manu's "talking animals," 20% of India's population), and even – if it could be conceived – for females (who, traditionally understood, must die and become a male-something in order to attain *moksha*). For in Baliraja, Savitribai found a luminary with a liberating voice, a person of virtue unimaginable. Listening to that worldvoice, she constructed an uncommon 19th-century Indian educational worldvenue, where education was universally available, child-sensitive, intellectually critical and socially reforming (Phule 2002b, 128–129).

With the above in mind, then, Phule's WV3 culture tree of India can be constructed from his writings (Figure 11.3).

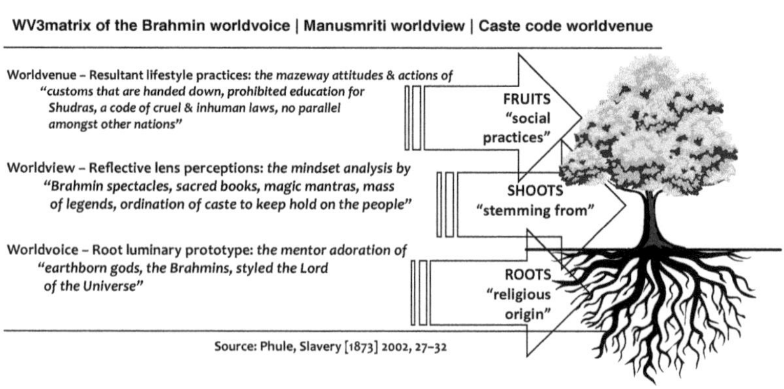

Figure 11.3 Phule's South Asian WV3 geo lifezone

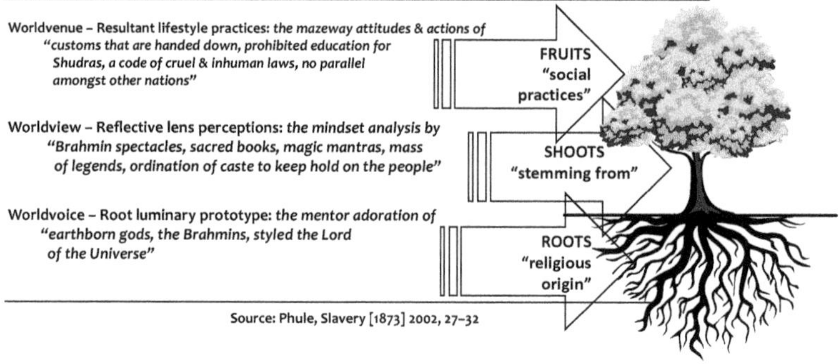

Conclusion

In WV3 terms, Phule saw his India as a whole. In his indigenous 19th-century vocabulary (Wolf 2010e), Phule saw the whole: he *located the worldvoice* in the Brahmins ("mythological legends" by "earthborn gods"), *found the worldview* to be consistently Manu-compatible ("Brahmin spectacles," "books to legitimize the caste system"), and *surveyed the worldvenue* as an everyday experience of a caste-coded-and-conducted geo lifezone "prison house": "this system…under which India has been groaning for many centuries past," "the chains of slavery…many customs traditionally handed down to us" by which "they totally prohibited education."

Phule's indigenous conclusion was that such a "system of despotism and priestcraft…can never create social unity," and "till a true unity is established, there will be no progress in this country" (Phule 2002b, 176, 178). His solution was to graft in the worldvoice of Baliraja (Wolf 2007a). For in the solitary truth of "Do to others what you would have others do to you," Phule envisioned the transformation of India's centuries-long stagnation.

Persistent issues being addressed by South Asian nations, illustrated here from Nepal and India, have provided case study examples where conceptual sap from religious roots produce discernible social fruits. Historically, Mahatma Jotirao Phule has provided a 19th-century comparative sociological reading of his own indigenous ground realities, focusing on the religiously rooted non-freedoms that have produced India's Sanskrit legacy of stern universal education prohibition.

Phule's writings might also be engaged for his WV3 prescriptions for how to change the reigning cultural matrix for those currently struggling with attempts at hybrid adaptations (Ramachandran 2004; Kumar and Oesterheld 2007; Kumar 2008; Sanger and Osguthorpe 2011; Alexander 2013; Brinkmann 2016). For Phule did not just wish for adaptations to change and adjust the "old Indian system of education [that] was non-universalistic, parochial and partisan." Many did that. Instead, Phule looked for an alternative with which to exchange that system. That he found in the Baliraja culture tree he saw growing among the British, the Americans and other culture trees: pleasant houses watered and built by Baliraja (Phule 2002b, 80, 88, 93). He and Savitribai set out to transplant those roots, shoots, and fruits with universal education for all the children of India (Wolf 2010b).

Surely then, the current concern of Nepal and others throughout South Asia over "social maladies stemming from religious origin" illustrates the long historical trajectory of the power of allegiances and the impact of ideas on social problems. And the compassionate and compelling voice of Phule still cries out against religious non-freedom traditions and the folk pedagogies that hamper universal education in the Indian social system. Deshpande's (2002a, 226) summary stands: Phule argues for "a monotheistic, humane, and benevolent system. That we as a people have not yet succeeded in doing this demonstrates the relevance of Phule."

Note

1 I only recently learned of the unfortunate news that Robert Edgerton passed away in July of 2016: http://www.anthro.ucla.edu/news/robert-b-edgerton-has-passed-away.

Bibliography

Abu-Lughod, Janet. 1989. *Before European Hegemony: The World System AD 1250–1350*. New York: Oxford University Press.

Afshari, Reza. 2001. *Human Rights in Iran: An Abuse of Cultural Relativism*. Philadelphia: University of Pennsylvania Press.

Ahmad, Omair. 2008. "Bronze Age Booming." *Outlook*, July 7. Accessed July 21, 2014. http://www.outlookindia.com/magazine/story/bronze-age-booming/237866.

Alexander, Robin. 2013. *Essays on Pedagogy*. London: Routledge.

Ambedkar, Bhimrao Ramji. 1946. *Who Were the Shudras?* Bombay: Thackers. AccessedJuly 30, 2016. http://164.100.47.134/plibrary/ebooks/Jagjivan%20Ram/(sno%207)jagjivan%20ram%201.pdf.

Ambedkar, Bhimrao Ramji. 2004. *The Essential Writings of B. R. Ambedkar*, ed. Valerian Rodrigues. New Delhi: Oxford University Press.

Amin, Samir. 2011. *Global History: A View from the South*. Cape Town: Pambazuka.

Anderson, James (ed.). 1955. *The World's Religions: Animism, Judaism, Islam, Hinduism, Buddhism, Shintoism, Confucianism*. London: InterVarsity.

Andrade, Suzanna, and Thom Wolf. 2009. "Savitribai Phule: You Owe Her, But Do You Know Her?" *Forward Press*, August.

Barzun, Jacques. 1981. *Darwin, Marx, Wagner: Critique of a Heritage*. Chicago: University of Chicago Press.

Baum, R. 1988. *Doctors of Modernity: Darwin, Marx, and Freud*. Peru, IL: Sherwood Sugden.

Bentley, Jerry. 1993. *Old World Encounters: Cross-Cultural Contacts and Exchanges in Pre-Modern Times*. New York: Oxford University Press.

Berger, Peter. 2011. "Introduction: Spiritual, Social, Human, and Financial Capital." In *The Hidden Form of Capital: Spiritual Influences in Societal Progress*, ed. Peter Berger and Gordon Redding. London: Anthem, 1–14.

Berger, Peter, and Gordon Redding (eds). 2011. *The Hidden Form of Capital: Spiritual Influences in Societal Progress*. London: Anthem.

Berzin, Alexander. 2006. "The Historical Interaction between the Buddhist and Islamic Cultures before the Mongol Empire." *The Berzin Archives*. Accessed August 3, 2016. http://studybuddhism.com/web/en/archives/e-books/unpublished_manuscripts/historical_interaction/pt2/history_cultures_08.html.

Berzin, Alexander. 2016. *Historical, Cultural, and Comparative Studies: Buddhism and Islam. The Berzin Archives*. Accessed August 3, 2016. http://www.berzinarchives.com/web/x/nav/n.html_1867868580.html.

Bista, Bikash. 2014. *National Population and Housing Census 2011* (*National Report*). Accessed July 21, 2014. http://cbs.gov.np/wp-content/uploads/2012/11/National%20Report.pdf.

Blackburn, Robin, and Raya Dunaevskaya. 2011. *An Unfinished Revolution: Marx and Lincoln*. London: Verso.

Boettke, Peter. 2011. "Spiritual Capital and Economic Development: An Overview." In *The Hidden Form of Capital: Spiritual Influences in Societal Progress*, ed. Peter Berger and Gordon Redding. London: Anthem, 29–39.

Bouquet, Alan. 1973. *Comparative Religions*. London: Penguin.

Braunthal, Alfred. 1979. *Salvation and the Perfect Society: The Eternal Quest*. Amherst, MA: University of Massachusetts Press.

Brinkmann, Suzanna. 2016. *The Role of Teachers' Beliefs in the Implementation of Learner-Centered Education in India*. PhD Dissertation, University College London.

Carrington, Philip. 1940. *The Primitive Christian Catechism: A Study in the Epistles*. Cambridge: Cambridge University Press.

Chowdhury, Prasenjit. 2006. "Blinkered Pastiche of a Cliché." *Hardnews*, November.

Chowdhury, Sagnik, Abantika Ghosh and Ruhi Tewari. 2015. "Census 2011: Hindus Dip to Below 80 Per Cent of Population; Muslim Share Up, Slows Down." *Indian Express*. August 27. Accessed August 2, 2016. http://indianexpress.com/article/india/india-others/indias-population-121-09-crores-hindus-79-8-pc-muslims-14-2-pc-census/.

Collier, Paul. 2015. *Exodus: How Migration is Changing Our World*. Oxford: Oxford University Press.

Courtois, Stephane, Nicolas Werth, Jean-Louis Panne, Andrzej Paczkowski, Karel Bartosek and Jean-Louis Margolin. 1999. *The Communist Black Book: Crimes, Terror, Repression*. Cambridge: Harvard University Press.

Dailyhunt. 2015. "Special Report: Maharashtra's 'Maha' Heritage Enriches Delhi's Grandeur" January 23. Accessed July 29, 2016. http://m.dailyhunt.in/news/india/english/hastakshep-english-epaper-hastaksh/maharashtras-maha-heritage-enriches-delhis-grandeur-newsid-45832664.

Das, Bijoyeta. 2014. "Nepal's Menstrual Exiles." *Al Jazeera*, February 10. Accessed July 1, 2014. http://www. aljazeera.com/indepth/features/2014/02/nepal-menstrual-exiles-201423131149488509.html.

de Blij, Harm. 2010. *The Power of Place: Geography, Destiny, and Globalization's Rough Landscape*. New York: Oxford University Press.

de Blij, Harm, Peter Muller and Jan Nijman. 2016. *Geography: Realms, Regions and Concepts*. New York: John Wiley.

Deshpande, Govind. 2002a. "Introduction, from The Book of Truth. Preface 1 April 1889." In Jotirao Phule, *Selected Writings of Jotirao Phule*, ed. and trans. Govind Deshpande. New Delhi: LeftWord, 226–227.

Deshpande, Govind (ed.). 2002b. *Selected Writings of Jotirao Phule*. New Delhi: LeftWord.

Devare, Aparna. 2011. *History and the Making of a Modern Hindu Self*. New Delhi: Routledge.

Dilworth, David. 1989. *Philosophy in World Perspective: A Comparative Hermeneutic of the Major Theories*. New Haven: Yale University Press.

Edgell, Alvin. 2003. "Globalization and Cultural Encounters." *International Third World Studies Journal* 14: 1–9. Accessed July 5, 2014. http://www.unomaha.edu/itwsjr/thirdXIV/Edgell.Globalization.14.htm.

Edgerton, Robert. 1992. *Sick Societies: Challenging the Myth of Primitive Harmony*. New York: The Free Press.

Edgerton, Robert. 2005. *The Balance of Human Kindness and Cruelty: Why We Are the Way We Are*. Lewiston, NY: Edwin Mellen.

East, William. 1965. *The Geography behind History: How Physical Environment Affects Historical Events*. New York: Norton.

Eisenstadt, Shmuel (ed.). 1986. *The Origins and Diversity of Axial Age Civilizations*. New York: State University of New York Press.

Emilsen, William. 2001. *Gandhi's Bible*. New Delhi: ISPCK.

Fellmann, Jerome, and Arthur Getis. 1990. *Human Geography: Landscapes of Human Activities*. New York: WCB Macmillan.

Ferguson, Niall. 2012. *Civilization: The Six Killer Apps of Western Power*. London: Penguin.

Freedman, David, and Michael McClymond. 2001. *The Rivers of Paradise: Moses, Buddha, Confucius, Jesus and Muhammad as Religious Founders*. Grand Rapids, MI: Eerdmans.

Gaestel, Allyn. 2013. "Nepal: Chaupadi Culture and Violence against Women." *Pulitzer Center*, February 5. Accessed August 1, 2014. http://pulitzercenter.org/projects/nepal-cultural-practice-women-rights-sexual-violence-chaupadi-migration-WHO.

Gellner, David. 2007. "Nepal: Towards a Democratic Republic." *Economic and Political Weekly*, May 19: 1823–1828. Accessed July 15, 2014. http://www.uni-bielefeld.de/midea/pdf/darticle2.pdf.

George, Rose. 2014. "How Can Sanitary Pads Be Made more Widely Available in Low-Income Countries?" *Pacific Standard*, April 24. Accessed August 1, 2014. http://www.psmag.com/navigation/health-and-behavior/can-sanitary-pads-made-widely-available-low-income-countries-79902/.

Goucher, Candice, Charles LeGuin and Linda Walton. 2004. "Religion and State: Buddhism, Christianity, and Islam." In *In the Balance: Themes in World History*. Boston: McGraw-Hill. Accessed July 21, 2014. http://www.learner.org/courses/worldhistory/support/reading_7_1.pdf.

Government of India, Ministry of Home Affairs. 2016. Accessed August 1, 2016. http://www.censusindia.gov.in/.

Graham, Gordon. 1997. *The Shape of the Past: A Philosophical Approach to History*. New York: Oxford University Press.

Guha, Ranajit. 2002. *History at the Limit of World-History*. New Delhi: Oxford University Press.

Gupta, Dipankar. 2004. *Ethics Incorporated: Top Priority and Bottom Line*. New Delhi: Sage.

Gupta, Natthulala. 2002. *Mahatma Jotiba Phule: An Educational Philosopher*. New Delhi: Anmol.

Hannan, Daniel. 2013. *Inventing Freedom: How the English-Speaking Peoples Made the Modern World*. New York: HarperCollins.

Harrison, Lawrence. 1985. *Underdevelopment Is a State of Mind: The Latin American Case*. Lanham, MD: University Press of America.

Harrison, Lawrence. 2000. *Underdevelopment Is a State of Mind: The Latin American Case*. Lanham, MD: Madison.

Harrison, Lawrence. 2008. *The Central Liberal Truth: How Politics Can Change a Culture and Save It from Itself*. New York: Oxford University Press.

Harrison, Lawrence. 2011. "Do Some Religions Do Better than Others?" In *The Hidden Form of Capital: Spiritual Influences in Societal Progress*, ed. Peter Berger and Gordon Redding. London: Anthem, 15–28.

Harrison, Lawrence. 2013. *Jews, Confucians, and Protestants: Cultural Capital and the End of Multiculturalism*. Lanham, MD: Rowman and Littlefield.

Hasan, Tariq. 2006. *The Aligarh Movement and the Making of the Indian Muslim Mind (1857–2002)*. New Delhi: Rupa.

Huntington, Samuel. 1996. *The Clash of Civilizations and the Remaking of World Order*. New York: Simon and Schuster.

Hussain, Nadia. 2011. "Chaupadi Pratha: Tradition or Torment?" *Restless Beings*, September 19. Accessed July 21, 2014. http://www.restlessbeings.org/human-rights/chaupadi-pratha-tradition-or-torment.

Ilaiah, Kancha. 2004. *Buffalo Nationalism: A Critique of Spiritual Fascism*. Kolkata: Samya.

Inglehart, Ronald, and Christian Welzel. 2005. *Modernization, Cultural Change, and Democracy: The Human Development Sequence*. Cambridge: Cambridge University Press.

Jadhav, Narendra. 2014. *Ambedkar: Awakening India's Social Conscience*. New Delhi: Konark.

Jaffrelot, Christophe. 1996. *The Hindu Nationalist Movement and Indian Politics: 1925 to the 1990s*. New York: Columbia University Press.

Jaspers, Karl. 1953. *The Origin and Goal of History*. New Haven: Yale University Press.

Jaspers, Karl. 1966. *Socrates, Buddha, Confucius, Jesus*. New York: Harvest.

Jensen, Ida, and Zalla Mandozai. 2014. *The Caste System in Nepal – According to the Youth*. Esbjerg, DK: Syddansk Universitet Esbjergat. AccessedJuly 25, 2014. http://static.sdu.dk/mediafiles/7/6/D/%7B76DA09E2-D87A-4F4A-ABC7-FCD175FE8A2F%7DEksempel_5%20sem_Nepal_Semesterprojekt.pdf.

Jha, Hari. 1997. "In God's Name: Community Activists Seek to End the Sale of Girls to Temples." *Hinduism Today*. Accessed August 3, 2016. http://www.hinduismtoday.com/modules/smartsection/item.php?itemid=4954.

Kahan, Alan. 2015. *Tocqueville, Democracy, and Religion: Checks and Balances for Democratic Souls*. Oxford: Oxford University Press.

Kakar, Sudhir, and Katharina Kakar. 2007. *The Indians: Portrait of a People*. New Delhi: Penguin.

Kaplan, Robert. 2013. *The Revenge of Geography: What the Map Tells Us about Coming Conflicts and the Battle against Fate*. New York: Random House.

Kaplan, Robert. 2015. *Asia's Cauldron: The South Pacific Sea and the End of a Stable Pacific*. New York: Random House.

Kapoor, Jaskiran. 2014. "Cycle of Change." *Indian Express*, July 31. Accessed August 1, 2014. http://indianexpress.com/article/cities/delhi/cycle-of-change/.

Keer, Dhananjay. 1974. *Mahatma Jotirao Phooley: Father of Indian Social Revolution*. Bombay: Popular Prakashan.

Khanna, Parag. 2016. *Connectography: Mapping the Future of Global Civilization*. New York: Random House.

Kumar, Krishna. 2008. *A Pedagogue's Romance: Reflections on Schooling*. New Delhi: Oxford University Press.

Kumar, Krishna, and J. Oesterheld (eds). 2007. *Social Change and Education in South Asia*. New Delhi: Orient Longman.

Lewis, Martin, and Karen Wigen. 1997. *The Myth of Continents: A Critique of Megageography*. Berkeley: University of California Press.

Madan, Gurmukh. 2010. *Western Sociologists on Indian Society: Marx, Spencer, Weber, Durkheim, Pareto*. London: Routledge.

Maharashtra Sadan. 2016. "History of Maharashtra Sadan."New Delhi. Accessed July 29, 2016. https://maharashtrasadan.maharashtra.gov.in/HistoryofmaharashtraSadan.html.

Mahbubani, Kishore. 2002. *Can Asians Think? Understanding the Divide between East and West*. South Royalton, VT: Steerforth.

Mahbubani, Kishore. 2013. *The Great Convergence: Asia, the West, and the Logic of One World*. Washington, DC: Public Policy.

Mahdavi, Majtaba. 2005. "Max Weber in Iran: Does Islamic Protestantism Matter?" Ottawa: Canadian Political Science Association. Accessed July 26, 2016. https://www.cpsa-acsp.ca/papers-2005/Mahdavi.pdf.

Mahto, Ram. 2012. *Research Report on Socio-Cultural Status of Other Backward Communities of Saptari and Siraha District*. Kathmandu: SIRF Secretariat. Accessed July 22, 2014. http://www.socialinclusion.org.np/new/files/Ram%20Narayan%20Mahato_1365494079dWhX.pdf.

Malik-Goure, Archana. 2013. *Jyotiba Phule: A Modern Indian Philosopher*. New Delhi: Suryodaya.

Malla, Uttam. 2012. *National Population and Housing Census 2011* (*National Report*). Kathmandu: Central Bureau of Statistics, Government of Nepal. Accessed July 21, 2014. http://cbs.gov.np/image/data/Population/National%20Report/National%20Report.pdf.

Mampatta, Sachin. 2015. "Four Out of Five Indians Will Still Be Hindu even when Muslim Population Peaks." *Live Mint*, September 16. Accessed August 2, 2016. http://www.livemint.com/Opinion/5bsICkXvl4t4hXSewk8bkN/Four-out-of-five-Indians-will-still-be-Hindu-even-when-Musli.html.

Mandal, Monika (ed.). 2014. *Indo-Nepal Relations*. New Delhi: KW.

Mangalwadi, Vishal. 2013. *Why Are We Backward? Exploring the Roots, Exploding the Myths, Embracing True Hope*. New Delhi: Forward.

Martin-Gorski, Darla. 2002. "Sick Societies and Islamic Nations." PHI 579 Religion: Revolt, Terrorism, and War. Buffalo: State University of New York at Buffalo. http://ontology.buffalo.edu/smith/courses01/papers/Gorski.pdf.

Massey, James. 2003. *Dr. B. R. Ambedkar: A Study in Just Society*. New Delhi: Manohar.

McGrath, Alister. 2007. *Christianity's Dangerous Idea: The Protestant Revolution – A History from the Sixteenth Century to the Twenty-First*. New York: HarperOne.

McNeill, William. 1963. *The Rise of the West: A History of the Human Community*. Chicago: University of Chicago Press.

McPherson, James. 2009. *Abraham Lincoln*. New York: Oxford University Press.

Meddeb, Abdelwahab. 2003. *The Malady of Islam*. New York: Basic.

Mehta, Pratap. 2003. *The Burden of Democracy*. New Delhi: Penguin.

Mehta, Vinod. 2014. "Mr. Modi, Time to Play Fast and Loos [sic]." *Times of India*, July 20. Accessed August 8, 2016. http://timesofindia.indiatimes.com/home/stoi/deep-focus/Mr-Modi-time-to-play-fast-and-loos/articleshow/38713223.cms.

Miklian, Jason. 2009. "Nepal's Terai: Constructing an Ethnic Conflict." *PRIO South Asia Briefing Paper # 1*. Oslo: International Peace Research Institute. AccessedJuly 5, 2014. http://file.prio.no/Publication_files/Prio/Nepal's%20Terai%20(South%20Asia%20Briefing%20Paper%201).pdf.

Mishra, Suresh. 2010. "Making of Panchayati Raj Institutions and Dr. Ambedkar." In *Socio-Economic and Political Vision of Dr. B. R. Ambedkar*, ed. Mishra Suresh. New Delhi: Concept, 211–222.

Mitchell, Joshua. 2013. *Tocqueville in Arabia: Dilemmas in a Democratic Age*. Chicago: University of Chicago Press.

Murphey, Rhoads. 1971. *An Introduction to Geography*. Chicago: Rand McNally.

Nasr, Vali. 2007. *The Shia Revival: How Conflicts in Islam Will Shape the Future*. New York: Norton.

National Discovery Channel. 2013. "Custom and Tradition of Nepal." February 6. Accessed August 1, 2014. http://www.nationaldiscoverychannel.com/2013/01/custom-and-tradition-of-nepal.html.

National Population and Housing Census 2011. 2012. Kathmandu: Government of Nepal National Planning Secretariat. Accessed August 10, 2016. http://cbs.gov.np/image/data/Population/National%20Report/National%20Report.pdf.

Nelson, Eric. 2010. *The Hebrew Republic: Jewish Sources and the Transformation of European Political Thought*. Cambridge: Harvard University Press.

Nemo, Philippe. 2005. *What Is the West?* Pittsburgh: Duquesne University Press.

Nolan, Patrick, and Gerhard Lenski. 2010. *Human Societies: An Introduction to Macrosociology*. Boulder, CO: Paradigm.

O'Hanlon, Rosalind. 2002. *Caste, Conflict and Ideology: Jotirao Phule and Lower Caste Protest in Nineteenth-Century Maharashtra*. Cambridge: Cambridge University Press.

Omvedt, Gail. 1976. *Cultural Revolt in a Colonial Society: The Non-Brahman Movement in Western India, 1873–1930*. Bombay: Scientific Socialist Education Trust.

Omvedt, Gail. 2008. *Seeking Begumpura: The Social Vision of Anticaste Intellectuals*. New Delhi: Navayana.

Parekh, Bhikhu. 2001. *Gandhi: A Very Brief Introduction*. Oxford: Oxford University Press.

Parrinder, Geoffrey. 1976. *Introduction to Asian Religions*. Oxford: Oxford University Press.

Parry, Jonathan. 1994. *Death in Banaras*. Cambridge: Cambridge University Press.

Parry, Jonathan. 2004. "Death and Cosmogony in Kashi." In *India's Religions: Perspectives from Sociology and History*, ed. Triloki Madan. New Delhi: Oxford University Press, 79–106.

Paudel, Sujata. 2011. "Nepal: Witchcraft as a Superstition and a Form of Violence against Women in Nepal." *Asian Human Rights Commission*. Accessed July 21, 2014. http://www.humanrights.asia/opinions/columns/AHRC-ETC-056-2011.

Peyrefitte, Alain. 1986. *The Trouble with France*. New York: New York University Press.

Phule, Jotirao. 1991a. *Slavery. Collected Works of Mahatma Jotirao Phule*, Vol. 1, trans. P. G. Patil. Mumbai: Education Department, Government of Maharashtra.

Phule, Jotirao. 1991b. *Selections. Collected Works of Mahatma Jotirao Phule*, Vol. 2, trans. P. G. Patil. Mumbai: Education Department, Government of Maharashtra.

Phule, Jotirao. 2002a. *Cultivator's Whipcord. Collected Works of Mahatma Phule*, Vol. 3, trans. Asha Mundlay. Mumbai: Education Department, Government of Maharashtra.

Phule, Jotirao. 2002b. *Selected Writings of Jotirao Phule*, ed. Govind Deshpande. New Delhi: LeftWord.

Ramachandran, Vimala. 2004. *Gender and Social Equity in Primary Education: Hierarchies of Access*. New Delhi: Sage.

Rao, Parimala. 2010. *Foundations of Tilak's Nationalism: Discrimination, Education and Hindutva*. New Delhi: Orient BlackSwan.

Rao, Raghavendra. 1993. *Babasaheb Ambedkar*. New Delhi: Sahitya Akademi.

Roche, Elizabeth and Nikita Mehta. 2014. "India Falls Short of UN's MDG Goals." *Live Mint*, July 16. Accessed July 22, 2014. http://blog.livemint.com/Politics/9VWB3A0iSrwG3Jrw5zt88J/India-falls-short-on-UNs-MDG-goals.html.

Rousseau, Jean Jacques. 1755. *A Discourse on the Origin and the Foundation of the Inequality among Mankind*. Accessed May 5, 2015. http://kms1.isn.ethz.ch/serviceengine/Files/ISN/28868/ipriadoc_doc/676F9B89-B107-4571-AF9F-C03D42C8264A/en/616.pdf.

Rubenstein, James. 2016. *The Cultural Landscape: An Introduction to Human Geography*. 12th ed. New York: Pearson Education.

Sanger, Matthew, and Richard Osguthorpe. 2011. "Teacher Education, Preservice Teacher Beliefs, and the Moral Work of Teaching." *Teaching and Teacher Education* 27(3): 569–578. http://dx.doi.org/10.1016/j.tate.2010.10.011.

Sangroula, Sangeet. 2014. "War on Social Evils: Interfaith Alliance to Take on the Ills of Society." *Republica*, June 30. Accessed July 1, 2014. http://e.myrepublica.com/2014/component/flippingbook/book/1645-republica-01-jul-2014/1-republica.html.

Schaeffer, Francis. 1969. *Death in the City*. Wheaton, IL: Crossway.

Shah, Ghanshyam. 2007. "Gujarat after Godhra." In *India's 2004 Elections: Grass Roots and National Perspectives*, ed. Ramashray Roy and Paul Wallace. New Delhi: Sage, 151–179.

Shain, Brian. 1996. *The Myth of American Individualism: The Protestant Origins of American Political Thought*. Princeton: Princeton University Press.

Shambaugh, David. 2013. *China Goes Global: The Partial Power*. New York: Oxford University Press.

Sharma, Aabhas. 2011. "Mayawati's Statues of Liberty." *Business Standard*, November 5. Accessed August 10, 2016. http://www.business-standard.com/article/beyond-business/mayawati-s-statues-of-liberty-111110500008_1.html.

Sharma, Jyotirmaya. 2011. *Hindutva: Exploring the Idea of Hindu Nationalism*. New Delhi: Penguin.

Sharma, Jyotirmaya. 2013. *Cosmic Love and Human Apathy: Swami Vivekananda's Restatement of Religion*. New Delhi: HarperCollins.

Sood, Vinay (ed.). 2005. *The Individual and Society: Essays, Stories, and Poems*. Delhi: Pearson Education.

Stevenson, Leslie, David Haberman and Peter Wright. 2012. *Twelve Theories of Human Nature*. New Delhi: Oxford University Press.

Strathern, Alan. 2013. "Why Are Buddhist Monks Attacking Muslims?" *BBC News Magazine*, May 2. Accessed July 21, 2014. http://www.bbc.com/news/magazine-22356306.

Stuenkel, Oliver. 2016. *Post-Western World: How Emerging Powers Are Remaking Global Order*. Cambridge: Polity.

Sutton, Peter. 2005. "Rage, Reason, and the Honourable Cause: A Reply to Cowlishaw." *Australian Aboriginal Studies* 2: 35–43. Accessed July 21, 2014. http://www.arts.kuleuven.be/ling/fest/cyp/sutton/2005aas.pdf.

Sutton, Peter. 2011. *The Politics of Suffering: Indigenous Australia and the End of the Liberal Consensus*. Melbourne: Melbourne University Press.

Tarnas, Richard. 1991. *The Passion of the Western Mind: Understanding the Ideas that Have Shaped our Worldview*. New York: Ballantine.

Taittiriya Brahmana. 2011. *Taittiriya Brahmana*. Accessed July 28, 2014. http://www.sacred-texts.com/hin/sbe48/sbe48167.htm.

Thakur, Shivesh. 1969. *Christian and Hindu Ethics*. London: Unwin.

Thapliyal, Sangeeta. 2014. "Perception of the Other – Myths or Realities." In *Indo-Nepal Relations*, ed. Monika Mandal. New Delhi: KW, 75–110.

The Economist. 2013. "Buddhism v Islam in Asia: Fears of a New Religious Strife." July 27. Accessed July 21, 2014. http://www.economist.com/news/asia/21582321-fuelled-dangerous-brew-faith-ethnicity-and-politics-tit-tat-conflict-escalating.

Troll, Christopher. 2013 [1979]. *Sayyid Ahmad Khan: A Reinterpretation of Muslim Theology*. New Delhi: University Institute.

Upreti, Bishnu. 2014. "Positioning India and Nepal in Contemporary Context: A Review of the Context, Dynamics and Issues." In *Indo-Nepal Relations*, ed. Monika Mandal. New Delhi: KW, 1–22.

Verma, Nirmal. 2000. *India and Europe: Selected Essays*. Shimla: Centre for the Study of Indian Civilization and Indian Institute of Advanced Study.

Wolf, Thom. 2007a. "Progress-Prone and Progress-Resistant Cultures: Worldview Issues and the Baliraja Proposal of Mahatma Phule." *Journal of Contemporary Social Work* 1: 1–52.

Wolf, Thom. 2007b. "Three Challenges for Buddhism of the 21st Century." In *Buddhism in the Contemporary World: An Ambedkarian Perspective*, ed. Bhalchandra Mungekar and Aakash Rathore. New Delhi: Bookwell, 29–48.

Wolf, Thom. 2008. *Phule in His Own Words*. New Delhi: University Institute.

Wolf, Thom. 2010a. "*Mahatma Phule on the History of Maharashtra and India. History Session – Maharashtra at 50: Ideas of India.*" New Delhi: Nehru Memorial Museum and Library Auditorium.

Wolf, Thom. 2010b. "Jyotiba Phule's View of History and the Social Reform Movement. From Gulamgiri to Asmita." *Talk*. New Delhi: Indian International Centre.

Wolf, Thom. 2010c. "Progress-Prone and Progress-Resistant Societies: Mariano Grondoña's Paradox and A Cultural Typology of Humane Development." *Talk*. Moscow: Finance and Budget Academy of the Finance Ministry of the Russian Federation.

Wolf, Thom. 2010d. *Phule: Apne Hi Shabdon Mein*. New Delhi: Aspire Prakashan.

Wolf, Thom. 2010e. "Phule's Fire." *Forward Press* (May): 22–24.

Wolf, Thom. 2011a. "Changing Education: The Changing Education: The 'Unusual and Unique' Worldvoice, Worldview, and Worldvenue of Jan Comenius and Savitribai Phule." *Journal of Applied Christian Leadership* 5(2): 78–104.

Wolf, Thom. 2011b. *Social Change and Development: A Research Template*. Srinagar: The Business School, University of Kashmir.

Wolf, Thom. 2011c. "Nepal and Switzerland: Two Different Trains, Two Different Bird Cages Part 1." *Forward Press* (December): 56–60.

Wolf, Thom. 2012a. "Nepal and Switzerland: Two Different Trains, Two Different Bird Cages Part 2." *Forward Press* (January): 58–62.

Wolf, Thom. 2012b. "WV3: Worldvoice, Worldview, Worldvenue." *Oikos Worldviews Bulletin* 12(1): 13–23.

Wolf, Thom. 2012c. "The Geo Zones." *Lecture 2*, Swallen Lectures. Berrien Springs, MI: Andrews University.

Wolf, Thom. 2012d. "Eight Contending Options." *Lecture 3*, Swallen Lectures. Berrien Springs, MI: Andrews University.

Wolf, Thom. 2012e. "Shivalinga: A WV3 Case Study." In *India: WV3 Voices, Views, and Venues.* New Delhi: University Institute, 22–24.

Wolf, Thom. 2013. "Abraham Lincoln and Jotirao Phule: The India Connection." *Forward Pres* (February): 47–49.

Wolf, Thom, and Suzanna Andrade. 2008. *Savitribai and India's Conversation on Education.* New Delhi: University Institute.

Yagati, Chinna Rao. 2002. "Education and Identity Formation among Dalits in Colonial Andhra." In *Education and the Disprivileged: Nineteenth- and Twentieth-Century India*, ed. Sabyasachi Bhattacharya. New Delhi: Orient Longman, 84–120.

12 Religious liberty in Brazil

Piecing the puzzle together through contemporary decisions

Katya Kozicki and William Soares Pugliese

1. Introduction

The matter of religious liberty is a nebulous one in Brazil. As religious liberty is guaranteed by the Brazilian Constitution (Article 5, VI) and by Brazil's ratification of the United Nations Universal Declaration of Human Rights (UDHR), an analysis of the most recent precedents should point to a broad understanding of religion.

This is not the case, however, if one examines decisions from Brazil's Federal Supreme Court. Apart from the traditional Catholic belief, religious liberty as granted by the Brazilian Constitution is not interpreted as broadly as it should be if the UDHR is to be taken into account, as the Declaration grants freedom of conscience and freedom of action. On the contrary, whenever a matter of religion reaches the courts in Brazil, the most common result is an answer limited by little knowledge of the matter: an answer that excludes many aspects of unorthodox religions from the realm of constitutional protection.

The purpose of this essay is to demonstrate the gap between the constitutional and statutory protection given to religious liberty, on the one hand, and the narrow understanding of religions by the courts, on the other hand. Therefore, the first part of this essay will present the constitutional guarantees related to religion, while the second part will examine a few decisions of Brazil's Federal Supreme Court that relate to religion.

In short, there is one major flaw in Brazil's definition of religious liberty: it understands religion by metaphysical belief instead of by what Ronald Dworkin calls "ethical independence" (Dworkin 2013). This right, which allows for freedom of conscience and freedom of action, without the need for a holy book or for a metaphysical explanation of the world, shall guide our approach to the theme.

2. The scope of religious liberty in Brazil founded on the Constitution and statutes

The Brazilian Constitution mentions the word "religion" or one of its synonyms a total of seven times. Right at the beginning of the document, freedom of conscience and freedom of belief are claimed to be fundamental rights. Furthermore, religious assistance in hospitals and other places of isolation is guaranteed. Article

5 also states that no one shall be deprived of any rights by reason of religious belief or political conviction. The text of the Constitution reads as follows:

> Article 5. All persons are equal before the law, without any distinction whatsoever, Brazilians and foreigners residing in the country being ensured of inviolability of the right to life, to liberty, to equality, to security and to property, on the following terms:
>
> VI – freedom of conscience and of belief is inviolable, the free exercise of religious cults being ensured and, under the terms of the law, the protection of places of worship and their rites being guaranteed;
>
> VII – under the terms of the law, the rendering of religious assistance in civil and military establishments of collective confinement is ensured;
>
> VIII – no one shall be deprived of any rights by reason of religious belief or philosophical or political conviction, unless he invokes it to exempt himself from a legal obligation required of all and refuses to perform an alternative obligation established by law.[1]

From the very beginning of the constitutional guarantees, freedom of religion and conscience are, or should be, protected by every political or state institution in Brazil. Moreover, by claiming that these liberties are inviolable and that no one shall be deprived of rights because of religious belief, Brazil should respect and treat all religions equally, despite the number of followers, philosophy, or any other criterion which is not offensive to the "terms of the law."

The Brazilian Constitution also prohibits state organizations from establishing or subsidizing religious sects or churches:

> Article 19. The Union, the states, the Federal District and the municipalities are forbidden to: I – establish religious sects or churches, subsidize them, hinder their activities, or maintain relationships of dependence or alliance with them or their representatives, without prejudice to collaboration in the public interest in the manner set forth by law.

Article 143 of the Brazilian Constitution allows followers of certain religions to require different services from those typical of the armed forces (which are compulsory for men, unless they are exempted):

> Article 143. Military service is compulsory as set forth by law.
>
> Paragraph 1. It is within the competence of the Armed Forces, according to the law, to assign an alternative service to those who, in times of peace, after being enlisted, claim imperative of conscience, which shall be understood as originating in religious creed and philosophical or political belief, for exemption from essentially military activities.

There is also a provision for optional religious education for children attending public schools.[2] The last topic on religion in the Brazilian Constitution, however, must be highlighted. The second paragraph of Article 226 determines that religious marriage has civil effects:

> Article 226. The family, which is the foundation of society, shall enjoy special protection from the State. Paragraph 1. Marriage is civil and the marriage ceremony is free of charge. Paragraph 2. Religious marriage has civil effects, in accordance with the law.

The first reading of Brazil's Constitution has but only one conclusion: there is broad freedom of religion and conscience in Brazil because people are allowed to choose whichever belief they prefer and because this choice has a wide range of positive effects, from military service to marriage. On the other hand, there is little reason to be concerned with prejudice because the state can only assign alternative services and cannot deprive anyone of any right, except for legal obligations. It is also important to remember that Brazil has ratified the UDHR. Therefore, statutes granting freedom of thought, conscience and religion are in effect in the country. It must be stressed, also, that in Brazil international treaties concerning human rights are to be treated as Constitutional Amendments.[3]

This legal frame granting religious freedom has usually been regarded as highly inclusive of all religions. For some Brazilian scholars, these constitutional guarantees in combination with the UDHR form a system which grants a right of religious liberty based on the following principles: i) autonomy and tolerance; ii) freedom of speech and religious freedom; iii) free exercise of religion; and iv) separation between church and state (Almeida 2006).

The first principle (autonomy and tolerance) must be understood in the sense that people have a right to choose their own beliefs and that the state will be politically tolerant, thus making it compatible with the ideals of equality and pluralism.[4] The second principle, of freedom of speech and religious freedom, aims to grant the right that every citizen may believe only in what is capable of convincing his or her own conscience, granting protection from anyone who wishes to impose their convictions, especially by force.[5]

By the free exercise of religion, the third principle, all citizens should be granted the right to make their own decisions concerning religious beliefs, which are not prohibited by the state. Therefore, Brazil's legal framework concerning religion allows, for example, Jehovah's Witnesses to refuse blood transfusions because the state must respect individual decisions grounded on equal consideration of the interests and values of the person.[6] All this is complemented by the fourth principle, that of separation between church and state.

This whole idea based on the four principles briefly described above seems to have been apprehended and improved by Ronald Dworkin (2013) in his *Religion without God*, when the right of religious liberty is described as the right for ethical independence (Kozicki and Pugliese 2013). In this sense, the description of the legal landscape of the Brazilian treatment of religious liberty appears to be one of the most inclusive, pluralistic and respectful of diversity. This, however, is not what is found when one descends from the statutes and studies some of the decisions held by the Brazilian courts. And it is to these decisions that we now turn.

3. Religious liberty and contemporary decisions

There are not many judicial decisions in Brazil that receive much treatment by the press. There are a few exceptions, however, and one of them is specifically related to the theme of this essay. To be covered by the press, the basic rule in Brazil is that the decision must be either highly innovative or highly retrograde. The decision taken on April 29, 2014, is a clear example of the latter.

At the beginning of the year, a few videos were posted on YouTube, a video streaming website now owned by Google, that criticized African-American religions, especially Umbanda and Candomblé, and said that their believers worshipped the devil and that the religions were related to witchcraft and drug use. The Public Ministry requested a preliminary injunction, arguing that the videos disseminated prejudice, intolerance and discrimination against African-American religions.

After looking into the request, a federal judge denied it, arguing that although Umbanda and Candomblé were "manifestations of religiousness" they did not have the "necessary traits of a religion, that is, a basic text (Koran, Bible, etc.)... hierarchical structure and...a God to be worshiped."[7] Thus, instead of reading the Constitution on its broadest protection for religious liberty, a judge denied religious status to two of the most typical religions from Brazil on the basis that they lacked a basic text and a God that is to be worshipped. With this understanding, there will be dozens of religions in Brazil that may be in danger of being excluded from legal protection. In less than a day, this decision had caused immense repercussions, with a lot of criticisms of the ruling being made on the Internet. The judge added a few clarifications, stating that the decision was not final and that there were religious traces in African beliefs, but he did not reconsider what was previously decided.

As unfortunate as this example is, many people had begun to take notice of a much bigger issue: despite all the constitutional protections of religious liberty, almost every belief that is not Catholic or Protestant tends to be treated with a lack of respect in the court system. Besides this particular case, there are many other examples relating to non-Christian religions that are not covered in any great detail by the press.

One of them is the number of suits filed against civil registries in Brazil that deny the effects of marriages that were sanctified via non-Catholic religious ceremonies. Again, Candomblé and Umbanda figure prominently in the suits, but they are joined by Spiritualism and Buddhism (and other religions). What this situation shows is that, although religious liberty is guaranteed by Brazil's Constitution, some aspects of the protections that it offers are what Karl Llewellyn has called "paper rules," not real rules (Llewellyn 2011, 27).

On another occasion, Brazil's Federal Supreme Court had to decide whether Masonry could be considered a religion under the Brazilian Constitution, a categorization that would give it a range of tax immunities. When deciding this case, it was pointed out that tax immunities should be interpreted with a restrictive view – contradicting the religious liberty guarantee. What the Federal Supreme Court argued was that Masonry, not having a theology, but only prescribing a way of life, could not be considered to have "temples of worship," and therefore was not immune from taxation.[8]

In this case, there seems to have been confusion between Dworkin's questions of science and of value:[9] the Federal Supreme Court only considered as a religion a cult of "scientific" nature – that is, a cult that offers a theistic explanation of reality, and that worships a deity. Any other manifestation of religion as a system of values without a godly figure would not be immune from taxation and therefore would not be considered to be an actual religion.

In this sense, besides Masonry, it could be argued that Buddhism is not a religion in Brazil – although the latter's status as a religion has never been questioned. Maybe Masonry is not a religion, as some of its members claim, in the usual sense of the word, but the argument used by Brazil's Supreme Court is dangerous in the sense that other religions might be considered mere "cults." If this is the case, it would not be simply tax immunities that these "cults" would not have, but the full range of protections provided in the Constitution.

Another case that deserves attention was also decided by Brazil's Federal Supreme Court.[10] Here, the Center of Religious and Jewish Education, along with some Jewish students, questioned a decision of the Court that had denied a request for the ENEM (Exame Nacional do Ensino Médio)[11] to be rescheduled. The test was supposed to happen on a Saturday morning, thus conflicting with every tradition that follows the Sabbath (Heb. Shabbat). What the students wanted was for the test to take place on any other day of the week.

Their main argument was founded on the Constitution, that "no one shall be deprived of any rights by reason of religious belief or philosophical or political conviction, unless he invokes it to exempt himself from a legal obligation required of all and refuses to perform an alternative obligation established by law" (Article 5, VIII cited above). They also argued that the ENEM was an imperative exam for anyone aiming to graduate. In this sense, it was mandatory, and the Jewish group requested that the test be rescheduled for another day of the week in order to maintain equality among candidates.

The Court argued that the state should promote a "free competition on the 'market of religious convictions'," and that the state should take positive actions in favor of religions. Despite confusing religion with a brand or a product, this was the most salient part of the decision. The following arguments stated that these positive actions are only legal if they maintain "the free flow of religious ideas and if there is proof that there is no other less restrictive means to achieve this aim."[12] Also, "one should also take care that the measure adopted encourages equal opportunities for religious denominations and not instead be a source of privileges or favors."[13]

In other words, to respect the Shabbat would be to grant a privilege to a certain religious group. To reschedule the exam would be a measure that would favor Jewish students. The judge who wrote the opinion also stressed that the rules governing the test already provided an alternative for sabbatarians: to confine candidates who so chose to fulfil the "guard day" and start the test after 18 hours of Saturday.[14]

This case shows that Brazil's Federal Supreme Court has considered religions to be players on a market of, probably, supernatural ideals. Therefore, the separation between church and state would mean that states should treat different religions as competitors for followers. This is absolutely outrageous because it suggests that rights of religious liberty are proportionate to a religion's "market share."

Furthermore, there is clear confusion between the guarantee that no one shall be deprived of rights by reason of religious belief with the misconception that a religion must not be a source of privileges for certain groups. What the Jewish students – and all sabbatarians for this matter – were aiming for was to take a test under conditions similar to those of any other candidate. This would be possible if the exam took place on Mondays, Tuesdays, Wednesdays or Thursdays, days that respected the traditions and beliefs of the Shabbat and all other religions. Instead, they were granted the right to be enclosed in a room for a whole day and, at night, to begin the test. This solution does not appear to be grounded in the legal framework designed to guarantee religious liberty in Brazil.

A few considerations about the understanding of religious liberty in Brazil shall now be presented, along with a brief analysis of the misreading of the Courts on the matter.

4. Flaws of the Brazilian understanding of religious liberty

Although the legal framework from Brazil's Constitution, supplemented by the UDHR, provides documents that protect and guarantee the right of religious liberty, the reality in Brazil seems quite the opposite. Rarely are cases on this matter actually taken to the Courts, but when they are, decisions seldom apply the constitutional statutes in the way they should.

In a way, it is possible to claim that there is religious liberty in Brazil. What this means, however, is that everyone is free to choose and follow the beliefs of any given religion, whether it is traditional or not. The state does not take part in this decision, but it does not help either, leaving citizens mostly subjected to Catholic and Protestant doctrines, which are the most common in the country. Therefore, what the Federal Supreme Court stated when deciding the ENEM case is actually true: religions are treated according to market rules, and this means the biggest religions are most likely to attract a higher number of followers. Liberty, thus, is available, but on these specific terms. There is no equal opportunity for people to be acquainted with each religion.

When one states that there is religious liberty in Brazil, however, there is a side that is not clearly noticeable at first sight, and once again it involves the state – or a lack of it. The constitutional provisions concerning religion state that there shall be no prejudice toward any religion, so that, despite people's differing beliefs, all shall be treated the same. This is true when the Constitution grants alternatives for military service, states that no one shall be deprived of rights by reason of religion, and even when the Constitution recognizes the validity of religious weddings.

Despite all of these provisions, what the decisions previously described show is that the constitutional text is not clearly understood and that, unfortunately, there is a major lack of respect for different religions in Brazil. In other words, people are free to choose and follow a religion, granted that it is a religion familiar to the state. The Umbanda case well demonstrates this, as the judge knew all the religious freedom guarantees from the Constitution, but did not know what a religion was. Evidently, when arguing that religions should have a foundational book, he was unfamiliar with almost every other religion outside of the popular beliefs from Brazil (Catholic and Protestant). Also, his claim that a religion must have a deity is almost naïve, revealing how little knowledge of the subject he had prior to the decision. This, however, must not be treated simply as a bad example that will not be repeated. This case reveals how little Brazilians know about diversity when it comes to religion.

This is also true for the second case. Masonry is not a religion in the sense of a "science" that tries to scientifically explain the universe and its mysteries, but it does state a group of values to be followed and a way of life to be had. In this sense, like many other religions, it has its followers and must be protected by the freedom of conscience clause.

The problems that Brazilians face when trying to validate a wedding performed in other temples or celebrated in different cults are also revealing. Even state officials such as Civil Registries have difficulty accepting that people may believe in anything else other than the teachings of the Catholic or Protestant churches. In this sense, an Umbanda wedding, or a Spiritualistic union, do not have the same value as a marriage in a church.

In Brazil, people have freedom of conscience and religion. The only problem is that, depending on what they believe, they will be treated differently. What is not realized is that this problem means, in reality, that there is no real religious liberty. The ENEM case is the perfect example: although there are few Jews in Brazil, their traditions are very well known, and although a remedy was offered to the sabbatarians, it was a bad one, as it violated their right to equality.

All of this shows that many of the mistakes made by Brazil's government and courts stem from one single flaw: the identification of religion with traditional Catholic/Protestant belief. These two major branches of the Christian faith, which together are responsible for almost 90% of the Brazilian population's creed, are taken as the role models for every religion: there is a single deity, the religion is based on a sacred book, and the traditions are well known and have been present in Brazil since its beginnings. Every other religion that is somehow different from this paradigm is not well comprehended and, because of this, cannot be properly protected by the state.

5. Conclusion

This brief description of Brazil's Constitution and discussion of actual cases aimed to demonstrate just how divergent the law on paper is from the law in reality. The short number of cases we discussed serve as proof of what we have argued – that while the Constitution envisages a plural and equal state in terms of religious liberty, what is found in reality is the complete opposite. Courts and state officials have difficulty dealing with religious traditions that are in any way different from the traditional beliefs in Brazil.

In short, the law on religious liberty in the books and in statutes is much more broad and protective than Brazilian law in action. The Brazilian Constitution can be interpreted as granting people the right to ethical independence in the sense defined by Dworkin (2013, 117): "[P]eople have a right to the free exercise of their convictions about life and its responsibilities." And scholars have also argued that the matter of religion must be considered so that respect and equal consideration can thrive in a multicultural reality (Pinheiro 2008, 122).[15]

What is seen when courts decide, however, is the opposite. Judges and Justices do not realize this multicultural reality and define religion in narrow terms, usually based on deities and sacred texts. This affects people's lives in many respects, from tax immunities to the validity of marriages. In addition, even when a religion is well known, courts have difficulty guaranteeing equal protection.

With this, courts play a restrictive role when they should do the opposite. Religious liberty in Brazil, according to its Constitution, should only be limited in narrow terms, in the sense of Dworkin's thought: "Religions may be forced to restrict their practises so as to obey rational, non-discriminatory laws that do not display less than equal concern for them" (Dworkin 2013, 135–136). What is limited, however, seems to be the definition of religion by the Judiciary Power.

This problem, although made explicit by judicial decisions, is not simply legal, in the sense that the law is incapable of handling all of the different religions followed in Brazil. The country has all the statutory tools for religious liberty to prosper. It is philosophical: the state's biggest challenge is to learn what a religion is and to abandon its focus on two religious traditions so that it can become a state of equality and pluralism.

Notes

1 The English version of the Brazilian Constitution cited in this paper is the official translation by Brazil's Federal Supreme Court. Accessed August 11, 2016. http://www.stf.jus.br/repositorio/cms/portalStfInternacional/portalStfSobreCorte_en_us/anexo/constituicao_ingles_3ed2010.pdf.

2 Article 210 of the English version of the Brazilian constitution reads as follows: "Minimum curricula shall be established for elementary schools in order to ensure a common basic education and respect for national and regional cultural and artistic values. Paragraph 1. The teaching of religion is optional and shall be offered during the regular school hours of public elementary schools."

3 Article 5, Paragraph 3, of the Brazilian Constitution.

4 "Ao se compreender a liberdade religiosa como direito que depende da virtude da tolerância em sentido político, os laços fundamentais que a unem com a igualdade e com o pluralismo se tornam evidentes. Todas as manifestações religiosas seriam toleradas, à exceção daquelas que defendessem e praticassem atitudes que violassem diretamente os direitos fundamentais dos outros cidadãos, o que revela um compromisso bastante forte com o pluralismo religioso. Além disso, a tolerância no sentido político também

se compromete com a igualdade entre todas as religiões, dada a sua independência das doutrinas substantivas de qualquer religião específica a respeito da postura com relação às outras religiões. O ponto de apoio da virtude da tolerância, politicamente compreendida, é justamente o reconhecimento da igualdade de todos enquanto membros livres e iguais da mesma sociedade política. Todas as religiões, assim, são iguais aos olhos da Constituição" (Almeida 2006, 72).

Free translation: "By understanding religious freedom as a right that depends on the virtue of tolerance in the political sense, the fundamental ties that unite it with equality and pluralism become evident. All religious events would be tolerated, except for those that defend and practice attitudes that directly violate the fundamental rights of other citizens, which reveals quite a strong commitment with religious pluralism. In addition, tolerance in the political sense is also committed to equality between all religions, given the independence of the substantive doctrines of any particular religion about the attitude toward other religions. The fulcrum of the virtue of tolerance, politically understood, is precisely the recognition of the equality of all as free and equal members of the same political society. All religions are thus equal in the eyes of the Constitution."

5 "Um dos significados mais lembrados do direito à liberdade de consciência é o reconhecimento de que é importante conferir aos cidadãos o direito de crer apenas naquilo que é capaz de convencer sua própria consciência, protegendo-os contra o proselitismo de qualquer um que busque, por meio da força, impor suas próprias crenças religiosas" (Almeida 2006, 51).

Free translation: "One of the most remembered meanings of the right of freedom of conscience is the recognition that it is important to provide citizens with the right to believe only in that which is able to convince their own conscience, protecting them from the proselytism of anyone who seeks through force to impose their own religious beliefs."

6 "Assim, fica claro que a autonomia e o livre exercício religioso também são componentes fundamentais do princípio da liberdade religiosa, capazes de justificar atitudes que muitos considerariam irracionais, mas que, para o fiel, são importantíssimas do ponto de vista de sua consciência moral e religiosa. O Estado, dessa maneira, precisa respeitar as decisões individuais, por mais que elas violem os valores éticos da maioria, por conta do fato de que, na medida em que a sociabilidade de uma democracia é fundamentada na compreensão da igual consideração pelos interesses e valores dos cidadãos, torna-se necessário reconhecer a responsabilidade moral de cada um para lidar com questões relativas à vida boa" (Almeida 2006, 77).

Free translation: "Thus it is clear that the autonomy and free exercise of religion are also key components of the principle of religious freedom, which is able to justify attitudes that many would consider irrational, but that for the faithful are very important from the point of view of their moral conscience and religion. The state thus needs to respect individual decisions, however they violate the ethical values of the majority, due to the fact that, to the extent that the sociability of a democracy is founded on the understanding of equal consideration for the interests and values of its citizens, it is necessary to recognize the moral responsibility of each to deal with issues related to the good life."

7 Translated from the original: "traços necessários de uma religião a saber, um texto base (corão, bíblia etc) ausência de estrutura hierárquica e ausência de um Deus a ser venerado" (Brasil Justiça Federal 2014).

8 CONSTITUCIONAL. RECURSO EXTRAORDINÁRIO. IMUNIDADE TRIBUTÁRIA. ART. 150, VI, C, DA CARTA FEDERAL. (...). ART. 150, VI, B, DA CONSTITUIÇÃO DA REPÚBLICA. ABRANGÊNCIA DO TERMO "TEMPLOS DE QUALQUER CULTO." MAÇONARIA. NÃO CONFIGURAÇÃO. (...). I – O reconhecimento da imunidade tributária prevista no art. 150, VI, c, da Constituição Federal exige o cumprimento dos requisitos estabelecidos em lei. II – (...) III – A imunidade tributária conferida pelo art. 150, VI, b, é restrita aos templos de qualquer

culto religioso, não se aplicando à maçonaria, em cujas lojas não se professa qualquer religião. IV – (...). (RE 562351, Min. RICARDO LEWANDOWSKI, Primeira Turma, 04/09/2012).

Free translation: "CONSTITUTIONAL LAW. EXTRAORDINARY APPEAL. TAX IMMUNITY. ART. 150, VI, C, OF THE FEDERAL CONSTITUTION. (...). ART. 150, VI, B, OF THE FEDERAL CONSTITUTION. SCOPE OF THE TERM "TEMPLES OF ANY DENOMINATION." MASONRY. NO CONFIGURATION. (...). I – Recognition of the tax exemption provided for in art. 150, VI, c, of the Federal Constitution requires compliance with the requirements established by law. II – (...) III – The tax immunity conferred by art. 150, VI, b, is restricted to the temples of any religious worship, not applicable to masonry, whose stores do not profess any religion. IV – (...)."

9 See, in this sense, arguments that state values are prior to gods (Dworkin 2013, 1–2) and that religion does not necessarily mean a belief in a god (Dworkin 2013, 6). From this, Dworkin reaches the conclusion that religions have two different parts, "science" and "value," and that values are not dependent on theism (Dworkin 2013, 22).

10 Brasil STF. 2009. AgR 389. Min. GILMAR MENDES, Tribunal Pleno. 03/12/2009.

11 ENEM is a national test for admission into universities, and is similar to the SAT in the United States.

12 Translated from the original: "livre fluxo de ideias religiosas e se comprovadamente não exista outro meio menos gravoso de se atingir esse desiderato."

13 Translated from the original: "deve-se também ter o cuidado de que a medida adotada estimule a igualdade de oportunidades entre as confissões religiosas e não, ao contrário, seja fonte de privilégios ou favorecimentos."

14 The proposal envisaged, historical considerations aside, the confinement of the candidates of the Jewish colony, as Min. Marco Aurélio highlighted: "Students of the Jewish colony, of memorable service to the country, would have to present themselves to be retained without communication for seven hours and, then, take the test which extends for four hours."

15 "[P]ermitindo uma convivência baseada no respeito e igual consideração a todos dentro de uma realidade multicultural." Free translation: "Allowing a life based on respect and equal consideration to everyone within a multicultural reality" (Pinheiro 2008, 122).

Bibliography

Almeida, Fabio Portela Lopes de. 2006. *Liberalismo político, constitucionalismo e democracia: a questão do ensino religioso nas escolas públicas.* LLM Dissertation, Universidade de Brasília.

Brasil Justiça Federal. 2014. Seção Judiciária do Rio de Janeiro. Ação Civil Pública n. 0004747-0004733.2014.4.02.5101. 29/04/2014.

Brasil STF. 2009. AgR 389. Min. GILMAR MENDES, Tribunal Pleno. 03/12/2009.

Brasil STF. 2012. RE 562351, Min. RICARDO LEWANDOWSKI, Primeira Turma. 04/09/2012.

Dworkin, Ronald. 2013. *Religion without God.* Cambridge: Harvard University Press.

Kozicki, Katya and William Soares Pugliese. 2013. "Religião sem Deus: uma questão de fé e valores" / "Religion without God: A Matter of Faith and Values." *Revista Direito e Práxis* 4: 319–342.

Llewellyn, Karl. 2011. *The Theory of Rules.* Chicago: University of Chicago Press.

Pinheiro, Douglas Antônio Rocha. 2008. *Direito, Estado e Religião: a constituinte de 1987/1988 e a (re)construção da identidade religiosa do sujeito constitucional brasileiro.* LLM Dissertation, Universidade de Brasília.

Index

For Product Safety Concerns and Information please contact our EU
representative GPSR@taylorandfrancis.com
Taylor & Francis Verlag GmbH, Kaufingerstraße 24, 80331 München, Germany

www.ingramcontent.com/pod-product-compliance
Ingram Content Group UK Ltd.
Pitfield, Milton Keynes, MK11 3LW, UK
UKHW011004180926
475701UK00004B/557

www.ingramcontent.com/pod-product-compliance
Ingram Content Group UK Ltd.
Pitfield, Milton Keynes, MK11 3LW, UK
UKHW011004180926
475701UK00004B/557

* 9 7 8 0 3 6 7 2 7 3 4 3 9 *